THE CIVIL WAR ON
HATTERAS

THE CIVIL WAR ON HATTERAS

THE CHICAMACOMICO AFFAIR AND THE CAPTURE OF THE U.S. GUNBOAT *FANNY*

LEE THOMAS OXFORD

Forewords by Dennis C. Schurr and R. Drew Pullen

Charleston · London

THE
History
PRESS

Published by The History Press
Charleston, SC 29403
www.historypress.net

Front cover: "The United States Steamer *Monticello* shelling the Rebel troops at Chicamacomico on their return from an unsuccessful attempt to cut off the retreat of the 20th Indiana Regiment towards Hatteras Lighthouse, October 5, 1861." This engraving from *Frank Leslie's Illustrated Newspaper*, November 2, 1861, was based on the false accounts of death and destruction found in the official report of U.S. Navy Lieutenant Daniel L. Braine of the *Monticello*. *Outer Banks History Center.*

Back cover: Rare photo of three Third Georgia Regiment soldiers from Company D, each wearing a blue Union overcoat captured from the Twentieth Indiana Regiment aboard the U.S. gunboat *Fanny* on October 1, 1861. Private Columbus C. Taylor, *far left*, was a member of the CSS *Curlew* gun crew, which fired on the *Fanny*. Taylor and James D. Jackson, *middle*, were both killed at Malvern Hill, July 1, 1862. James H. Porter, "detailed for railroad service," was discharged January 1862. The photo was taken near Richmond during the winter of 1861–62. *Museum of the Confederacy.*

First published 2013

Manufactured in the United States

ISBN 978.1.60949.898.6

Library of Congress CIP data applied for.

To My Father
Gunnery Sergeant Douglas Ray Oxford Sr., U.S. Marine Corps (Retired)
Korea–Vietnam
1935–2007

Contents

CONTENTS

Foreword

*T*he *Civil War on Hatteras: The Chicamacomico Affair and the Capture of the U.S. Gunboat* Fanny is Lee Oxford's first book. It comes at an exciting time given our nation's observance of the sesquicentennial of the Civil War. Through comprehensive research and engaging narrative, the author presents a vivid picture of a chapter of Civil War history not previously told in such detail. It is especially illuminating for anyone seeking to understand the role that the Twentieth Indiana Volunteer Infantry played while on the shores of eastern North Carolina. Very little has been written about their early journey to the Outer Banks. After a little over a month, they would depart Hatteras with a bad taste in their mouths that they would long remember—of sand, salt water and nor'easters, not to mention encounters with the Third Georgia Infantry and the Ninth New York (Hawkins Zouaves).

Lee Oxford and I first met in 2001 while he was doing research at the Outer Banks History Center in Manteo, North Carolina. He learned through my then-fiancée—KaeLi Spiers (now Schurr), curator of the center—that I was a collector of the Ninth New York Hawkins Zouaves and asked if I could recommend research related to this regiment, which I was pleased to do. As I listened to Lee's enthusiasm, I knew that he would be going on a very long journey. Over the next seven years, we stayed in contact, and I followed his progress with great interest and respect.

During the fall of 2008, the Flags Over Hatteras Civil War on the Outer Banks Sesquicentennial Committee was formed. Working under the auspices of the Friends of the Graveyard of the Atlantic Museum, the group orchestrated a series of events to commemorate those that occurred at Hatteras Island in August through October 1861. In the course of four years of planning and presenting Flags Over Hatteras, the group would have many collegial debates, but one decision that was quickly reached by overwhelming consensus was that we would design a weeklong series of three key events: a descendants "VIP Blue-Gray" reunion, a conference featuring a mix of national and regional speakers and a living history program geared to the general public.

In the spring of 2010, I contacted Lee about being a guest speaker during our "VIP Blue-Gray" reunion and conference. By then, we had enlisted three Civil War luminaries for the conference, Dr. James McPherson, Dr. Craig Symonds and Edwin Bearss. Lee's immediate response was, "Of course!" We then wondered whether the three had ever been together in the same room at once. Another year would pass.

On August 22, 2011, Flags Over Hatteras was set to begin. Nearly ninety descendants converged on Hatteras Village from all over the country, including Lee Oxford; his wife, Stacy; and a delegation of twenty-six others representing the Twentieth Indiana Volunteer Infantry. The first day of the reunion was memorable, exceeding all expectations of planners and attendees alike. Lee contributed two talks on the second day of the reunion, the "Capture of the *Fanny* and the Chicamacomico Races" and the "POWs of the *Fanny* and Chicamacomico."

It seemed that the stars and the moon were perfectly aligned, or so we thought. But "Old Man Weather" had a different idea. Out in the Atlantic, Hurricane Irene was gaining strength and threatening to make land fall somewhere along the southeastern seaboard. By the morning of the second day of the reunion, it had become obvious that Hatteras Island was in the storm's path and a tough call had to be made. The conference and living history program would have to be postponed, and hurricane preparations went into full swing. In hindsight, that difficult decision was the right one. Irene would do major damage to much of Hatteras Island and leave it largely cut-off from the world for many months that followed.

It would be April 26, 2012, before Flags Over Hatteras would reconvene. By then another event had been added—Lee Oxford would lead with a presentation in Rodanthe, "Capture of the *Fanny* and the Chicamacomico Affair," sharing his extensive research for the first time with the community in which it all happened. That talk and his presentation at the conference, "Camp Live Oak: Capture of the *Fanny* and Subsequent Chicamacomico Affair, October 1–5, 1861," were both well received as they revealed much that was previously unknown even to this learned audience.

I admire these works more than I can easily say. Through his extensive research, Lee Oxford has been able to shed new light on the accounts of the Twentieth Indiana's trials while stationed at Camp Live Oak and on Hatteras Island. Come along on a journey to the Outer Banks of North Carolina of 150 years ago and experience an aspect of our history that is largely unknown. *Civil War on Hatteras: The Chicamacomico Affair & the Capture of the U.S. Gunboat* Fanny is a must read for anyone interested in the people and places of our great country.

DENNIS C. SCHURR
Manteo, Roanoke Island
North Carolina

Foreword

My first contact with Lee Oxford occurred in the spring of 2010 at the Atlantic Coast Cafe in Waves, North Carolina. Dennis Schurr, a fellow member of the Flags Over Hatteras, Civil War on the Outer Banks Sesquicentennial Committee, had invited me to meet him at this restaurant, located on Pamlico Sound, in order to introduce me to Lee Oxford.

Our committee was interested in planning a Civil War sesquicentennial event for the tri-villages of Salvo, Waves and Rodanthe. We hoped to have Lee Oxford speak at this event. I had heard from both Dennis Schurr and another researcher, Mel Covey, that Lee was doing research on the capture of the federal gunboat *Fanny* and the Chicamacomico Races in order to write a book on the subjects. Both of these Civil War events occurred near the location of this restaurant in October 1861.

Mel Covey and Dennis Schurr had both expressed a very favorable impression of Lee Oxford and the depth of his research in advance of this meeting. The restaurant was a pleasant setting in which to meet Lee and for all of us to sit around a table to discuss events that occurred here 150 years ago.

The longer I listened to Lee share about his research the more I was impressed with the depth and scope of his efforts. Because I had done research on these two events for my book, *The Civil War on Hatteras Island*, I was familiar with much of the primary source material and knew how limited it was. It seemed to me that Lee was really determined to leave no stone unturned in researching every detail of these little-known events of the Civil War.

The committee followed up on this breakfast meeting by inviting Lee to be a presenter at our Flags Over Hatteras Sesquicentennial Civil War Conference in Hatteras Village the last week of August 2011. Our event was disrupted by Hurricane Irene but was finally completed in April 2012. The quality of Lee's talks and scholarship was right up there with some of the nationally known participants such as Dr. James McPherson, Dr. Craig Symonds and Dr. Edwin Bearrs. We were proud and honored to have Lee Oxford speak at our event.

I just finished reading the advanced manuscript of *The Civil War on Hatteras: The Chicamacomico Affair and the Capture of the U.S. Gunboat* Fanny. I come away with an even more favorable opinion of Lee Oxford and the quality of scholarship presented in this book.

R. DREW PULLEN
Buxton, Hatteras Island
North Carolina

Preface

This study of two Civil War "firsts," the capture of the U.S. gunboat *Fanny* and the Chicamacomico Affair on Hatteras, grew out of a casual inquiry into the imprisonment of my grandfather's grandfather, who was taken captive on the *Fanny* on October 1, 1861. My cousin David Oxford had been researching our family history for a number of years and posted some information online about the *Fanny* capture of our paternal ancestor Elias Oxford, a private with the Twentieth Indiana Regiment, while aboard the small transport steamer in those early months of the rebellion. I thus became aware, for the first time, that I had an ancestor who served during the Civil War. My deep appreciation goes to David for keeping our Oxford family history alive and for encouraging me in my own research.

I soon became interested in identifying specifically the seventy-three Union men and boys, mostly of the Twentieth Indiana Regiment of Volunteers, captured aboard the *Fanny* and in the Confederate assault that followed at Camp Live Oak, the brief encampment of the Twentieth at the north end of Hatteras Island. I had never been to the Outer Banks and had certainly never heard of Live Oak or Chicamacomico, the little group of villages on Hatteras Banks where the communities of Rodanthe, Waves and Salvo exist today. I quickly realized that relatively little had been written concerning these two engagements. The little that was available was largely based on the same few reports, and those were full of factual errors. Those errors continue to be repeated to the present.

I became particularly focused on locating other descendants of the *Fanny*/Chicamacomico prisoners of war (POWs). The first family I located included the great-granddaughter of a Twentieth Indiana musician. Nancy Andrews Muenchausen had posted information about her ancestor John Henry Andrews on the website of Indiana Civil War historian Craig Dunn. We discovered that our ancestors were apparently friends throughout their service and captivity and perhaps even before the war. So I drove to Danville, Illinois, to meet Nancy and her brother John H. Andrews in 2008, which proved an exciting reunion that we each certainly treasure.

This book is the first half of a much longer story originally intended for a single volume. For a number of practical reasons, the account of the 224 days of captivity in Rebel prisons for the seventy-three *Fanny* and Chicamacomico POWs will have to wait for a future work. The account of their captivity and their lives after imprisonment and the war is a rich one.

I have been particularly fortunate in receiving the encouragement and support of so many people over the years of my research. Craig L. Dunn's regimental history of the Twentieth Indiana, *Harvestfields of Death: The Twentieth Indiana Volunteers of Gettysburg*, was the first account I read of my ancestor's capture and the events surrounding it at Chicamacomico. Craig's website, www.civilwarindiana.com, also made available to me an extensive archive of Twentieth Indiana photographs, which included a number of the key players in my research and even a handful of the POWs.

I sense I have been warmly received into a new family of Outer Banks friends and historians as a result of my research. Early help came from KaeLi Schurr, curator of the Outer Banks History Center on Roanoke Island. In addition to the significant archive of source material related to the Civil War on the Outer Banks and Roanoke Island, KaeLi also connected me with Dennis Schurr, who was then her fiancé. Dennis is a collector and an expert on all things Ninth New York (Hawkins Zouaves). Since 2003, KaeLi and Dennis have gone over the top in providing material, making connections with other historians and setting up speaking opportunities. Many a phone call to or from Dennis began with him asking, "How's your book coming?" Drew Pullen, author of *Portrait of the Past: The Civil War on Roanoke Island North Carolina* and *Portrait of the Past: The Civil War on Hatteras Island North Carolina*, has been a great inspiration as well. Though not a Hatteras native, he married one and has been relentlessly committed to telling the island's story. Thanks to Hatteras natives Mel Covey and Danny Couch, who have both been uncovering and preserving Civil War history on the island for quite a while. Bruce Long is another early contact turned friend who has constantly challenged me to dig deeper. Bruce has eagerly shared his ever-growing wealth of knowledge and information on the Civil War and Coastal North Carolina with me personally and through his website, http://ncsquadron.wordpress. com/. Thanks to Ben Callahan and Vickey Cline of the Eastern Cabarrus Historical Society; Charles MacDonald; Joseph Schwarzer, director of the Graveyard of the Atlantic Museum at Hatteras; the Flags Over Hatteras Committee; Wanda Stiles, curator of the Museum of the Albemarle; and Richard W. Lawrence, North Carolina's deputy state archaeologist.

Special thanks go to Bob and Wendy Mooers of Gateway Books in Hebron, Maryland, for opening to me their archive of antiquarian newspapers, where I first discovered Elias's name in a prisoner list on the front page of the *New York Herald*, of October 14, 1861. My friend Karen Needles of the Lincoln Archives Digital Project, www.lincolnarchives.us, will never know how much the access she made available to me at the National Archives meant to my research. Thanks to Johnnie Pearson, author of *Lee and Jackson's Bloody Twelfth*, for transcribing the Third Georgia memoirs of adjutant William W. Turner. Thanks to Clyde Wiggins III for making the transcripts of his Third Georgia ancestor, A.B. Spencer, available before his own book, *My Dear Friend*, was published. Thanks to Don D. Worth for his website, www.3gvi.org, which has been absolutely invaluable, as well as for his personal assistance in locating images for me at the Georgia Capitol Museum. Thanks to Jill Severn, curator of the Georgia Capitol Museum, for taking swift action on my behalf.

Thanks to *Fanny* POW descendant Clif Hinds for the stories, photos and friendship you have extended these past years. Thanks as well to POW descendants Nori Muster, Adrienne Inglis and Mary Ellen Sackett Wills for providing family information, photos and more.

Special thanks to Dr. John Gilcrest Barrett of Lexington, Virginia, for his personal encouragement over the phone and for his book, *The Civil War in North Carolina*, published when I was still a small boy catching tadpoles behind my house in Craven County.

I also want to thank my brother, Doug, who has passionately taught history for many years in Garrett County, Maryland, and has been an inspiration for me to "press on." Thanks to my pastors, Jonathan and Linette Willey, for their friendship and the continual reminder that "I can have what I say." Thanks to Dennis Burke, as well, for his willingness to provide some quick but timely help in navigating my contract.

My wife, Stacy, has been cheering me on for quite a few years now. She has given me permission to be "absent," whether at home or away, in order to do research, write or meet with other historians. Stacy has not appeared tired of hearing my newest discoveries, and without her support and confidence, this volume would never have become a reality.

This study is dedicated to my father, Gunnery Sergeant Douglas Ray Oxford Sr.

LEE THOMAS OXFORD
Salisbury, Maryland
March 2013

"These and Similar Trophies"

The flag of the Congress and the sword of the officer commanding at the time of her surrender are at this Department, together with the flag and sword of the gunboat Fanny, *captured by Flag-Officer Lynch in October last; and I submit for your consideration the propriety for safe-keeping of these and similar trophies.*[1]
—Confederate Secretary of the Navy Stephen R. Mallory report to Confederate President Jefferson Davis, March 11, 1862

The flag of the USS *Congress* and the sword of the officer commanding at the time of its capture were trophies of a decisive Confederate victory at the Battle of Hampton Roads on March 8 and 9, 1862. The first day of the battle ended as the bloodiest day in United States naval history up to the December 7, 1941 Japanese attack on Pearl Harbor.[2] The ironclad CSS *Virginia (Merrimack)*, on its first day out of Norfolk Navy Yard, destroyed two wooden-hulled Union warships in an effort to bring an end to the Union naval blockade. The first was the twenty-four-gun sloop of war USS *Cumberland*, followed by the fifty-gun sailing frigate USS *Congress*. The *Cumberland* fell prey to the *Virginia*'s 1,500-pound iron ram attached to the ironclad's bow. The *Congress* later perished under a rain of fiery hot shot ordered by the *Virginia*'s commander, Flag Officer Franklin Buchanan. The following day the Union ironclad USS *Monitor* was thrown against the *Virginia* in history's first battle between steam-powered ironclad warships. Wooden warships thus became effectively obsolete in this single battle.

"The Sinking of the '*Cumberland*' by the Iron Clad '*Merrimac*' Off Newport News Va. March 8th, 1862," by Currier & Ives. *Library of Congress.*

Late in the evening of March 9, 1862, the flag of the USS *Congress*, a "bunting flag of very fine quality and large size," having become a trophy of the Confederacy, was unrolled before President Jefferson Davis at the Executive Mansion in Richmond.[3] The trophy was hand-delivered by Lieutenant John Taylor Wood, Gun Captain of the CSS *Virginia.*

Wood was also grandson of President Zachary Taylor and nephew of Confederate president Jefferson Davis.[4] Following the engagements of March 8 and 9 and the return of the ironclad *Virginia* to Gosport in the early afternoon of the second day,[5] Flag Officer Buchanan called Wood to his bedside at the Norfolk Naval Hospital. Buchanan lay seriously wounded by a Minié ball, which had passed through his left thigh and grazed the femoral artery.[6] Though suffering, Wood later recalled, the commodore dictated a brief report, including "the return of the ship and the result of the two days' fight, and directed me to proceed to Richmond with it, and the flag of the *Congress*, and make a verbal report of the action, condition of the *Virginia*, etc."[7]

The flag of the USS *Congress*, when unrolled, was found saturated in blood. First Lady Varina Howell Davis wrote, "I took hold of it and found it damp with blood, and retired to my room sick of war and sorrowful over the dead and dying of both sections."[8] Some of that blood certainly flowed from the mortal wound of Confederate navy lieutenant James Langhorne

Tayloe of the CSS *Raleigh*, as he received it the afternoon of March 8 at 4:30 p.m.[9] The young officer had gathered the prize flag around him in preparation to quit the burning *Congress*, having seized the colors under a flag of truce, as ordered by Flag Officer Buchanan.[10] After Wood's visit, Tayloe, like Buchanan, lay in a bed at Norfolk Naval Hospital where he would succumb to his wounds in the early morning hours of March 11.[11]

Prior to serving aboard the CSS *Raleigh*, Tayloe, an 1860 Naval Academy graduate, had commanded another small gunboat, the CSS *Fanny*, until earlier in the year. The *Fanny* was a small propeller steamer, a former Union gunboat captured in a brief engagement at Hatteras the previous October. Under Flag Officer

Master James Langhorne Tayloe, Confederate States Navy. This is Tayloe's 1860 graduation photo from the U.S. Naval Academy yearbook. Tayloe commanded the CSS *Fanny* from the time of her capture until she was scuttled in the Battle of Elizabeth City, February 10, 1862. *Nimitz Library, U.S. Naval Academy.*

William F. Lynch, a Rebel squadron, later known as "the Mosquito Fleet," consisting of three shallow-draft gunboats, captured the *Fanny* in the coastal waters of North Carolina's Pamlico Sound on the afternoon of October 1, 1861. The flag and the sword of the officer in command of that Union gunboat were preserved as well, in accordance with naval custom.

Tayloe, an officer serving in Lynch's small but growing squadron operating in the environs of Roanoke Island, had been forthwith given command of the newly acquired propeller. As a Rebel gunboat, the CSS *Fanny* took its last stand with Lynch's "Mosquito Fleet" off Cobb's Point just southeast of Elizabeth City, North Carolina, on February 10, 1862. The *Fanny* was run aground and burned, on Flag Officer Lynch's orders, a rather inglorious end to an otherwise seemingly insignificant vessel. Tayloe, having been recently promoted to lieutenant, was transferred to the CSS *Raleigh*, on which vessel

"Second day's action at Hatteras inlet," August 29, 1861. U.S. gunboat *Fanny* as General Benjamin Butler's flagship leads (from right to left) USS *Wabash*, USS *Minnesota*, U.S. Tug *Adriatic*, USS *Cumberland* and USS *Susquehanna* during Hatteras Invasion. Drawing by Alfred R. Waud. *Library of Congress.*

Stephen R. Mallory, secretary of the navy, Confederate States of America. *Library of Congress.*

he served during the Battle of Hampton Roads.

The flag of the U.S. gunboat *Fanny* and sword of the Union commander at the time of its October 1, 1861 capture were probably with Tayloe among his effects at the Norfolk Naval Hospital or were readily available to John Taylor Wood on the afternoon of March 9, 1862, prior to his mission to Richmond. Wood carried the trophies of the former U.S. gunboat *Fanny* with him to Richmond along with those of the USS *Congress*. The question of who was the officer in command of the *Fanny* on the afternoon of her capture, October 1, 1861, and thus, whose sword was presented to Jefferson Davis by John Taylor Wood, will be answered toward the end of this study.

The capture of the U.S. gunboat *Fanny* proved significant to the Confederacy in that it was the first Confederate capture of an armed Union vessel of war. The *Fanny*'s flag and sword were symbols of that Civil War naval first. In the wake of this October 1 capture, the CSS *Fanny*, having been fitted out for Lynch's squadron, took part in yet another Civil War first three days later on October 4, 1861. The first amphibious assault by combined forces of the Confederate States army and navy initiated what was first known as the "Chicamacomico Affair" and later became popularly known as the "Chicamacomico Races."

Captain John Taylor Wood, Confederate States Navy. Lieutenant and gun captain aboard CSS *Virginia* at Battle of Hampton Roads. *U.S. Naval Historical Center.*

These two Civil War firsts, the capture of the U.S. gunboat *Fanny* and the subsequent Chicamacomico Affair at Hatteras Island during the first week of October 1861, were each significant and symbolic naval victories for the Confederacy. Significant also was just how near the Twentieth Indiana Volunteer Regiment, a "Fighting 300 Regiment," came to being captured en masse the evening of October 4, 1861, on Hatteras at Big Kinnakeet, North Carolina. Perhaps more significant, though, beyond the symbols of swords and colors, are the lives and destinies of the seventy-three Union prisoners of war taken in these two engagements. These were all common men who paid an uncommon price to maintain the union of their homeland and to distinguish themselves in the eyes and hearts of their countrymen back home.

Private John H. Andrews, Twentieth Indiana. Shown here in August–September 1861, in the original gray uniform, holding an altered smoothbore musket. *Nancy Andrews Muenchausen and John H. Andrews Collection.*

Chapter One

"Every Case Is a Tragic Poem...A Pensive and Absorbing Book If Only It Were Written"

E very one of these cots has its history—every case is a tragic poem, an epic, a romance, a pensive and absorbing book, if it were only written," wrote Walt Whitman, essayist, poet and volunteer nurse, reflecting on the Union soldiers suffering in makeshift hospitals in and around the nation's capital during the second year of the rebellion.[12] One of the best of those provisional hospitals Whitman visited was the Indiana Hospital, originally established in September 1861 to care for the "sick soldiers at Washington City belonging to Indiana reg'ts."[13]

Confined to two wings of Washington's Patent Office Building, the Indiana Hospital was also widely known as "the Patent Office Hospital." The edifice Whitman appreciated as "that noblest of Washington buildings"[14] was modeled by architect Robert Mills after the Parthenon of Athens. Situated on an entire city block between Seventh and Ninth Streets, and F and G Streets, the Patent Office rose halfway between the scaffolding of the unfinished Capitol dome to the east and the president's house down Pennsylvania Avenue to the west. The Patent Office was a ten-block walk, just over a mile, from the Baltimore & Ohio (B&O) Railroad depot and the nearby Soldiers' Rest, where Union soldiers were quartered and fed a warm meal while waiting to be carried south, sent to the rear, reassigned to skeleton regiments or discharged and sent home.

Private John Henry Andrews, recently of Rossville, Illinois, and a musician from the Twentieth Indiana Regiment's Company H, made the thirty-minute trip from the Soldiers' Rest to the Indiana Hospital

Model room located inside the Old Patent Office Building in Washington, D.C. In 1861 and 1862, this room was used as part of the Patent Office Hospital, also known as the "Indiana Hospital." *Library of Congress.*

Union soldiers' bunks in Patent Office, 1861. *Harper's Weekly.*

just a few days following his arrival in Washington from the heart of the Confederacy. Andrews accompanied his company comrade Private Elias Oxford who suffered with advanced symptoms of typhoid fever and had orders from the Sanitary Commission for immediate admission to the hospital.[15]

Private Andrews and his Hoosier friend were among hundreds of Union POWs recently removed from Richmond's Libby tobacco warehouse prison at daybreak on Monday, May 12.[16] That same morning, in the North, the *New York Herald* ran a headline announcing, "Norfolk Is Ours!" Norfolk and Gosport Navy Yard had fallen into the hands of the Federal government on the evening of May 10 after a combined operation of the Union army and navy, an operation designed by President Lincoln himself. Federal war vessels had begun looking farther up the James River, then, putting additional and intense pressure on Richmond. The Confederates wanted to rid themselves of prisoners, particularly the sick, considered a draw on resources and excess baggage in the event of a full Rebel retreat from Richmond.

Some 885 paroled prisoners of war boarded two Rebel flag-of-truce steamers, the *Curtis Peck* and the *Northampton*, which stood waiting along the James River at Richmond. Several dozen of the paroles signed in advance on

May 1, including those of Andrews and Oxford, were for Twentieth Indiana men, along with eleven Hawkins Zouaves, all who had been captured on Hatteras Island in two engagements the previous October.[17]

Steaming down the James from Rocketts Landing, past Drewry's Bluff in the early light of dawn, the ships carrying the released prisoners hove within sight of the USS *Port Royal* by 6:30 a.m.[18] and soon thereafter in view of the Union ironclads *Galena* and *Aroostook* just below Jamestown. Twenty or more miles up from Newport News, Virginia, nearing Hardy's Bluff, the soldiers caught a good look at the Federal ironclads *Naugatuck* and *Monitor* and stood in disbelief as the *Monitor* refused a reply to the Rebel batteries of Fort Huger, which opened up on it from the bluff: "The prisoners gave her three cheers; and in response to a question, asking why he did not silence the batteries, the officer commanding replied that they had more important work to do up river." At Newport News the paroled Union prisoners first heard of the Confederate evacuation of Norfolk and the Navy Yard and of the scuttling of the CSS *Virginia*, which the men were still calling by its former Federal name, *Merrimack*.[19] The prisoners recalled having passed the *Merrimack* at Gosport Navy Yard upon their departure from Norfolk Jail to Richmond by train the previous October, more than two-hundred days earlier.

The parolees headed up the Potomac from Fort Monroe for Washington on May 14,[20] arriving in the evening at their temporary quarters, a "long low building constructed for the use of soldiers" at the Soldiers' Rest near the B&O station.[21] Having taken an oath not to take up arms against the Confederacy again in exchange for their freedom, the men readied to be paid and mustered out.[22]

The May 14 homecoming to the nation's capital splendidly punctuated Private John Andrews's twenty-fifth birthday. Private Oxford, though, was in failing condition on arrival. He had experienced symptoms similar to influenza earlier, prior to release from Libby Prison. Food and water in the Southern prisons during the war were often contaminated by raw sewage through various means, which apparently happened at Libby within a couple weeks of Oxford's release. Typhoid's early stage fever and rash gave way day by day to blurred vision, increased diarrhea, a tender distended abdomen and finally "muttering delirium." Death was just a step away. By the time the Sanitary Commission wrote its orders, it was too late for the primitive medicines to have any curative effect. On Sunday, May 18, Private Andrews brought Oxford to the Patent Office in what the surgeon described as "a morbid state." Oxford's illness was so advanced that he was unable to give his age, place of birth, marital status or residence. Andrews later provided some minimal information, noting he thought Oxford was married and that his next of kin resided in Iroquois County, Illinois.[23]

Private John Henry Andrews was already intimately acquainted with the atmosphere of death and the contagious diseases that hasten its coming. Both of Andrews's parents died in the summer of 1847 at the immigration depot and quarantine station of Grosse Isle, in Gulf of St. Lawrence in Quebec. Andrews's family was English, and his father, Vincent, was a sergeant in Her Majesty's Coldstream Regiment of Foot Guards. The Second Battalion Coldstream Guards were sent to Lower Canada (Quebec) in 1838 to support troops there in the suppression of the rebellion, or Patriots' War, stirred up at the end of 1837 by radical French-Canadian leaders, such as Louis-Joseph Papineau. It seems Sergeant Vincent Andrews and family arrived in the British colony late in 1839, two years after John's birth in Southwark, Surrey. John's younger sister was born in September 1839 onboard the ship between Portsmouth and the Canadas. The Second Coldstream left Canada in 1842, however, and returned to England. The Andrews family stayed in the colony, though, moving to Grosse Isle, where Vincent served as a nurse, or "surgeryman," fighting the 1847 typhus pandemic, with ship after ship arriving daily, filled with dead and dying Irish immigrants. By July 1847, typhus claimed Vincent and his wife, Mary Ann, and orphaned John, at the age of ten, along with a younger sister and brother. Such was Private Andrews's early education in death and disease, which cultivated in him a lifelong sensitivity and nurturing spirit toward the sick and dying.[24]

Andrews and Oxford—both of the Twentieth Indiana Regiment's Company H, and both captured on the U.S. gunboat *Fanny*—had stuck it out together throughout their nearly ten months in service to the Union cause. All but two months of that service since their capture at Hatteras was spent in the Rebel prisons of Norfolk, then Richmond and Columbia, South Carolina. By late February, the POWs were back in Richmond and, in March, were among the first to walk through the doors of the newly opened, and later notorious Libby Prison. Private Andrews had spent every day of those nearly eight months in confinement together with his comrade and now sat devotedly with Oxford in those final hours of his life, which was fading within the marble-tiled halls of the Patent Office. Andrews doubtless found the medical facilities in the North and West Halls of the Patent Office much the way Walt Whitman did, as a *strange, solemn, and, with all its features of suffering and death, a sort of fascinating sight…filled with high and ponderous glass cases crowded with models in miniature of every kind of utensil, machine, or invention it ever entered into the mind of man to conceive, and with curiosities and foreign presents. Between these cases were lateral openings, perhaps eight feet wide, and quite deep, and in these were placed many of the sick; besides a great long double row of them up and down through the middle of the hall…Then there was a gallery running above the hall, in which there were beds also. It was, indeed, a curious scene at night when lit up. The glass cases, the beds, the sick, the gallery above and the marble pavement under foot; the suffering, and the fortitude to bear it in the various degrees; occasionally, from some, the groan that could not be repressed; sometimes a poor fellow dying, with emaciated face and glassy eyes, the nurse by his side, the doctor also there, but no friend, no relative—such were the sights but lately in the Patent office.*[25]

The miniatures on display in glass cases throughout the halls of the hospital were a most curious assortment of machines, tools, instruments and contraptions, mostly made after the 1836 Patent Office fire, which destroyed the original Patent Office, its records and models. The United States government, in the nineteenth century, required applicants for patents to submit a made-from-scratch model, no larger than twelve-inches square, along with a detailed drawing of the specifications of the machine. The result was thousands of these handcrafted models housed in tall glass cases lining the corridors. Included were Samuel F.B. Morse's telegraph register of 1849, along with cook stoves and nautical instruments, mousetraps and steam engines, propellers and tobacco cutting machines. Each model was a means for Private Andrews to "visually turn back time." Each could conjure visions of things and events that had broken into his world since the previous summer. The joy of wearing fresh and new Union blue had been snatched away at Hatteras Banks aboard the propeller steamer *Fanny* off Chicamacomico and then on the lonely overcrowded floors of Liggon's and Libby's tobacco warehouse prisons of Richmond and the cramped county jail of Columbia, South Carolina. Private Andrews, as he sat beside his dying comrade in those last hours, had time to reflect on how truly and wonderfully strange it was just to be home again on his adopted Union soil.[26]

Chapter Two

"I'm But a Stranger Here"

The Twentieth Indiana Volunteer Infantry Regiment arrived at Fort Monroe the morning of September 25 and immediately pitched tents on "a field of frost." The regiment camped only one night at the fort, though, before receiving orders for Hatteras. There was no time to investigate Hampton or the fort itself.[27] The Twentieth broke camp the next morning and was steaming south to Hatteras Inlet by nightfall.

The men of the Twentieth, though, were not walking as tall as they might. Commander of the Department of Virginia, Major General John E. Wool noted on their arrival at Fort Monroe from Baltimore that the regiment was "badly armed" with old altered muskets, about 150 of which were actually unfit for service.[28]

Raised as a "rifle regiment," the Twentieth Indiana discovered in Indianapolis in July that all but two companies would receive outdated Harpers Ferry smoothbore muskets. At the outbreak of the war, there were simply not enough new Springfield rifles to supply so many troops. The Twentieth instead was issued the old 1795-design Springfield flintlocks altered to use percussion caps in 1842 at the Harpers Ferry Armory. Each altered musket fired a single cartridge containing one .69 caliber ball and three buckshot each.[29]

Only two Twentieth Indiana companies received Springfield Model 1855 rifles in the initial issue. These were Captain John Van Valkenburg's Company A and Captain John Wheeler's Company B, the right and left flanks of the regiment.[30] The Springfields were consistently accurate in battle

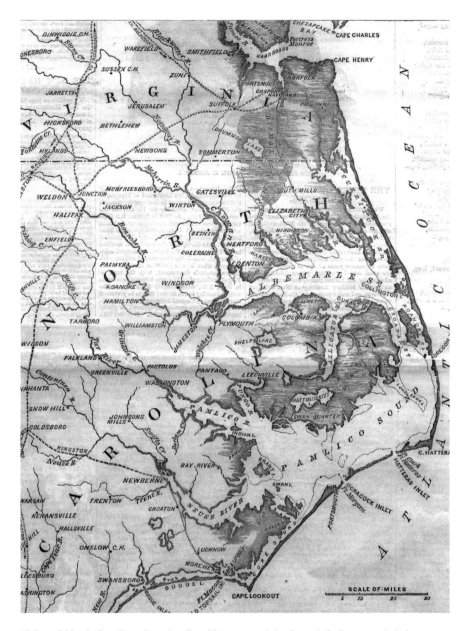

"Map of North Carolina, Showing Fort Hatteras and the Sounds It Commands." *Outer Banks History Center.*

at up to three-hundred yards with a .58 caliber Minié ball and, in the hands of a skilled sharpshooter, could be accurate up to one thousand yards.[31] One of the Twentieth's two rifle companies were favored the night of August 6 with the thrill of firing off a few shots at secessionists attempting to set fire to the Northern Central Railroad bridge spanning the Gunpowder River north of Cockeysville, Maryland.[32]

Wool ordered the Twentieth's "unfit" Harpers Ferry muskets traded in for old Confederate muskets, which had been surrendered by the Seventh North Carolina troops at Fort Hatteras on August 29.[33] This was not a significant improvement but certainly is an indication of the wretched condition of the original smoothbores. Wool held the regiment's departure until it was also adequately supplied with overcoats, trousers, boots and other army necessities.[34]

While in Indianapolis, the men of the Twentieth had been issued poor-quality, gray uniforms, with jackets that had "rounded corners and a braided edge," all made of material that wore out quickly. The officers' uniforms, however, were regular army blue.[35] Company musicians, like Private John Andrews, drummer for Company H, initially were issued the standard gray, as well. Later, in mid-September in Cockeysville, each musician, along with the recently mustered regimental band, received a new uniform which "set them off."[36] Each musician went into Baltimore to purchase his twenty-three-dollar uniform, returning with pride, ready to play at dress parade.[37] They wore blue cashmere pants with black strips down each leg, "a deep black frock coat, brass buttons and regulation caps." It was said the musicians presented "a fine appearance with a little brass in their buttons and a small amount in their instruments and considerable in their 'faces.'"[38]

At 5:00 p.m. on Thursday, September 26, 1861, the "Tall Twentieth," under the command of Colonel William Lyons Brown, formed a line on the beach at Fort Monroe, Virginia. It marched to the wharf, ready to board the iron-hulled, side-wheeled transport steamer, *S.R. Spaulding*, which waited there, steam up.[39] President Lincoln had declared that day "a day of humiliation, prayer, and fasting for all the people of the nation."[40] Accordingly, Flag Officer Louis M. Goldsborough sent a copy of his orders that suspended "duties on board the vessels under [his] command…and that divine service be performed on board each one having a chaplain attached to her at the hour of half past 10 o'clock a.m." to each vessel at the port of Hampton Roads, including the *S.R. Spaulding*.[41] It could certainly be expected that the military chaplains would see to it prayers were offered to God asking for Union success in battle.[42]

Private John H. Andrews, Twentieth Indiana. Camp sketch of Andrews, drummer of Company H, in a new musician's uniform, September 1861. *Nancy Andrews Muenchausen and John H. Andrews Collection.*

The colonel of the Twentieth Indiana, William Lyons Brown, was a forty-three-year-old Mexican War veteran. At the outbreak of the Mexican War, thirty-one-year-old Brown had been commissioned Second Lieutenant of the Cass County Volunteers, a company of the First Regiment of Indiana Volunteers. Together with the Second and Third Regiments, the First

Regiment was part of the Indiana Brigade under Brigadier General Joseph Lane. Unlike the Second and Third Regiments of the Indiana Brigade, though, the First Regiment never saw battle during the Mexican War. Brown, like another young First Indiana Regiment second lieutenant, Lew Wallace, spent most of his Mexican War service on garrison duty along the Rio Grande as General Zachary Taylor's rear guard.

William L. Brown, "banker, merchant, farmer, soldier," was also known to have been a devout Presbyterian. Brown's Indiana farm, which he named "Chapultapec," overlooked the Wabash River at the mouth of Fitch's Glen and was the envy of Logansport. The native Ohioan's parents had four sons, all but Brown Presbyterian ministers.[43] While Brown was holding garrison duty at Cockeysville, his younger brother, Frederick Thomas Brown, chaplain of the Seventh Ohio Volunteers, was making headlines in Rebel newspapers. Chaplain Brown had crossed enemy lines blindfolded under a flag of truce following the Battle of Cross Lanes, (West) Virginia, in the attempt to care for the Union dead and wounded of his regiment. His requests, contained in hand-delivered communiqués, were refused by Confederate brigadier general John B. Floyd, and Chaplain F.T. Brown, leaving his Buckeye brothers to the care of Rebel surgeons and interment, returned to Union lines.[44]

Colonel Brown's Twentieth Indiana, on the front end of its service to the Union during August and most of September, had had all of the guard duty it could stand and was itching to see action. Headquartered at Cockeysville, Maryland, it guarded the sixty-five bridges up and down the Northern Central Railroad from Harrisburg to Baltimore. First Lieutenant Erasmus C. Gilbreath, Company I, recalled, "We drilled a great deal and worked ourselves into a fair state of discipline."[45] The Twentieth was particularly watchful of sabotage by Confederate sympathizers. Never having had the opportunity to fire its altered smoothbore muskets at anything more threatening than the trees, cows, barns and rocks around Cockeysville, the regiment was ready to get into battle and test its mettle.[46]

Three companies of the Twentieth Indiana were ordered to wait at Fort Monroe under the command of Lieutenant Colonel Charles D. Murray and meet up with the regiment at Hatteras after a few days.[47] These included both "rifle companies," Companies A and B, and a third, Company G, commanded by Captain Nathaniel Herron.[48] The baggage for the advance seven companies of the regiment was stowed, and due to the large number of troops to embark, there was the "usual delay." Finally, that evening, the *Spaulding* shoved off. As one Indiana soldier wrote that night aboard ship, "The paddles moved, and away we are, off into the enemy's rear, way down in Carolina."[49]

This experience of ocean travel was a new one for many of these Indianians. Regimental musician Jonathan H. Main wrote home to friends, "I thot [*sic*] when I got on board that I would like to be in a storm but before I got off I thot that I would rather not." For some, it was the first time they had ever seen the ocean. The calm of the night was only interrupted by the rhythmic rotation of the steamer's paddle wheel and the periodic explosion of practice artillery fired from Fort Monroe, back in the distance. Main marveled at the sights of the mid-Atlantic waters: "Schools of little fishes were circling about the surface of the water, porpoises plunging to and fro, flying fish darting around."[50]

Others of the Indiana regiment, however, had already experienced the thrill of ocean travel. Scottish-born immigrant Private Robert A. Inglis, a young man of sixteen, had already spent several years at sea, and had already experienced the dangers of Hatteras waters. One of Bob Inglis's earliest memories was standing on the veranda of the Globe Inn in West Cowes on the Isle of Wight. There, on August 22, 1851, Inglis, age six, watched the presentation of the Royal Yacht Squadron's "One Hundred Guinea Cup" to the winning racing yacht *America*, in the first race of what later became known as the "America's Cup."[51] In 1852, at age seven, Inglis and his family moved from the Isle of Wight to Philadelphia.[52] Inglis wrote later that his stepmother "found it pleasant to make things very unpleasant for me," and the following year Bob ran away to sea. In January 1861, Inglis, then fifteen, was working on a small "coasting schooner," which wrecked near Hatteras. Young Inglis made his own way north to Maryland, but things were "strained," he said, due to Lincoln's election. He watched a slave couple sold off, the man to one place and the woman to another. Making a comment, he was "termed a "D—D Abolishnest [*sic*]," and then soon left for Indiana to work in the fields, but instead joined Company C of the Twentieth Indiana.[53]

Similarly, Private Charles Henry White, of Captain George W. Geisendorf's Company H, went through the ordeal of a long ocean voyage while emigrating from Europe. Charles "Weidt" changed his name to "White" in April on his enlistment. Weidt's father had died just a year after Charles's 1838 birth in Mecklenburg, Germany, forcing the boy and his mother into a destitute existence in servitude to a nobleman there. In November 1856, however, Louisa Weidt with eighteen-year-old Charles exhausted her savings to get on a ship and find freedom in America. Mother and son worked for a LeRoy, New York farmer for over a year. Then in the summer of 1859, Charles Weidt, along with many other German immigrants, looked west to the wheat fields of Illinois. Working for an Oxford, Indiana farmer only weeks after the fall of Fort Sumter, Charles gave in to a surge of patriotism and was caught up in the winds of war.[54]

The *Spaulding* pushed on through the ocean swells and just after 8:00 p.m., moved past the Virginia capes, the shore gradually fading into the dark Atlantic night.[55] Private Edmund M.B. Hooker of Company H wrote in the moment, "The ship, as she plunges through the water, leaves long trails of light in her wake, caused by the phosphoric matter in the water."[56] With the soldiers strewn pell-mell about the deck, Sergeant Theodore M. Bartlett of Company I grew introspective. He wrote:

> *My sensations on finding myself really afloat on the great ocean were of a nature not easily described. The scenery around me, the crowded decks of the vessel, the distracted state of our once happy country which had been the occasion of my wanderings, and more than all, perhaps, anxiety for the welfare of the loved ones at home, furnished abundant material for thought and contemplation.*[57]

Clouds began to form, but starlight peeked through occasionally, reflecting off the swells. The moon had not yet risen. The ocean had not been churning, but the gentle ups and downs and to-and-fro rocking stirred the stomachs of quite a few young men. As the breezes picked up and the night sky showed a little more of a coming storm, the *Spaulding* pitched. By midnight, a full gale was blowing.[58] Sergeant Bartlett's stomach was unaffected, so he amused himself in the seasickness of his fellow soldiers:

> *They were spread out as thickly as they could lie, both above and below, while those who were compelled to relinquish the contents of their headbaskets, had to stumble over their prostrate companions to the side of the ship—the latter generally being too sick to remonstrate. I pitied the poor fellows, but could do nothing for them except to laugh at their miseries.*[59]

Winds became stiff, and a real danger of widespread seasickness showed before daybreak. The officers of the Twentieth holed up in the dining cabin until 4:30 a.m. Finally venturing on deck, they discovered that most of the men were deathly seasick and their conditions only getting worse. Thus the night of Thursday, September 26 passed, and as morning dawned, the ship continued to pitch so violently that moving about on deck was near to impossible except for the most experienced of the old tars on board: "The

Above: U.S. steamer *S.R. Spaulding*, Union troop transport. Drawing by Alfred R. Waud. *Library of Congress*.

Left: *Hatteras Light*. Drawing by Edwin Graves Champney. *Outer Banks History Center*.

spewing among the land-lubbers aboard was now really serious and many of the boys affirmed that they had vomited so hard as to throw up the pegs in the soles of their shoes." By 9:00 a.m., the 150-foot tower of the Hatteras Lighthouse showed itself on the cape, and the excitement onboard was running about as high as the breakers. A full-on gale had brewed, and things were getting quite nasty. It was all the Hoosiers on deck could do to keep from being swept overboard. It is said that "no beacons in the world excite stronger or more conflicting emotions in the breast of the mariner than the…flashing white light of Hatteras." But the Hatteras light was darkened, not flashing at all, its "first order" Fresnel lens having been spirited away mid-summer by the Rebels.[60]

Two large vessels came into view at the inlet, and the sailors told the men that they had just come alongside Forts Hatteras and Clark, captured recently from the Rebels. The storm brought waves breaking completely over the neck of sand separating the two forts. The *Spaulding*'s pilot knew his business and "entered the Inlet when it was a sheet of foam…the channel not to be distinguished." The captain of the Union tug USS *Ceres* later told Twentieth Indiana captain James M. Lytle of Company I that he had watched the *Spaulding* coming in for about two hours, expecting at any moment for the ship to come apart. Captain Lytle was informed that it was only the "experience and coolness" of the pilot of the *Spaulding* that saved the ship from "going to pieces." This was "one of the roughest passages ever encountered" by the *Spaulding*. Coastal residents, well acquainted with seasonal storms, said that of all the hurricanes experienced at that latitude, this was the most severe ever.[61]

Soon after the arrival of the *Spaulding*, the USS *Susquehanna* arrived and anchored just outside the bar, bringing with it two small captured prizes.[62] The *Susquehanna*, commanded by U.S. Navy captain John S. Chauncey, had been sitting outside the bar at Hatteras the day previous, intercepting vessels attempting to run the Union blockade, and had also witnessed the *Spaulding*'s arrival in the storm. In a report on his return the morning of the twenty-eighth, Chauncey described the angry nature of the hurricane the Hoosiers had survived the previous night:

> *Yesterday, a heavy gale springing up from the southeast making this a very exposed anchorage, I judged it prudent to proceed to sea during the violence of the gale. I remained on the inner edge of the Gulf Stream during last night, it blowing very heavy from southeast, and afterwards from the southward and westward, the gale being a rotary one. I was enabled*

to escape its violence by standing to the southward, while the gale was proceeding to northward and eastward. This morning, the weather having moderated, I returned to this anchorage.[63]

The *Spaulding* cleared the channel and anchored in the sound at 10:00 a.m.[64] In the safety of the Pamlico, a relieved Private Hooker noted, "Our ship headed for the breakers, just grazed the bar, and we are anchored abreast of Fort Hatteras, in the Inlet, just beyond a sandy point."[65] A group of soldiers found comfort in singing while the storm raged and the side-wheeler pushed itself across the bar. Their selection was "I'm But a Stranger Here," a favorite, new to their hymn books back home. Indeed, though many were immigrants of German, Swiss and British birth, the Hoosiers were all strangers there on the sandy shores of North Carolina's Outer Banks.

What though the tempests rage, Heaven is my home;
Short is my pilgrimage, Heaven is my home;
And time's wild, wintry blast, soon will be over, past,
I shall reach home at last—Heaven is my home.[66]

Fort Clark was but a few hundred yards from where the regiment anchored. The Indiana soldiers could see the "fort" and were not impressed, except to wonder how the breastwork could have withstood the recent two-day Federal bombardment that defeated the Confederates. The fortification was nothing more than sand covered with turf and a few guns mounted on top, without bombproof casements.[67]

The steam sloop USS *Pawnee* was also lying safe inside the bar, just eighty yards from Colonel Brown's troops in the *Spaulding*.[68] The *Pawnee*'s commander was fifty-two-year-old, Irish-born Stephen Clegg Rowan, a seasoned navy officer, veteran of the Mexican War and more recently, a participant in Major General Benjamin F. Butler's successful expedition to Hatteras. Rowan stood as the U.S. Navy commander of the inlet. Several smaller steamers and one or two man-of-wars also lay just outside the safety of the inlet.[69]

Colonel Brown went to shore in a launch just after 10:30 a.m. to obtain his orders. The colonel soon returned with another younger colonel from New York whom Captain Lytle quickly assessed to be a "very cool and deliberate man."[70]

Chapter Three

"To-night I Shall Start for Chicamacomico"

R ush Christopher Hawkins was the young and flamboyant colonel of
the Ninth New York Volunteers, also known as "Hawkins Zouaves."
Colonel Hawkins's regiment was "one of four Zouave regiments" originating
from the state of New York. Zouave regiments were styled after the French
light infantry units that fought in French North Africa and were easily
recognized by their uniforms: short open jacket, baggy trousers and fez.
Hawkins's men wore a dress uniform of "deep blue cloth with scarlet sash,
fez and trimmings."[71]

The Zouave colonel had turned thirty on September 14, only two weeks
before the *Spaulding*'s arrival, and had been placed in command at Hatteras
Inlet by Major General Benjamin F. Butler, who had steamed back north on
August 30 following his successful invasion.

A native of Pomfret, Windsor County, Vermont,[72] Rush Christopher
was the only son of Lorenzo Dow Hawkins and Maria Louisa Hutchinson.
The Hawkinses and the Hutchinsons were each regarded as a distinguished
"Old Family" of Pomfret.[73] The Hutchinsons had moved from their native
Connecticut to the "valley of the Upper Connecticut" on July 4, 1776. On
"that memorable day," the family moved to what became "the Hutchinson
farm," just "two miles from the court-house in Woodstock."[74]

Hawkins's paternal grandparents were native Rhode Islanders and,
like the Hutchinsons, were migrants to Pomfret in the mid-1770s. Dexter
Hawkins was among the first to sign the Freeman's Oath in April 1778
after Vermont had become an independent state. He served with Colonel

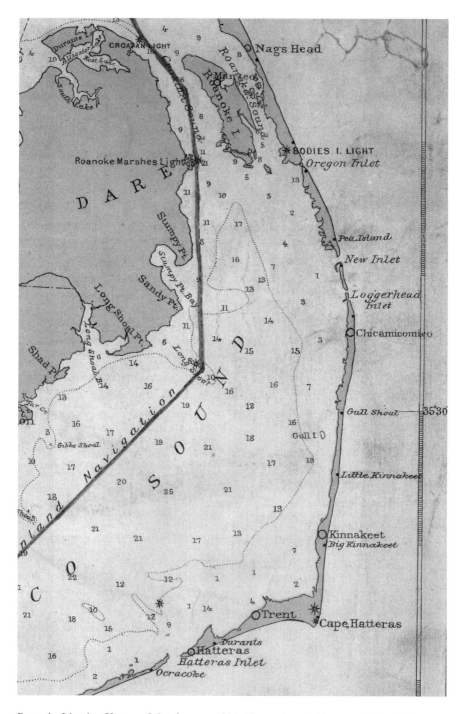

Roanoke Island to Hatteras Inlet, from an 1855 Albemarle and Chesapeake Canal Map. *Office of Coast Survey, NOAA.*

Archibald Crary's Regiment of the Rhode Island Brigade from 1777 to the close of the Revolutionary War. Dexter Hawkins's house "at the crotch of the roads," where young Rush spent his early years, was the "Saturday and Sunday halting-place for the old soldiers of Pomfret and several of the nearby towns." Veterans of the Revolutionary War and the War of 1812 among his relatives and other Pomfret locals stood out in Rush Hawkins's early childhood memories. Dexter Hawkins also served as Pomfret's Representative to the Vermont General Assembly from 1818 to 1821 and again in 1823. It appears Rush and his parents lived on Dexter Hawkins's farm until Lorenzo's unexpected death in 1840.[75]

Young Rush Hawkins was a voracious reader, his great-grandmother having taught him the alphabet and then to read by the age of six. Hawkins claimed to have read his first full book, *The Life of Sir William Wallace*, at the age of seven. Though Hawkins received a "scanty education" through the local school, by his early teens, he had read "all the things boys read," such as *Arabian Nights*, *Robinson Crusoe* and many of the English poets.[76]

A month before Rush's ninth birthday, his father died suddenly while away in St. Louis. Louisa Hawkins moved the family into the nearby Woodstock home of her grandmother's brother, former Vermont Supreme Court chief justice Titus Hutchinson. Judge Hutchinson's library "was the mecca for all the scholarly folk for miles around." From the age of nine, Rush enjoyed daily access to Uncle Titus Hutchinson's library, which only fed his appetite for fine books and literature.[77]

Judge Hutchinson was the son of Reverend Aaron Hutchinson. Reverend Hutchinson was a 1747 graduate of Yale College and was considered "one of the most learned men of his day," having earned advanced degrees from both Yale and Harvard and honorary degrees from Princeton and Dartmouth. Reverend Hutchinson "was a learned and accomplished classical scholar and the first Congregational clergyman to settle in the middle section of Eastern Vermont." Pastor of the Congregational churches in Pomfret, Hartford and Woodstock, Hutchinson's memory was so developed that "it was a saying that if the New Testament should be lost, he could repeat it in [entirety]."[78]

Judge Hutchinson's house on the square in Woodstock was more than simply a home to an extraordinary library. When Rush and his mother moved from Pomfret to Woodstock, the judge was becoming increasingly active in Vermont's anti-slavery movement and the early formation of the Liberty Party. Hutchison was Vermont's Liberty Party candidate for governor in 1841. In 1843, the former chief justice gave an address declaring slavery unconstitutional. The judge's home, while Hawkins lived there, was used as a station along the Underground Railroad. Beginning in the 1840s, escaped slaves from the South were concealed in the home after having been secreted through a hidden tunnel that ran from the Kedron Brook to beneath the Woodstock square and directly to Hutchinson's home.[79]

Young Rush Hawkins was particularly moved as a boy in the 1830s and 1840s by the summer parade "marchings of Captain Partridge and his cadets" through the streets of Pomfret. Alden Partridge, in 1819, founded the "American Literary, Scientific, and Military Academy," the nation's oldest private military college, at Norwich, Vermont (now Norwich University at Northfield, Vermont). "This was one of the summer events," Hawkins recalled, "which excited the boys and filled many among them with a desire to become soldiers."[80]

The boy's imagination was awakened by the pomp and the military display, particularly of Partridge's uniform. Hawkins, reminiscing a year before his death about the root of his military passion, wrote that "Captain Partridge with his wonderful, black varnished horse hide hat, adorned with a high plume of red, white and blue feathers—the whole so stiff and erect showing how completely it was fitting ending to a strong and upright man, earnest in all affairs and a true soldier."[81] The inspiration for Colonel Rush Hawkins's French North African–styled Zouave uniform and cap topped with a high white plume of feathers (as seen in the 1861 Mathew Brady photograph) was certainly Captain Alden Partridge.

Rush Hawkins, just shy of fifteen in September 1846, conspired with three other Pomfret-Woodstock boys to run away, enlist in the military and join the Mexican War. Hawkins and the other boys "began to hear and read about the fighting along the Rio Grande and some of the young men and boys of my native town who were mostly descendants from soldiers of the Revolution talked about going to war."[82] The other boys eventually backed out, but headstrong Hawkins, intending to enlist as a drummer, told the Boston recruiter he was eighteen and had the blessing of his parents. The recruiter, unconvinced, told him to "go home and grow up!" To shake off the rejection, Hawkins left the recruiting office, borrowed some finer clothes, had his likeness taken and sent the daguerreotype to his mother. By September 1848, at age seventeen, Hawkins had indeed grown. He went to the Boston recruiting office and was enlisted by Captain William Eustis under the name "Christopher R. Hawkins."[83] "Being a good horseman," Hawkins was mustered in and sent to Carlisle Barracks in Pennsylvania for a month, assigned to the Second Dragoons.[84]

The search to uncover Hawkins's true Mexican War service and his life before the Civil War is a difficult one. Hawkins, in his later years, looked back and gave his service only a brief nod, playing it down by stating that he "took to the field, lived under canvas, smelt burning powder, next year was discharged for disability, contracted in the service and never became a hero. But it was enough, the seed had been rooted and ever since I have loved the army." Elsewhere, Hawkins recorded, after training at Carlisle, the Second Dragoons went down to the Rio Grande. He said, without detail or elaboration, "I was in the army nine months. Then I was taken sick, very sick. I went to New Orleans and was sick there." Hawkins, indeed, spent only a couple months in the service. Zouave historian Matthew J. Graham has a correction to his book, by "Colonel Hawkins," which states that Hawkins "was not in the service until 1848, after active hostilities between the armies had ceased."[85]

Hawkins's own account is quite different from those that wished to distinguish him before the public early in his Civil War career. In some New York City newspapers, reports were released following Hawkins's successes at the Battle of Roanoke Island, in which he was said to have served in the same Mexican War unit as Major General George B. McClellan. The fabricated accounts revealed Hawkins had joined

> *the corps of Cadet Sappers and Miners, organized at West Point, and followed Gen. Scott from Vera Cruz to the city of Mexico. He was often under fire, and at the storming of the city (in the celebrated charge of a mile and a half across the causeway, at the head of which was a powerful battery raking the whole distance) he was wounded in the leg by a spent ball. This, however, did not prevent him from entering the city with the storming column.*[86]

Hawkins remained in New Orleans from Christmas 1848 until the Fourth of July 1851. Not much, if anything is known about those two and a half years, except what Hawkins tells: "It was my Red-Letter Day in Bohemia! I studied singing and music, I sang in the chorus supporting Jenny Lind and had one grand good time." Hawkins took part in a musical company of men, calling themselves the "Wandering Musicians" in which he sang and played cello. Hawkins admitted, "During those years I grew up."[87]

Rush Hawkins returned to Woodstock in 1851 and said, "My own mother did not know me. There was a great family council. What should be done with me? I had been floating around so long, dangling between heaven and earth without getting anywhere. What should be done with me?"[88]

It was decided Hawkins should move to New York City and make a go at becoming a merchant. Attempts at selling dry goods failed miserably, ending with Hawkins punching his boss in the nose. Hawkins then began studying law. His great-uncle, Judge Titus Hutchinson in Woodstock, "the leading abolitionist of the community," wrote Hawkins a letter of introduction to Horace Greeley. Hawkins recalled Greeley saying to him, flatly, "'There is no room for you here. New York is overcrowded. Go West, young man.' And I went West." Hawkins traveled two years as a debt collector in Chicago and St. Louis and throughout the Midwest.[89]

Hawkins finally returned to New York and began working for his cousin's law firm. That same year, 1855, Hawkins started "attending book sales, buying chiefly American history and Elizabethan drama." At the age of twenty-four, Rush Hawkins purchased his first "fifteener" at a Nassau Street bookshop in New York City. "Fifteeners," in the language of book collecting, are books printed prior to 1501 and are early examples from the first presses with moveable type.[90]

Colonel Hawkins, the young adventurer, lawyer and erudite book collector in private life, settled in and made New York his home. In June 1860, he married Annmary Brown. Raised and educated in Rome and Geneva, Annmary was the daughter of the former U.S. consul-general to Rome and granddaughter of Nicholas Brown II, the man for whom Brown University is named.

In July 1860, the "Hawkins Zouaves" was first "formed as a company with its namesake as its leading spirit; and, before the first year of [Rush and Annmary's] married life had passed, Civil War had broken out and the Zouaves had been mustered into service." On April 15, 1861, President Abraham Lincoln issued Proclamation 80, which called forth the militias of the Union states—totaling seventy-five thousand troops—to put down the rebellion of the Confederacy and, as a first service, "repossess the forts, places, and property which have been seized from the Union." Rush Hawkins left New York for Albany at 11:30 p.m. It is often told that "he appeared at the governor's office so early the next morning that he was the first New York citizen to offer himself or a company to the Union." The company of Zouaves became "the nucleus of a regiment, and the leader was appointed colonel."[91]

The Hawkins Zouaves were at Newport News on August 25, 1861, when "Special Order No. 13" was issued by General Wool from Fort Monroe explaining Major General Ben Butler's plans to "prepare eight hundred and sixty troops for an expedition to Hatteras Inlet, North Carolina, to go with Commodore Stringham, commanding home squadron, to capture several batteries in that neighborhood." The "batteries" to be captured were Forts

Hatteras and Clark, the control of which allowed the Rebels to hold Hatteras Inlet and thus the inland waterways of coastal North Carolina.[92]

Known in the newspapers of the day as the "Butler Expedition," the combined operation of the Union army and navy was under the command of both Butler and Commodore Silas H. Stringham of the U.S. Navy Atlantic Blockading Squadron. The vessels of the U.S. Navy involved were: the USS *Minnesota* (Commodore Stringham's flagship), the USS *Wabash*, the USS *Cumberland*, the USS *Monticello*, the USS *Susquehanna* and the USS *Pawnee*. The U.S. Revenue Service cutter *Harriett Lane* and the U.S. Army armed tug *Fanny* also participated, the latter as Butler's army flagship. U.S. Army forces included 500 soldiers of the Twentieth New York Infantry Regiment under Colonel Max Weber; 220 Zouaves from Companies C, G and H of the Ninth New York Volunteer Infantry; roughly 100 men of the Naval Brigade; and the balance were officers and men of Company B of the U.S. Second Artillery. This totaled approximately 880 ground forces.[93]

The expedition left for Hatteras Banks on August 26, with Colonel Hawkins and his three companies aboard a transport, arriving off the forts the morning of the twenty-seventh. The Zouaves attempted a perilous landing in the surf from the transports along with the Twentieth New York, though only 345 men of the 860 troops made it to shore. These included sixty-eight men of the Ninth New York Company G, with their captain Edward Jardine, and a portion of the Twentieth New York Infantry. Meanwhile Commodore Stringham was "hotly engaging the forts" using "a system of attack peculiarly his own." Stringham kept his vessels in motion while discharging broadsides when abreast of Forts Hatteras and Clark. Captain Jardine took command of the vulnerable force that had made the landing. The following day, August 29, the Confederate command, under Flag Officer Samuel Barron, accepted Butler's terms of surrender onboard his flagship, the U.S. transport *Fanny*, and later formally signed those articles of capitulation aboard Stringham's flagship, the USS *Minnesota*. Remarkably, there were no Union deaths, despite the poorly executed amphibious assault, the first of the Civil War. Captured were "715 prisoners, 1,000 stand of arms, 30 pieces of cannon."[94]

Colonel Hawkins, having finally landed all 220 Zouaves of Companies C, G and H, along with the other land forces of the expedition, "by virtue of rank…assumed command of the land forces at Hatteras on August 30th, making his headquarters at Fort Clark, while Colonel Max Weber, with part of the 20th New York, was stationed at Fort Hatteras."[95] Butler returned north that day to carry news of the success to Washington. That afternoon,

Hawkins later related, a delegation of Hatteras citizens "waited upon me, and placed in my hand a paper, a copy of which is herewith inclosed [*sic*]":

To the COMMANDER OF THE FEDERAL FORCES AT HATTERAS INLET:

DEAR SIR: We, the citizens of Cape Hatteras, do ask of your honor that you will allow us to return to our homes and property and protect us in the same as natural citizens, as we have never taken up arms against your Government, nor has it been our wish to do so. We did not help by our votes to get North Carolina out of the Union. Believing that your clemency will not allow you to treat us as rebels, who have always been loyal citizens, we do earnestly request, for the sake of our women and children, that you will comply with our wishes, as we seek protection from your honor.
Yours, very respectfully,

CITIZENS OF HATTERAS.

P. S.—Please let us know by the bearer what we can depend upon.[96]

Hawkins reported on September 7 that he "agreed verbally to give them all the necessary protection against the vigilance committees which infest all parts of the State, and are organized for the purpose of suppressing Union sentiments and pressing men into the service of the Confederate Army, and to afford them such other protection as may appear necessary." Colonel Hawkins began creating an atmosphere of friendship and trust with the native islanders. Nearly all the males took the oath of allegiance within ten days of the Union occupation. A number of these men were willing to act as Federal spies and carry information about Rebel movements from the mainland back to Hatteras. The colonel expressed to Wool that he was "over-anxious" about putting into action his plan for the protection of the loyal inhabitants on the Outer Banks. Hawkins also seemed to be aware within the first week of his command that Wool was making plans to send a general officer south to take command at Hatteras, and thus, someone less concerned than he would derail his campaign for the welfare of the Bankers. Hawkins requested, "that I may be allowed to continue in the work which I have commenced. These people who look to me for protection I have already taken a very deep interest in; I sympathize with them in their misfortunes, and would do anything for them in my power. I fear that if I am superseded the promises I have made will not be carried out, and that the measures I have commenced will fall to the ground."[97]

Hawkins was quickly convinced that the Confederates had retreated to Roanoke Island, fortifying it with the intention of launching an immediate offensive against Hatteras. He foresaw an amphibious landing at the north of the island near Chicamacomico as the Confederates' first objective. This would be followed by a march south some twenty-five miles, culminating in the destruction of the Hatteras Lighthouse.[98] Hawkins believed Confederate command of the Croatan Channel, the link between the Pamlico and Albemarle Sounds, was a clear and present danger to Union control of the Hatteras Inlet and traffic in and around Pamlico Sound. Hawkins from the first days of his command at Hatteras was concerned about how slow the government was in following up on the success of Butler's expedition. The young colonel complained to and even instructed the veteran Wool, "The ball moves too slowly; one success should follow another in quick succession."[99]

So-called "intelligent contraband" had informed Hawkins of Rebel gunboat movements up and down the Pamlico, beginning within the first week of Union occupation at Hatteras. These black "contraband" informants—escaped or liberated slaves who had attached themselves to Union regiments—served whatever role most significant to the Federal cause. So persuaded was Hawkins of an imminent assault that he sent a September 7 report to Wool suggesting immediate action.[100]

Major General Butler, immediately following his report to Lincoln at Washington, informed Wool "by a unanimous vote the Cabinet approved of holding the forts at Hatteras."[101] Late the night before that cabinet meeting, Butler entered Washington, arriving at the president's house after 1:00 a.m. Together with Assistant Secretary of the Navy Gustavus V. Fox, Butler woke Lincoln. The president, as Butler retold the story, came out in his nightshirt to receive the news of the Butler's victory at Hatteras on August 28 and 29. Being that it was the first real success of the Union in the war, emotions were high, and Butler recounted:

> *Everybody knows how tall Lincoln was, and he seemed very much taller in that garment; and Fox was about five feet nothing. In a few hurried words, without waiting for any forms or ceremonies, Fox communicated the news, and then he and Lincoln fell into each other's arms. That is, Fox put his arms around Lincoln about as high as his hips, and Lincoln reached down over him so that his arms were pretty near the floor apparently, and thus holding each other they flew around the room once or twice, and the night*

shirt was considerably agitated. The commanding general was entirely overcome by the scene, and lying back on the sofa roared with the most irresistible Merriment.[102]

Concerning the administration's decision to hold Hatteras Inlet, a response from General Wool to Secretary of War Simon Cameron, dated September 4, was again personally delivered by Butler in which Wool stated that only 812 Union "rank and file" were at the inlet following the August 29 surrender of Forts Hatteras and Clark. Wool was not familiar with Colonel Hawkins and noted, "How well they are commanded, being volunteers, I am unable to say, from the circumstance that I have not been long enough acquainted with the officers to pronounce upon their ability or efficiency to command." Wool needed Secretary Cameron's "views" on how to keep and defend the inlet. More troops would be necessary, and more first-rate, light-draft steamers would also be required. If the inlet was to be held, though, Wool opined, certainly "it will depend on the Navy." Cameron, without delay, gave a definitive decision to Wool the following day, stating, "Your letter of September 4 is received. The position at Cape Hatteras must be held, and you will adopt such measures, in connection with the Navy Department, as may be necessary to effect the object. Your letter has been referred to the Commander-in-Chief, who will give detailed instructions."[103]

Hawkins, meanwhile, continued chasing his obsession with convincing General Wool of the "importance and necessity of immediate action." He needed Wool's agreement and wanted the general to convince the Lincoln administration to authorize immediate preemptive action in the face of the obvious aggressive intentions of the Rebels occupying Roanoke Island. Hawkins's September 7 report to Wool laid down five proposed counter movements: occupy Roanoke Island at once; station a small force at Beacon Island that commands the mouth of Ocracoke Inlet; shut out all commercial traffic with New Bern and Washington, North Carolina, by stationing two or three light-draft steamers between the Neuse and Pamlico Rivers; station a minimum of eight light-draft gunboats in the Pamlico Sound; and occupy Beaufort as soon as possible. The report further states that "seven thousand men judiciously placed upon the soil of North Carolina would, within the next three weeks, draw 20,000 Confederate troops from the State of Virginia." Hawkins's report was not received by Wool until September 13, along with another September 11 report. Wool forwarded these reports the same day to Lieutenant General Winfield Scott with his own request for more troops for Forts Monroe and Hatteras and an artillery officer for

Hatteras. Wool also noted the recall from Hatteras of the five hundred men of the troublesome Twentieth New York under Colonel Max Weber.[104]

General Wool's early plan to supersede Colonel Hawkins's command at Hatteras Inlet with a general officer immediately after the Hatteras Invasion was revealed in a *New York Times* report from Fort Monroe dated September 8 but appearing in print on September 13.[105] That same day, September 13, Wool reported to Lieutenant General Scott that Brigadier General John Fulton Reynolds was ordered to Hatteras to take command. Wool was preparing to send Reynolds south, in fact, the following day, September 14, along with the two remaining Hawkins Zouaves companies under Major Edgar Kimball. Little did Wool know that on September 12, headquarters had called Reynolds back to the Army of the Potomac, orders Wool received only hours before Reynolds was to board a steamer at Fort Monroe en route for the Outer Banks.[106]

General Wool could not delay increasing troop levels at Hatteras Inlet and so, without waiting for specific orders, took the initiative, sending Hawkins five of the remaining seven companies of the Ninth New York, under command of Lieutenant Colonel George F. Betts. The troops arrived at the inlet on September 10. Companies B and K, however, remained behind at Newport News with Major Edgar A. Kimball.[107] The five companies of Hawkins Zouaves under Colonel Betts rejoined the detachment of their fighting Zouave brethren who had served gallantly to take Hatteras Island back from the Confederacy. The New York Ninth could once again shout its motto with a united and reinforced confidence: *Toujours pret!* (always ready).[108]

The companies' arrival came at a perfect time. Hawkins needed "an advance post, for the purpose of checking any approach of the enemy by land." Therefore, soon after Betts's arrival, Hawkins created another encampment only two miles north of Fort Clark on the sound side. Sending four companies with Betts, Hawkins named the encampment Camp Wool in honor of the "old General." Zouave pickets were thrown out north, extending Hawkins's view another two miles beyond the new encampment. By September 19, Hawkins reported the increased Federal strength on Hatteras to be 946 officers and men.[109]

General Wool also sent a single company of the First U.S. Artillery, Battery C, commanded by Captain Lewis O. Morris to Hatteras. Morris, a fourteen-year veteran, was not a West Point graduate but, coming from a military family, had received an army commission. (His father had been killed in the siege of Monterey during the Mexican War.)[110] Captain Morris also served during the closing months of the Mexican War; however, he

Major Edgar A. Kimball, Ninth New York (Hawkins Zouaves). Kimball seated in carriage in this rare shot taken either at Newport News, Hatteras or Roanoke Island, 1861–2. *Dennis C. Schurr Collection.*

never served in battle, reaching his regiment at Vera Cruz just as it was moving out of Mexico.[111]

Rush Hawkins attempted a second time to drive home the urgency of his counter-offensive strategy on September 17, describing the industry of the Confederates immediately following the Union capture of Fort Hatteras. The Confederates, Hawkins explained, had mustered a large number of troops on Roanoke Island, troops that had been busy mounting seventeen heavy artillery pieces. In addition, they had obstructed the Pamlico and Neuse Rivers to prevent Union advances on New Bern and Washington, North Carolina. During this same period, Fort Macon had been strengthened with additional heavy guns. Hawkins was sensing the shifting balance of power over the Pamlico Sound and again urged the recommendations made in his earlier September 7 report to Wool, an immediate response and additional troops to reinforce the inadequate Union presence on Hatteras.[112]

General Wool strongly approved Hawkins's plan and forwarded Hawkins's communiqués of September 17 and 21 to Winfield Scott on September 22.[113] Wool informed Winfield Scott that two companies were available for Hatteras, but he would wait for Scott's response to Hawkins's reports. General Wool had been short on troops at Fort Monroe since sending additional forces earlier to Hawkins and had already written a letter directly to President Lincoln, explaining he had hoped to send more troops to Hatteras but had not been able to do so. Winfield Scott responded very quickly as is indicated by Assistant Secretary of War Thomas Scott's September 24 memo, which stated, "Two regiments leave Baltimore for Fort Monroe September 24, p.m. The Navy Department, I presume, will furnish boats as desired."[114] One of those two regiments was the Twentieth Indiana, headquartered at Cockeysville, Maryland.

On the evening of September 21, at Cockeysville, Adjutant Israel N. Stiles was animated, calling the full Twentieth regiment to dress parade. The adjutant read Scott's orders "in a voice clear and piercing as a bell," for the regiment to report to Fort Monroe for movement south:

> *This regiment is now under orders to march immediately. The good name already acquired by this regiment will be to each one, officer and man, a stimulus, until we exceed in all that is glorious in arms—until this accursed rebellion is wiped away, and our beloved country again smiles in the happiness, the prosperity, and blessings of peace.*[115]

Colonel Hawkins's successes with the loyal citizens on Hatteras and the support of the "old General" for his Hatteras defense plans "won a handsome reputation" for him back in Newport News and Fort Monroe. Ninth New York major Edgar Kimball wrote to Hawkins from Newport News, congratulating him on his progress since taking command: "If reports are all true, I'll soon have the pleasure of addressing you as Brigadier instead of Col...which those who know you—know you deserve—& believe me none will be more happy to congratulate you than your humble servant."[116]

"Two fugitive apprentices" visited Hawkins on the morning of September 21. They had lived with Samuel Jarvis on Roanoke Island for eight years and were well known by some of the Hatteras locals. Jarvis, "an ardent secessionist," had been talking openly to his family the previous few days in front of his servants. Jarvis, they said, had frequent contact with the colonel of the Georgia regiment on Roanoke Island and was privy to a plan of attack by the Rebels on Hatteras Island. It seems one of these apprentices from Roanoke Island was a relative of a Hatteras man who had taken an oath of allegiance and had become a Union informant. Hawkins's suspicions of an imminent attack were finally validated.[117]

A Rebel assault was imminent, according to the informants. They said there were at that time

1,500 troops on the island: 1,400 Georgians and 100 North Carolinians. The latter were formerly at Oregon Inlet. One thousand more North Carolina troops were to land there yesterday [September 20] from Norfolk, and more are expected every day, until their whole number will amount to 8,000; then they are to land, hang the people who have taken the oath of allegiance, blow up the light-house, and retake the forts.[118]

Hawkins knew the Confederates had accumulated some six or seven shallow-draft tugs and a sufficient number of flatboats and barges to make a successful amphibious landing. The colonel argued such a landing could succeed only at Chicamacomico, the northernmost village on Hatteras, which sat just below Loggerhead Inlet. Hawkins made immediate preparations to defend the site and its loyal people:

To-night I shall start for Chicamacomico for the purpose of selecting a suitable ground for a camp, after which I shall return and send up all the force I have to spare, with two pieces of artillery. This force will be encamped there permanently, unless otherwise ordered by yourself. I know that there is great objection to separating so small a command as mine, but these people, who have taken the oath of allegiance, must be protected, though at the cost of every life under my command. What may not be said of a government which is too weak or unwilling to protect its own loyal subjects against its own rebels?...I hope you will send me at least 1,000 men within the next four or five days, and one or two rifled guns, if you have them to spare.[119]

Colonel Hawkins knew he could not act soon enough to prevent a Rebel landing. His intentions were ultimately twofold: protect the loyal natives who had taken an oath of allegiance and prevent the surprise of a large troop landing and their subsequent march down the island.[120] Hawkins needed the force of a regiment placed at Chicamacomico as soon as possible in order to bring his intentions into reality. The colonel was unaware at that time that the Twentieth Indiana had received orders that same day in Cockeysville, orders that would fortunately send them to Hatteras within one week.

While Colonel Hawkins prepared for the anticipated Confederate attack, U.S. Navy commander Stephen Rowan was also taking decisive measures to prevent a Rebel foothold in the Pamlico and along the adjacent waterways. He sent his own detailed report to the secretary of the navy, Gideon Welles, dated September 20. Rowan reported on the various Rebel defenses being erected in the region of Hatteras Island and the Pamlico Sound. He reported that Colonel Rush Hawkins had informed him on September 14, that the Confederates were carrying away the abandoned Rebel guns from Fort Ocracoke on Beacon Island, located at Ocracoke Inlet. In an effort to prevent farther movement of the artillery but without any small U.S. Navy steamers of light draft at his disposal, Rowan had requested from Colonel Hawkins use, for the first time, of "a small steamer belonging to the quartermaster's department." This "small steamer" was the *Fanny*. Together with a launch from the USS *Pawnee* on September 16 the *Fanny* steamed to Beacon Island under command of regular navy lieutenants James G. Maxwell and Thomas Henderson Eastman to prevent the Confederates from carrying off the guns. Maxwell and Eastman were to destroy whatever guns remained. The Naval Brigade also assisted, having remained at the inlet since the invasion. Then, after raising the stars and stripes above Fort Ocracoke, Maxwell and Eastman saw to it that the twenty-two naval guns there were "broken" and the fort left in ruins.[121]

The U.S. Army transport *Fanny* had gained fame as Butler's army "flagship" during the Hatteras Invasion, though it was ridiculed by a *Boston Journal* correspondent who wrote that the *Fanny* rolled "about like a tub" during the invasion. The *Fanny*, formerly the civilian steamer *Philip T. Heartt*, was an iron-hulled barge built in 1845 in Philadelphia to run the Chesapeake and Delaware Canal between Philadelphia and Baltimore,[122] It was converted to a propeller steamer of 145 tons, 115 feet long and 18 feet wide in 1860. A $100-a-day U.S. Army quartermaster charter, it had been under command of U.S. Navy lieutenant Peirce Crosby since early August, before and during the invasion and then shortly thereafter.

Gideon Welles, U.S. secretary of the navy. *Library of Congress.*

Left: Commander Stephen C. Rowan, United States Navy. *Library of Congress.*

Below: USS *Pawnee. U.S. Naval Historical Center.*

The identity of the U.S. gunboat *Fanny* has not always been clear. About July 1, navy lieutenant Peirce Crosby went to Philadelphia on behalf of the army quartermaster and chartered a steamer, then named *Fanny*, from the Philadelphia Transportation Company. The services of civilian Captain John H. Morrison of Brooklyn, New York, and his civilian crew of five were included as part of the charter agreement and traveled with the steamer from the beginning. On the arrival of that chartered steamer, named *Fanny*, at Fort Monroe, it was hastily armed as a gunboat with two brass rifled guns, one six-pounder James gun and one nine-pounder Sawyer rifled cannon.[123]

Soon afterward, the gunboat gained some prestige in various expeditions of the Eastern Shore of Virginia and as the August 3 carrier of aeronaut John LaMountain's reconnaissance balloon at Hampton Roads. In early August, however, the steamer was disabled and her crew transferred to the steamer *Philip T. Heartt* along with the sign bearing the original steamer's name, *Fanny*, which had been on her stern. Therefore, the U.S. gunboat *Fanny*, which was Butler's flagship at the Hatteras Invasion (and which would be captured in the Pamlico Sound later), was not the same tug (though named *Fanny*) used by LaMountain on August 3, and called history's "first aircraft carrier." The "original" *Fanny*, after repairs, took on the name "*H. Burden*" and began running between Annapolis and Baltimore.

Ominous reports of expected Rebel assaults at various places on the island were on the increase. Rowan, at one point, was given information by Colonel Hawkins that an attack was to occur the night of September 20. Rowan explained the situation in his report to Welles, written earlier on the day of the supposed attack. The Confederates, Rowan explained, were expected to move down from Roanoke and Oregon Inlet by land and make a night attack. Rowan, wanting to make a concerted defense with Hawkins, asked him for permission to use the *Fanny* again as a gunboat, as he had a few days earlier at Beacon Island. Rowan planned to arm and equip the tug and a launch, preparing them to skirt the beach and "open fire" in case of an attack.[124] Hawkins also informed Wool in his September 19 report, "I shall meet the rebels when they attempt to land with a force of 700 on shore, and the steamer *Fanny*, with three ship's launches, on the water, carrying 200 men and five guns."[125]

Captain John Chauncey of the *Susquehanna* also reported to Flag Officer Stringham on September 20, referencing discussions he had had with both Hawkins and Rowan concerning defending Hatteras from this probable attack from Roanoke Island. Chauncey related that both he and Rowan had been alerted by Hawkins concerning news of an imminent attack on the village of Chicamacomico and a Rebel plan to march south and destroy the tower of the already darkened Hatteras Lighthouse. Chauncey's recommendation, like Rowan's, was an immediate combined operation of army and navy forces at the inlet, but Chauncey suggested proceeding to Stumpy Point. Stumpy Point was on the western shore of the Pamlico but north of Chicamacomico about twelve miles. Chauncey's plan was to wait and surprise the Confederate squadron and its landing craft from behind as it attempted an assault on Chicamacomico, destroying all Rebel craft loaded with troops before they landed. Chauncey suggested Hawkins also place one company at Hatteras Lighthouse along with a howitzer for defense. In addition, Chauncey had located appropriate anchorage inside Hatteras Cove for support vessels.[126] This feared Rebel attack on the night of September 20 never materialized.

Rowan also laid out in his September 20 report to the navy secretary the strategic importance of a Union-held Roanoke Island. He stressed that it was "the key to Norfolk" and with it the government would command Albemarle Sound, the Neuse and Pamlico Rivers and make a hold on Hatteras Inlet a much easier task. A proper defense, Rowan concluded, would require several well-armed, light-draft gunboats of five feet and under and a couple not over seven feet draft for use inside and outside the Sound.[127] Gideon Welles later only gave a passing formal acknowledgement of Rowan's concern about Roanoke Island and maintaining Union command of the coastal waterways inside the Outer Banks. This acknowledgement was communicated in a September 25 commendation letter from Welles. The navy secretary was giving a nod for a job well done in destroying Fort Ocracoke. But in reference to Rowan's strategic concerns, Welles only remarked that Commander Rowan's communiqué had been "received and read with interest."[128] Secretary Welles later, in a brief memo well circulated in the newspapers, categorically denied any recollection of or familiarity with the navy's employment of the army transport *Fanny* for these combined operations.[129] Rowan was unaware that two days earlier Welles had already increased the number of shallow-draft steamers available to his squadron.

Prior to Rowan's report, Gideon Welles had ordered an increase to the number of steamers and tugs at Hatteras by four. On September 18, Welles sent word to Rowan that two steamers and the two tugs *Ceres* and *General Putnam* had been ordered to join his squadron at Hatteras Inlet.[130] The *Ceres* and *General Putnam* were both assigned to the Atlantic Blockading Squadron that day. It would be the incoming flag officer's duty, though, to assign those tugs to Hatteras. Welles's order, which also included an additional two tugs for the Pamlico Sound, would buoy Hawkins's hopes of being able to fulfill his promises of protecting the island and its loyal citizens.

The navy tugs USS *Ceres* and USS *General William G. Putnam* arrived at the inlet just a few days ahead of the Twentieth Indiana Regiment: the *General Putnam* on Monday, September 23, and the *Ceres* on Thursday, September 26. Commodore Goldsborough, the incoming flag officer, on September 23, the day he took command of the Atlantic Blockading Squadron, gave orders to Acting Master Jared L. Elliott to proceed with the USS *Ceres* from Hampton Roads to Hatteras Inlet. Elliott, in command of the *Ceres*, was to report "to the senior naval officer for such duty as he may require of you." Commander Rowan was not satisfied, though, with the gunboats. The small wooden tugs were, in his words, "wretchedly fitted out and the *Ceres* is not half manned."[131]

The USS *Ceres* was built as a side-wheel merchant steamer at Keyport, New Jersey, in 1856. The wooden-hulled, 150-ton tug was 108 feet long and 22 feet wide, with a shallow draft of just over 6 feet and a top speed of about nine knots. Newly acquired by the navy on September 11, the *Ceres* was ordered to report to the Atlantic Blockading Squadron on September 18 and to Hatteras on September 23. The USS *General Putnam was* a 149 ton wooden-hull tug. This side-wheel steamer was built in 1857 at Brooklyn, New York, as a civilian tug under the original name *William G. Putnam*. The Union navy purchased the steamer in July 1861, renaming it *General Putnam*, often called simply "*Putnam*." The *Putnam* was 149 tons and smaller than the *Ceres*, only 103 feet 6 inches in length. At 22 feet wide, *Putnam* had a draft just over 7 feet and cruised at seven knots.[132]

Immediately on the arrival of the *General Putnam*, Rowan sent out navy lieutenant Thomas Eastman with the tug on a reconnaissance of Ocracoke Inlet on Tuesday, September 24. Eastman reported the fort was still smoldering, a week after being set ablaze, and all was quiet. The Rebels had arrived the day after the destruction of Fort Ocracoke and its guns and had taken away the anchor chain from the destroyed lightship when they could find nothing else to salvage.[133]

On Friday, September 27, Colonel Rush Hawkins, along with Twentieth Indiana Colonel William Brown, boarded the *Spaulding*, still at anchor in Hatteras Inlet, carrying with him a certain "characteristic pomposity."[134] Most people detected it immediately. Prior to giving Colonel Brown his orders in orientation with the officers of the Twentieth, the colonel passionately communicated the cruelties expressed by the Rebels toward the Union-loving natives of Hatteras and the Pamlico's western shore. Hawkins related a galling account of an old War of 1812 veteran named John Sadler who hoisted the stars and stripes over his house at Swan Quarter, at the mouth of the Pamlico River. Ignoring Sadler's past service, a "committee called on him and arrested him, shaved his

head, and absolutely tarred and feathered the poor old man."[135]

Hawkins's orders for Colonel Brown would send the Twentieth Indiana up the Pamlico Sound the following day to "Loggerhead Inlet," where it was to erect fortifications necessary for the defense of the island.[136] The orders were then communicated to the ranks of the regiment, who were told they would not land there at Hatteras Inlet. Instead, they would run up the Pamlico Sound some forty miles and throw up a new fort, or battery, "to prevent pirates and privateers from running into the Sound, and thus escaping from Uncle Sam's cruisers."[137]

The *Spaulding*, which carried the Twentieth Indiana to Hatteras from Fort Monroe, provided regular transport between Fort Monroe and points south. A much lighter craft, though, would have to be acquired to transport the Hoosier regiment to their new station at Chicamacomico at the north end of the Pamlico Sound. At the time the regiment received its orders north to

Top: Colonel William Lyons Brown, Twentieth Indiana. *Craig Dunn Collection.*

Left: Major General John Ellis Wool, commanding U.S. Army Department of Virginia at Fort Monroe. *Library of Congress.*

Colonel Rush Christopher Hawkins, Ninth New York (Hawkins Zouaves). *Library of Congress.*

Loggerhead Inlet, however, high winds from the tail end of the gale rendered it unsafe for the smaller steamers and flatboats to be brought out to transfer the troops and equipment.[138] The transfer of baggage from the *Spaulding* would have to wait until later that Friday, September 27 evening, and the transport of the Indiana regiment to Chicamacomico, below Loggerhead, would have to wait yet another day.

Chapter Four

"We Feel As If We Stand upon Our Native Soil of the Union"

Three armed steamers—the *Fanny*, *Ceres* and *General Putnam*—were brought alongside the *Spaulding*, late the night of the twenty-seventh, and the majority of the Twentieth's baggage was transferred. At midnight, the troops were safely transferred from the *Spaulding* to the shallow draft steamers, except seventy-five men who were loaded on launches towed behind the tugs. At noon on Saturday, with only two days' rations and a few tents for the short term, the flotilla was out of sight, steaming northeast inside the Pamlico Sound toward Chicamacomico.[139]

More than thirty of the Twentieth Indiana, under the charge of Quartermaster Isaac W. Hart, remained aboard the *Spaulding*, however, to keep watch over the remaining baggage, quartermaster goods and commissary stores.[140] They would catch up with the regiment in a few days. This detachment included, in addition to the quartermaster, one sergeant, two corporals, twenty-four privates and four citizens attached to the regiment from Indiana, Maryland and Pennsylvania. A commissary captain brought the number to thirty-three officers, men and citizens.

The three gunboats bearing the bulk of the Indiana regiment and their baggage arrived south of Loggerhead Inlet at dusk on Saturday, September 28. The day had been "delightful; the sound was as smooth and bright as a mirror." Captain James M. Lytle remarked, "Never saw Colonel Brown more animated." With the Pamlico Sound being quite shallow along much of the island, the steamers anchored more than two miles from the beach in little more than seven feet of water. Colonel Brown, Colonel Hawkins,

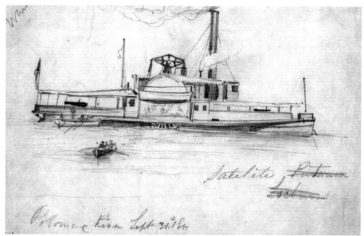

Major Benjamin H. Smith and Adjutant Stiles hastily took a "lighter," and headed to shore. The regimental band, traveling together in the forward steamer, played "Yankee Doodle" by order of Colonel Hawkins, assuring the loyal Bankers this was a Federal landing party. The Twentieth, excited by the reality of getting onto the field of action, gave their colonel three cheers and "pronounced him a brick." One private remarked that the Twentieth "is the 1st Indiana regiment that has penetrated so far south, and we feel as if we stand upon our native soil of the Union."[141]

There were Hatteras men fishing along the sound where the regiment was preparing to land. Thinking the Indiana troops were Confederate soldiers, the weatherworn natives turned and ran, then waved small white "flags of truce" from the safety of the live oak. Brown immediately sent out a reconnaissance party with a detailed map of the area surrounding Chicamacomico. The group soon returned, having located the village of Chicamacomico with little difficulty due to the cartographers' decision to "give [it] almost as large a place on the map as it occupies on the sand." "Chicamacomico" is a Coastal Algonquin, or Croatan Indian, word meaning "place swept over." Many say in the native Croatan tongue it means "place of sinking down sand." Not surprisingly then, pointing to the native references in the word, today "geologists recognize the site as an ancient overwash inlet—meaning the ocean has previously broken and separated the island in the exact location of Chicamacomico…this area experiences some of the worst storm surge, erosion and flooding with each passing storm."[142]

Leaving Hawkins on shore, Colonel Brown returned to the gunboats and by 10:00 p.m. commenced the landing of men and equipment. Brown decided the regiment would land on launches, seventy-five men to each. The process of landing some 550 men after dusk in this manner was an especially slow one, as the "distance at which the steamers lay from the shore [made] discharging a cargo off this landing a tedious business." However, "the boys went at it with a will." In the shallow sound, the launches could come within only a few hundred yards of the beach. The men found themselves jumping in, taking the baggage on their backs and wading the remaining distance to

Opposite, top: USS *Ceres*. From larger drawing including the USS *Susquehanna* by Alfred R. Waud. *Library of Congress*.

Opposite, middle: USS *General Putnam*. Mislabeled "USS *Satellite*." The *Satellite* was the identical sister to the *Putnam*. Drawing by Alfred R. Waud. *Library of Congress*.

Opposite, bottom: U.S. gunboat *Fanny*. Drawing by Alfred R. Waud. *Library of Congress*.

shore. It became a game, and the soldiers cheered as they trudged through the Pamlico mud throughout the night. At 8:00 a.m. on Sunday, September 29, the regiment had made it on shore, safely and without incident.[143]

The Twentieth Indiana encampment was quickly named Camp Live Oak, evidenced by their letters written the first day or two of arrival. A small wooden windmill at the site ground corn for the islanders and "slightly broke the dead level landscape." There was a twenty-acre thick of pine trees providing shade from the hot coastal sun. Grapes, persimmons and figs also grew in vast quantities. Green grass covered the "soil of fair quality," and potable water was abundant, making this an enviable location compared to those of Forts Hatteras and Clark to the south.[144]

How different were the Hoosiers' impressions of Hatteras from those of the Hawkins Zouaves. Ninth New York Sergeant Augustus Dusenberry of Company C wrote from Fort Clark, complaining, "The Fort is built upon a peninsula of sand, mosquitoes and flies being the principal productions." Dusenberry put it quite plainly, stating Hatteras "is the most barren place I ever saw."[145]

A Hatteras Island house, circa 1862. *Brimley Collection, State Archives of North Carolina.*

Colonel Brown estimated the Chicamacomico settlement to have included about fifty families.[146] The island population at Chicamacomico was "sparse," though each family had "from nine to nineteen children." Hatteras folks were "of simple habits, living on corn-meal, fish, oysters, pork, and tea made from the leaves of the yapon shrub; but they had to have a little money for clothing and tobacco. To obtain this they cut and sold the live-oak and the cedar." Chicamacomico, like the settlement south at Kinnakeet, had large

A Hatteras Island windmill, circa 1862. *Brimley Collection, State Archives of North Carolina.*

groves of trees, and in the thickest part, typically on the Pamlico Sound side, people built their homes. These were one- or two-room board shanties or log cabins with a small garden close by—"all that the Hatteras islander ever aspired to."[147] The Banker houses were furnished "principally with the furniture from wrecked vessels, that they have gathered together from time to time."[148]

Though not numerous, the Outer Bankers at Chicamacomico were "Union men from the stump." Meeting the locals living around the newly established Indiana encampment confirmed to Brown what Colonel Hawkins had already told him about the strong Union sentiment in this part of North Carolina.[149]

Sabbath morning rose on this Eden, and all were mindful of what they understood at the time to be 1,500 Rebels entrenched just twenty-five miles north on Roanoke Island, a shorter distance than to Hatteras Lighthouse in the opposite direction to the south.[150] Hawkins, though, knew troop levels could have grown to at least 2,500 a week earlier with more troops arriving daily. The total force was expected to soon be nearly 8,000.[151] This more complete intelligence on increased Rebel troop levels was withheld from Colonel Brown and the officers of the Twentieth Indiana prior to deployment at Chicamacomico. "Intelligent negroes" coming into the Union Camps from Roanoke Island also brought additional news of some two to three hundred Negro laborers who had done much of the work in throwing up two batteries, which were intended for commanding the channel between the Albemarle and Pamlico Sounds.[152]

"Secesh" was dug in at Roanoke Island and overrunning the Currituck Sound and adjacent areas, striking terror into the hearts of the isolated native Carolinians of the region. Colonel Brown, meanwhile, was anxious about the artillery Hawkins promised. Officers of the Twentieth naively breathed threats that the Rebels could expect trouble when, not if, the guns arrived. Captain Lytle understood from Hawkins that twenty-five thousand men at Fort Monroe would be on the way any day and "in less than six days the whole coast from Sewell's Point, as far as a rebel can be found," would be cleared of Rebel troops.[153]

Rush Hawkins, before leaving Live Oak, pumped up Brown's officers with a glorious expectation of General Wool's sweep south within six days. At Live Oak, the Twentieth dreamed of its assault on Roanoke Island, capturing it in a glorious victory that the folks back in Indiana would soon hear about. Lytle, an official correspondent for his hometown paper, the Valparaiso, Indiana *Republic*, wrote home in awe of the privileged placement the Twentieth was enjoying so early in its career. "Little did we expect," Lytle wrote, "when we left our quiet homes, that we would be in advance of the many thousands of brave men sent from the noble Hoosier State, but we are determined to prove worthy the position (now very important) we hold; cut off from civilization as we are."[154]

Fortifications were a first priority at Live Oak, though Hawkins also communicated his intentions to establish another camp a distance to the North beyond the encampment.[155] Hawkins's anticipation of a grand sweeping Federal strike was clear in what he initially communicated to the Hoosiers, who were now encamped within spitting distance of the swelling Confederate menace on Roanoke Island.

Hawkins's estimates of Union troops that were then available to Wool at Fort Monroe were grossly inflated, which helped ease the agitation Brown and his officers sensed being so far from Forts Hatteras and Clark without artillery or rifles. As the Twentieth understood the situation, Colonel Hawkins intended to immediately send up artillery to the Hoosiers, which would enable them to support their position until they completed their entrenchments. On completion, "they were to be supplied with heavy guns and reinforcements as fast as additional forces might reach" the inlet.[156]

Sunday morning after unloading, the *Fanny* and the *Ceres* returned to the inlet, leaving the *General Putnam* alone at anchor off the camp. Brown posted pickets along the sound watching the coast after learning the lay of the land. Having employed local help for reconnaissance, Brown reported, "Two small sail boats manned by reliable citizens and men from the regiment coasted up the shore."[157]

Rush Hawkins was zealous to protect the loyal islanders, but the colonel was accused of a lack of discretion in revealing his plans to those who had taken the oath of allegiance. Navy commander Rowan, at least once, expressed his concern over Hawkins's lack of prudence and his open conversations with islanders he trusted. In Rowan's September 13 report to Flag Officer Silas H. Stringham, the commander stated abruptly, as a rather unconnected thought, "I think Colonel Hawkins makes a mistake in allowing the oath-of-allegiance people to visit him. There is a class of men north of them who obtain all the information they want and carry it to the troops at Oregon Inlet."[158]

Leaks of sensitive information flowed freely and consistently through northern newspaper reports as well. Reports from the inlet on October 1 revealed Hawkins was "making preparations for formidable operations against the rebels upon the arrival of reinforcements."[159] Though it is not certain that anyone later blamed Hawkins's imprudent revelations for the *Fanny* capture and the Chicamacomico Affair, this weakness was evidence of Hawkins's lack of tactical expertise, a "mistake" as Rowan called it.

Colonel William Lyons Brown was a conscientious soldier and took the responsibility for the lives and safety of his men as a sacred trust. Standing on a narrow spit of sand on Hatteras looking north, he weighed the strength of the 550 effective men of the Twentieth at Live Oak against what he thought were only 1,500 Rebel troops north on Roanoke Island. Brown contemplated the hell that could be thrown against his precarious position, a perilous forty miles north of Fort Clark and Hawkins's Zouaves, more than thirty miles from the nearest Zouave picket.

On arrival at Live Oak, Brown made careful inquiries of Hawkins about this position below Loggerhead Inlet, questioning the location's advantages and disadvantages for the defense of the Indiana regiment. Offensive strength was a secondary issue at this point. Having assessed the situation, Brown was not at all comfortable with his position. Three of his companies, including his only two rifle companies, were still back at Fort Monroe awaiting transport to Hatteras, and he did not believe his present seven companies could hold the position without artillery. Hawkins reassured Brown with a promise of two pieces of rifled cannon and two gunboats, with a third gunboat to be sent soon thereafter.[160]

Hawkins, while making promises to Brown, had only two pieces of field artillery, apart from the two guns already aboard the *Fanny*, available to him as commander of land forces at Hatteras. Two boat howitzers had been taken off the USS *Minnesota* with the landing party during the Hatteras Invasion a month earlier. The howitzers, not battle ready, remained at Fort Clark under Hawkins's command, though navy property. One of the gun carriages had a broken wheel and required replacement. Ammunition was short, nearly non-existent, as most of it had been wetted down in the botched amphibious landing on August 28, the first day of the invasion of Hatteras by Butler's forces above the inlet.

Commodore Goldsborough had already given Commander Rowan approval for keeping the guns at the inlet if needed instead of returning them to the *Minnesota*. Goldsborough was even willing to supply fresh ammunition for both pieces.[161] Hawkins delayed a formal request to Goldsborough, however, until September 28. He believed that General Wool also planned to send one or two rifled guns filling a request from a week earlier.[162] No artillery, however, was forthcoming and neither were any trained gun crews. The Naval Brigade had been called back north with the return of the *S.R. Spaulding*.

Chapter Five

"In Honey and Clover up to Their Eyes"

O n Sunday afternoon, September 29, Sergeant Theodore M. Bartlett and the other Hoosiers aboard the *Spaulding* wondered what had delayed the transports' return from Chicamacomico. Unaware of the long-drawn-out landing at Live Oak, the men expected the return of the tugs hours earlier. Bartlett, feeling like a prisoner onboard, uncomfortable after seventy-two hours confinement in cramped quarters, wrote in a letter home, "How much longer we shall remain on board, I can not tell."[163] Late in the afternoon, two of the three steamers were finally spotted as they cruised south with Colonel Hawkins.[164] Commander Rowan had earlier given orders for the *General Putnam* to stay behind after unloading at Chicamacomico and to blockade the Croatan Sound.[165] The nine-pounder Sawyer rifle had been transferred from the *Fanny* to the *General Putnam* to serve in the event trouble appeared.[166] Following this transfer, the *Fanny* only had its single six-pounder rifled James gun when it returned to the Inlet.

The detachment of the Twentieth on the *Spaulding* expected to board the *Fanny* and *Ceres*, as the tugs hove in sight, and commence the forty-mile Pamlico cruise at once. The orders to board did not come, though, and the remnant of thirty-three officers, men and citizens stayed yet another night aboard the *Spaulding*. The officers felt no need to inform the men of the reasons for the delay, so all they could do was wait.[167]

The four men waiting from Company C included Privates George W. Clark, John Helsel, Robert A. Inglis and Abel O'Blenis. Company F had two privates in the detachment, John A. Comingore and Henry C. Wilkinson.

Seven men of Company I included Sergeant Theodore M. Bartlett and Privates Napoleon Baum, Hiram Hyde, Swiss-born John Muster, John N. Jones, Jacob Rice and John W. Sparks.

Company H corporal James A. Meek remained with Privates James C. Kerns, Elias Oxford, Frank B. Peirsons, William Wendle, John H. Andrews, Frederick P. Sackett, Charles White[168] and Lucius L. Bennett. Andrews and Sackett were both company musicians—Andrews a drummer and Sackett a fifer. Bennett, a six-foot, twenty-two-year-old farmer, was showing signs of measles and was left on ship until the regimental surgeon Orpheus Everts could establish a camp hospital at Chicamacomico.[169]

Corporal Calvin W. Keefer of Company K was with four privates, including Michael Casper, Van Buren Hinds, Noah E. Kelley and James B. Smith. Mike Caspar "was not well at the time." While at Camp Belger in Baltimore guarding the Northern Central Railroad line, Caspar contracted measles and was recovering on the *Spaulding*. Caspar, twenty-six, was born in Coblenz, Germany, the son of a French father and German mother. The short, five-feet-five, blue-eyed blond immigrated to the United States in 1846.[170]

Private White wrote a number of long, news-filled and wholesome letters home during his early months in the army. (He had learned to speak, read and write English fluently in just a few years.) Though only twenty-three, he made certain his mother was cared for back in LeRoy, New York. White also wrote to John Prentice, the farmer who employed his mother and who had obviously become a trusted friend of the woman and her son. White had written from camp in Indianapolis before the regiment formed and asked Prentice's wife, Sarah, to "please encourage Mother and tell her not to greave [*sic*] nor worry herself because I am a privateer." He signed one letter, "Charles H. Weidt, Privateer," before mustering in with the Twentieth.[171]

White's patriotism as a new immigrant soldier ran high, as evidenced in the flair with which he began his letters home: "Up, up with that flag, upon Sumter again. It shall wave when all traitors are down as fall of fort Sumter." Several times, White wrote of his willingness to pay the ultimate price for freedom: "I have volunteered to fight for my Country and willing to put down Traitors at resk [*sic*] of my life, we have come to enjoy our freedom in this happy Country."[172] Just weeks before leaving for the seat of the war, Charles White ended his note to John Prentice: "I like American liberties and I will fight and die for it."

Two cooks who had attached themselves to the regiment at Cockeysville remained with the regimental baggage on the *Spaulding* as well. Both William

Letter of Private Charles H. Weidt (White) dated July 1, 1861, at camp in Indianapolis, Indiana. White was expecting companies to form in "Col. Brown's regiment" the following week. This original letter was submitted as a supporting document by Louisa Weidt in her dependents' pension application. *National Archives.*

Vogel (alternatively spelled Vagel and Vogler) of Cockeysville and Joseph Chaffer of Chester County, Pennsylvania,[173] were cooks for Company G, Captain Herron's company, which had been held at Fort Monroe. A free "colored boy" named J.H. Edwards from Dulaney Valley, in Baltimore County near Cockeysville, was also among those serving the Twentieth who remained. Sutler's clerk Hugh Watson stayed with the sutler's stores onboard. (The sutler for the Twentieth Indiana, a Mr. Speakman, had left his entire inventory and all cash to run his business with Watson.)[174] Commissary of Subsistence John Clark, stationed at Fort Hatteras, was onboard with intentions personally to accompany the commissary stores to Live Oak. Captain Clark had been the editor of the *Boston Courier* newspaper before the war.[175]

The situation at the inlet was changing rapidly. Commander Rowan received orders from Flag Officer Goldsborough a few days earlier to have

Private Henry Parent Pearsall, Twentieth Indiana, Company I. Captured on the retreat from Camp Live Oak. *Pearsall Family Collection*.

Sergeant Charles W. DeMotte, Twentieth Indiana, Company I. Captured during the retreat from Chicamacomico. (Interesting side note: DeMotte's uncle, William H. DeMotte [with whom Charles lived and worked until enlisting in the Twentieth], was an eyewitness to the Lincoln assassination. The Illinois State Historical Association published his seven-page account, *The Assassination of Abraham Lincoln*, in 1927.) *Ted Yungclas Collection*.

the USS *Pawnee* at the Washington Navy Yard on October 5. Secretary of the Navy Gideon Welles had ordered the *Pawnee* to other duty.[176] Goldsborough, though, wanted Rowan to stop at Hampton Roads for a meeting, if possible, along the way.[177] Rowan, commanding the naval squadron at Hatteras, found these new orders placed him in a bind in a number of ways.

Endeavoring to follow orders and get to Washington by October 5, Rowan found it necessary to ensure there was proper oversight of navy property at the inlet in his absence. He also was attempting to respond in a timely and effective manner to the very real threat of a Rebel invasion of the Pamlico Sound that had been communicated to Rush Hawkins through escaped slaves from Roanoke Island. Rowan was also having issues with Captain Chauncey concerning the command of the inlet and in particular of the two new tugs, *Ceres* and *General Putnam*. Rowan assumed both tugs were placed under his direct command because he was the one who had requested them from Goldsborough. Acting Master Elliott's orders were specifically to report with the USS *Ceres* "to the senior naval officer [meaning Commander Rowan] for such duty as he may require of you."[178] Captain Chauncey, though, seemed to think that he had greater immediate need of the tugs because of his numerous recent captures of prize vessels attempting to run the Union naval blockade.

The *Pawnee* was inside the bar and had a seven-foot draft. Rowan needed to wait until conditions were right to get safely over that eight-foot-deep obstacle on his departure for the Washington Navy Yard. Commander Rowan was anxiously waiting to cross the bar with the *Pawnee* and carry out his orders from Flag Officer Goldsborough to arrive at Alexandria on or before October 5.

As outgoing navy commander of the inlet, Rowan was also dealing with a severe shortage of midshipmen who could take command of the various steamers inside and outside the bar at Hatteras. Immediately, Rowan needed to assist Colonel Hawkins in completing the deployment of the Twentieth Indiana Regiment at the north end of the island at Chicamacomico. Because of this shortage of navy midshipmen and other officers available at the inlet, Rowan was not able to supply Hawkins with direct navy assistance in taking the army-chartered gunboat *Fanny* north to Chicamacomico with the quartermaster supplies, commissary stores and remaining Twentieth Indiana troops and baggage.

On September 29, the Hoosiers had been left at Camp Live Oak with only two days' rations in anticipation of the remaining stores arriving within that time. Tuesday, October 1, would be "day three," and the seven companies would be running short of food and water. Though there was a good potable water source for the villagers at Chicamacomico, it was not a consistent and adequate supply of fresh water sufficient to supply seven companies. Food and water had to be brought regularly from Baltimore by steamer. It was important to allow no further delay and get the regiment their supplies no later than the end of the day on Tuesday. That morning, expecting the supply steamer at any time, a Hatteras correspondent reported the Hoosiers, at present, were "in honey and clover up to their eyes…delighted with the beautiful country they are now in possession of and which they have no idea of giving up."[179]

The *Fanny* finally left the inlet at 6:00 a.m. on October 1 for Camp Live Oak. The rifled canons that had been originally mounted on the tug's bow and stern were to be hastily manned by artillery crews from the Ninth New York. The *Fanny*, though was presently short one gun. The Sawyer rifle was with the *General Putnam* and would be transferred again upon their meeting later in the day. The *Fanny*, fully loaded, lumbered up the Pamlico Sound, and civilian captain John Morrison anchored in eight feet of water off Camp Live Oak around 1:00 p.m.[180]

Chapter Six

"A More Hair-brained Expedition Was Never Conceived"

A crisis was looming over the coastal waters of North Carolina when Confederate flag officer French Forrest, commander of the Gosport Navy Yard, ordered forty-eight year-old Commander Thomas Triplett Hunter, a Virginian by birth,[181] to take "command of the expedition for the defense of the inlets of North Carolina." On August 28, Forrest ordered Commander Hunter, nicknamed "Tornado,"[182] south immediately, along with any military troops Brigadier General Benjamin Huger may attach to his command. Brigadier General Huger had Confederate infantry command of the Department of Norfolk, with defensive responsibilities for North Carolina and southern Virginia. Huger's headquarters was at Norfolk. Hunter, in command of this "combined operation" of the Confederate army and navy, was to be "guided by circumstances," as Forrest ordered. Forrest then directed "should you meet with Flag Officer Barron, you will cooperate with him."[183]

Brigadier General Huger walked into Camp Gwynn, outside Gosport Navy Yard on that same afternoon of August 28 and informed the Third Georgia Volunteers, and their colonel, Ambrose R. Wright, that four companies of the regiment were moving to Roanoke Island.[184] Years later, it would be noted as a matter of regimental pride that "as thus constituted this was the first organized regiment of Georgians that stood upon the soil of Virginia to hurl back the threatened invasion of that noble old Commonwealth. They arrived upon the banks of the beautiful Elizabeth river before the secession of the State, and organized amid the smoldering fires and crumbling walls

Map of Roanoke Island. Adapted from the "Map of the Battlefield of Roanoke [Island]."
Office of Coast Survey, NOAA.

of Gosport Navy Yard."[185] Intelligence gathered, the Georgians were told, indicated that the twelve Union troop transports, seen near Ocean View a couple days earlier "would land their cargoes of Yankees" at some unknown location.[186] It was crucial to provide immediate defense for Roanoke Island, the sounds and channels and, thus, the "backdoor" to Norfolk against what appeared to be a threatened Union amphibious invasion from the south.

Colonel Ambrose Ransom Wright, familiarly known as "Rans," was a thirty-five-year-old lawyer and politician in private life.[187] Rans Wright was not hard to identify across a room. The heavy beard worn to his chest and his long hair combed back behind his ears set him apart. Though born in Louisville, Jefferson County, Georgia, Wright's Virginia roots were what brought his regiment north to the aid of the state so early in the rebellion. Wright's father, Ambrose Wright, a Virginian, served as a major of a Virginia militia regiment in the War of 1812.[188] His grandfather served in the Revolutionary War. Rans Wright, a political moderate prior to the election of Abraham Lincoln, was a member of the Georgia delegation that traveled to Maryland earlier in 1861 to convince the legislature to secede from the Union. In May 1861, Wright enlisted

Top: Flag Officer French Forrest, Confederate States Navy, commander of Gosport Navy Yard. *Library of Congress*.

Right: General Benjamin Huger, Confederate States of America. General Huger (who pronounced his name "ooh-ZHAY") was then a brigadier general commanding forces at Norfolk, Virginia. *Library of Congress*.

Colonel Ambrose Ransom "Rans" Wright, Third Georgia Volunteer Infantry. This sketch was produced after promotion to brigadier general and major general in 1864. Wright's brigade in A.P. Hill's corps at Gettysburg had the distinction of penetrating the farthest into the Union defenses on Cemetery Ridge on July 2, 1863. *Library of Congress.*

as a private in the Third Georgia and was quickly elected colonel.[189] The colonel's son, Private William Ambrose Wright, seventeen, left school in May 1861[190] to enlist with his father as a private in the Third Georgia Volunteers, Company G, the Confederate Light Guards.[191]

Third Georgia adjutant William W. Turner was more than skeptical about the odds of four companies up against twelve transports full of Union troops. "A more hair-brained expedition was never conceived," Turner wrote in his diary. Huger, though, expected the Georgians to arrive in advance of the flotilla, throw up breastworks on Roanoke Island and meet the Federals when they arrived. Neither Brigadier General Huger nor Flag Officer Forrest had any idea what was already transpiring at Hatteras Inlet against Confederate-held Forts Hatteras and Clark. Adjutant Turner wrote parenthetically in his journal, "I would remark here, that I afterwards found this apparent thoughtlessness, carelessness, recklessness, or whatever it may be termed, was characteristic of General Huger. Strange it was, too, for he appeared kind, good-hearted, and a perfect gentleman. But such is the inconsistency of man."[192]

The long roll sounded early at Camp Gwynn at 3:00 a.m. on August 29, cutting that night's sleep quite short.[193] Brigadier General Huger had promised transports would be waiting at the Navy Yard Wharf at 10:00 a.m. Four companies of the Third Georgia, the First Battalion, had received orders for active service and prepared rations for ten days and procured the necessary entrenching tools the previous evening. The battalion included companies C, E, G and K—the Dawson Greys, the Governor's Guard, the Confederate Light Guards and the Athens Guards, respectively.[194]

The First Battalion of the Third Georgia Volunteers[195] shoved off at 2:00 p.m. after several delays.[196] The CSS *Kahukee*,[197] commanded by Midshipman James L. Tayloe, towed two open barges with all four companies of Georgians, twenty guns and two rifled cannon packed on board the steamer and barges.[198] Commander Hunter, in the CSS *Raleigh*, accompanied the First Battalion and the *Kahukee*. The *Raleigh* was towing an armed launch, commanded by Captain William Harwar Parker, fitted out with a howitzer and sails for use on the Albemarle and Pamlico Sounds. Captain Parker was aboard the uncrewed vessel, ordered by Commodore Samuel Barron to bring the armed launch at Hatteras.[199]

Third Georgia's Company E, Governor's Guard, was fortunate to be aboard the *Kahukee* despite minimal cover and limited "comforts." The other three companies were not so lucky, aboard open barges towed in the rain the first day of slow travel south.[200] Private Alva Benjamin Spencer, of Company C, Dawson Greys, was among the less fortunate and wrote home, "The first day and night it rained incessantly and we were compelled to lay down and sleep with our blankets wet."[201] Adjutant Turner noted that there was no protection from the elements on the barges except in the suffocating holds. Not much better was found on the *Kahukee* where Adjutant Turner slept in "the coal bin, on muskets, camp stools, &c."[202] A change in weather came on the thirtieth and those who slept with wet blankets, like Private Spencer, "dried them in the sun's scorching rays."[203]

Private Spencer described the beauty of Roanoke Island, though, in a letter to "My dear friend:"

On our passage we passed through some most beautiful canals. The scenery was the most beautiful I've ever seen. On each side, the canal was covered with the most interesting, soul inspiring shrubbery imaginable. The beautiful windings of the rivers, and their different colored waters all tended to render the scene one of deep interest to those who had never seen such before.[204]

Hunter's flotilla stopped "at several places along the [Chesapeake and Albemarle] canal, and at landings on the Croatan river [*sic*], but got no news." However, soon a "schooner under full sail for Edenton" was met, and news of the fall of Fort Hatteras in the Union invasion of August 28 and 29 was received. The schooner, Hunter discovered, had on board several officers of the Seventh North Carolina Regiment who had escaped the invasion and the capture that followed.[205] Commander Hunter then slowed the *Raleigh* and came alongside the *Kahukee* to speak with Midshipman Tayloe as the sun was going down on August 30. Hunter told Tayloe, "There are four Federal steamers firing into Fort Oregon… the enemy has taken possession of Hatteras…you must go down to the marshes and anchor there, tonight." Tayloe was doubtful he could make it to the marshes that evening but thought perhaps by the next morning. The Georgians, en route to the marshes, spotted yet another schooner with a smaller boat alongside. The captain of the schooner boarded the *Kahukee*, explaining what had transpired over the two previous days in the loss to the Union of Forts Hatteras and Clark.

> *The fort at Hatteras being a small one, was not capable of holding the thousand men there, and many of them were behind it. The enemy landed, proceeded to the rear, and took possession of a small battery, thus cutting off retreat in that direction, while the Federal vessels bombarded from the front.* [206]

Colonel Wright, having received the news of the fall of Fort Hatteras, went aboard the *Raleigh* with Commander Hunter for a meeting, the *Raleigh* having been hovering protectively close to the *Kahukee* that evening. Additionally, a Seventh North Carolina captain from the schooner bound for Edenton they had met earlier went aboard. He reported that when attempting to rejoin his company at Fort Oregon, he saw his garrison was under fire from Federal vessels, and so he returned to Roanoke Island. Having heard this captain's account, Hunter ordered Midshipman Tayloe to take a defensive position with the *Kahukee* at the marshes south of Roanoke Island. Adjutant Turner recorded, "The result [of the meeting] was, [Commander Hunter] put a gun on one of our barges, and some men were detailed to man it. [Commander] Hunter then moved off to send a dispatch to Norfolk, while we cast anchor." The Third Georgia established a watch for Federals through the night, and hung a lantern viewable only from the North, hoping later to lead Hunter back to their position. A Union attack on Fort Oregon was hourly anticipated from Hatteras. Commander Hunter immediately revised his expedition's mission from one that included reinforcing and supporting the garrisons at Forts Hatteras and Clark to one of defense and protection, specifically of Roanoke Island and the Croatan and Albemarle Sounds, from further advances north toward Norfolk.

Hunter left for Fort Oregon late the evening of August 31, with the Seventh North Carolina captain, to retrieve the guns and the three remaining companies of the Seventh garrisoned there. Meanwhile, the Third Georgia's First Battalion waded to shore back at Roanoke Island, soon after Hunter's departure, at a place on the Croatan Sound where the shipping channel was quite wide and established a camp. However, Colonel Wright and Commander Hunter quickly "agreed it would be folly for this handful of men—our four companies—to remain here, so entirely at the mercy of the large force that may come up." The channel was so wide that even with a battery established, Federal gunboats could pass and cut off the four Georgian companies encamped there, separating them from Norfolk and "leaving [them] to starve." As soon as Hunter returned from Oregon Inlet, the Georgians expected to board the barges again, and move farther north— where the channel was narrower and the position more defendable—and wait for updated orders from Brigadier General Huger.[207]

The balance of the Third Georgia, the Second Battalion,[208] consisted of Companies A, B, D, F and H, under command of Lieutenant Colonel James S. Reid.[209] The Second Battalion started for Roanoke Island separately on August 30, aboard steamers CSS *Empire*, CSS *Curlew* and CSS *Junaluska*, along with two barges and a few schooners, the *Curlew* being the newest acquisition of the Rebel navy. Soon after Commander Hunter left for Fort Oregon in the *Raleigh*, the First Battalion welcomed the arrival of its Second Battalion brothers from Norfolk. It was 2:00 a.m. on September 1,[210] and the adjutant procured "a little row boat and went off to them."[211]

The Third Georgia was back together as a complete regiment and initially landed near Pork Point, where both battalions pitched tents creating Camp Hope and began working night and day "constructing a most formidable battery." Camp Hope was soon renamed Camp Rescue, as the mission of the forces on Roanoke Island had taken a new direction.[212]

The CSS *Junaluska*, a seventy-nine-ton, iron-hulled screw steamer, was considered the "fleetest" available. The *Junaluska* was built in Philadelphia in 1860 and purchased by the Confederate navy at Norfolk earlier in 1861. It had been assigned to duty in the coastal waters of Virginia and North Carolina.[213]

The *Junaluska* took a cruise toward Fort Hatteras and Fort Oregon soon after the Second Battalion arrived in the early morning darkness of September 1. On board the *Junaluska* were Colonel Wright and Adjutant

Turner,[214] accompanied by Major Augustus H. Lee and Captain John F. Jones of Company H along with ten of Jones's men.[215] Colonel Wright, concerned that perhaps Commander Hunter and the CSS *Raleigh* had become drawn into an engagement, soon discovered Hunter's vessel four miles from Fort Oregon and all quiet around Oregon Inlet. Adjutant Turner concluded the captain's story concerning the Union gunboat attack on Oregon was "a fabrication, concocted in his frightened imagination." The Third Georgia officers and men made a bold attempt to row a boat from Hunter's steamer the four miles to Oregon Inlet but were unsuccessful and reluctantly returned to the *Junaluska* and back to Roanoke Island. To their dismay, the infantry officers were informed, on their return, that the Third Georgia would stay on Roanoke Island for an indefinite period of time to fortify it, as well as possibly another point on the western side of the Croatan Sound.[216]

Commander Hunter, along with Captain Parker, was invited on arrival at Fort Oregon on August 31 to a "council of war."[217] Lieutenant Joseph W. Alexander, commanding the CSS *Raleigh*, was also invited to advise and observe, but not to vote. The captain who accompanied Hunter and Parker to Oregon overnight called the council. He was Captain Daniel McDonald Lindsey from the Seventh North Carolina Volunteers, Company H, the Currituck Atlantic Rifles. Captain Lindsey was in command of the garrison at Fort Oregon. Lindsey, having witnessed[218] the fate of his officers and comrades at Fort Hatteras, called the council to decide a course of action, including possibly the garrison's evacuation.[219] Captain Lindsey had been ordered to Fort Hatteras by Seventh North Carolina colonel William F. Martin to attend a court martial there, where Lindsey narrowly escaped capture. Second Lieutenant William Glover, Company L, State Guards of Pasquotank, had been left in command at Oregon in Lindsey's absence. Glover was found, on Captain Lindsey's return, "making preparation to resist an attack, which was hourly expected."[220]

Commander Hunter presented to the "council" his orders from Flag Officer French Forrest, dated August 28, 1861, "to assume command of the expedition for the defense of the inlets of North Carolina." The current situation was certainly the kind of "circumstances" Forrest foresaw when he scratched out those orders to Hunter. Captain Lindsey was also informed of Commander Hunter's command over the Third Georgia infantry troops at Roanoke Island and other ground forces under Brigadier General Benjamin Huger.[221]

Lindsey convened the "council of war," with Hunter invited only by virtue of being "commander of the expedition for the defense of the North

Above: Flag of the State Guards of Pasquotank, Company L, Seventh North Carolina Volunteers. This company, as one of three companies not captured at Hatteras on August 29, 1861, reformed as the Seventeenth North Carolina Company L (First Organization) and flew this flag during the Battle of Roanoke Island. William C. Dawson of this regiment hid this flag remnant in his clothing when the company was captured. *Museum of the Albemarle.*

Right: Captain John Bartlett Fearing, Seventh North Carolina Volunteers, Company L, State Guards of Pasquotank. *Museum of the Albemarle, J. Howard Stevens Collection.*

85

Carolina inlets," though he remained a non-voting participant. Present at this council, "consisting of all the Commissioned Officers of the Companies at the Post," were: Third Lieutenant Isaac L. Sawyer, Company L, the State Guards of Pasquotank; Second Lieutenant William Glover and Third Lieutenant Charles G. Elliott, Company F, the John Harvey Guards; and Second Lieutenant B.I. Shannonhouse, Third Lieutenant Thomas H. Gilliam and Second Lieutenant E.J. Mercer of Company H, the Currituck Atlantic Rifles. Also present was Third Lieutenant William Perkins Walston of Company G, Gratiot Luke's independent company, the North Carolina Defenders. Twenty-five men of Luke's company who escaped capture at Hatteras had made it to Oregon that afternoon. Chief engineer, Colonel Elwood Morris, designer of Fort Oregon and the assistant engineer, C.R. Barney, also participated.[222]

The decision was made to evacuate Fort Oregon entirely and immediately. Lindsey, Mercer and Morris were the dissenting votes against evacuating.[223] All guns and public property of the state and the Confederacy were to be removed. Reasons for evacuating without a fight were several: the power of the Federals to cut off all supply lines; very limited ammunition stores; exposure to attack from both land and sea; and overall isolation of the island. Colonel Morris,[224] "very loth [sic] to abandon it,"[225] together with Lindsey and Mercer, voted against evacuating the fort. Morris, seeing several months of work wasted, argued that "the evacuation…was not justified by any military necessity."[226]

Years later Captain Parker reflected on that council and wrote, "After the fall of Hatteras, [Fort Oregon] became of absolutely no importance. The principal entrance to the sound being open what earthly reason could there be for holding the other two? I do not think the Federals occupied the forts at either Oregon or Ocracoke Inlets during the war—they had no occasion to!"[227]

Commander Hunter ordered the evacuation of the garrison post haste when the war council adjourned,[228] but Colonel Elwood Morris, a dissenting voter, strongly encouraged the garrison to not recognize the navy commander's authority over infantry troops and instead "hold the fort." The garrison consisted of the three Seventh North Carolina companies, each having roughly sixty-five to seventy-five men, totaling some 207 officers and men. These companies were: Company H, the Currituck Atlantic Rifles, Captain D. McDonald Lindsey; Company F, the John Harvey Guards, whose captain, Lucius Junius Johnson, was away and captured at Hatteras; and Company L, the State Guards of Pasquotank, Captain John Bartlett Fearing.[229] In addition were the twenty-five men of the North Carolina

Defenders under command of Third Lieutenant Walston,[230] bringing the total to 232 North Carolinians in addition to the Eighth Regiment. The evacuating garrison fired the buildings upon departure but neglected to take the remaining artillery pieces.[231] Hunter immediately sent dispatches explaining the status of Fort Oregon to Flag Officer French Forrest at Gosport via Captain Parker, who left his armed launch behind in the able hands of Boatswain Charles H. Hasker.[232]

The garrison had abandoned Fort Oregon by early Monday morning, bringing off three of the guns on a barge. The barge was not adequate to carry the load, however, and the three pieces were lost in the Pamlico Sound. Hunter flew into a rage over the lost guns, which he had intended to put in place at Pork Point. Adjutant Turner revealed that Hunter "indulges in very strong expletives concerning those who lost them." Colonel Morris in the meantime went to Roanoke Island looking for Colonel Wright. Morris, acknowledging Wright as "chief in command" of infantry troops, attempted to persuade the colonel to hold Fort Oregon, against the conclusion of the "council of war." Adjutant Turner wrote later that night that Morris "seems to have a horror of the idea that his work should be abandoned." Wright's officers agreed, believing he was indeed "the senior officer, and in command of all the land forces on, and around the island." Even still, the Colonel acknowledged the authority of Hunter against the appeals of the engineer, who finally left the island after being told Wright did not intend to listen to his argument.[233]

The Fort Oregon controversy, between Hunter and the Seventh, continued to fester, though, and some of the Third Georgia troops soon began to take sides in the controversy against the commander. Private A.B. Spencer, for one, blamed the evacuation of Fort Oregon and its garrison of North Carolina volunteers on Hunter, stating that "the North Ca. Soldiers…their deserting it [Fort Oregon] was all caused by [Commander] Hunter of the Con. Sts. Navy, as grand a coward as ever lived. He almost compelled them to evacuate it, and then published a report that these troops acted cowardly."[234]

Adjutant Turner also reported things were not going smoothly in bringing the garrison of Seventh North Carolina Troops back from Oregon Inlet: "Every thing [*sic*] has been in confusion there." Commander Hunter received expressed orders from Flag Officer Forrest to take command of both the navy and army as they related to this expedition for the defense of the inlets of North Carolina. Because Flag Officer Barron had been captured at Hatteras, Hunter did not feel obligated to cooperate with anyone else for the moment.[235]

On Monday, September 2, a detachment of fifty Georgians of Company H went back to Fort Oregon with the major to remove the remaining guns for installation at Pork Point. The engineer had tools enough for only one hundred men and started construction on the Pork Point battery right away on the morning of September 2. The work began around the clock in shifts of one hundred men at a time.[236]

Captain John Bartlett Fearing, of Company L—the State Guards of Pasquotank—also escaped capture at Fort Hatteras on August 29, having spent two days under the ferocity of the Federal bombardment, first at Fort Clark and then at Fort Hatteras. Fearing, however, did not return to Fort Oregon in time for the council of war. Each of the captains of the three Seventh North Carolina Volunteers companies that garrisoned Fort Oregon had been called to the court martial at Fort Hatteras, as Lindsey previously related to Hunter. Only Captain Johnson, of the John Harvey Guards, however, was captured. Fearing's name is on none of the lists of Hatteras prisoners, but he was later captured at the Battle of Roanoke Island.[237]

Flag Officer Forrest at Gosport was from the outset of the Hatteras crisis preparing Commander Hunter to take immediate offensive action against the Union forces at the inlet and in the Pamlico Sound. Initial reports received by Forrest on the condition of Union gunboats in the sound led Forrest, on September 4, to send a message to Hunter about continuing the defenses at Roanoke Island and informed him of the weaknesses of the Union hold on the Pamlico Sound. One strong gunboat, Forrest calculated, could "drive everything from the Sound in the neighborhood of Hatteras." A lieutenant who had escaped capture at Hatteras reported to Forrest that the Union tugs inside the inlet were unarmed and were "badly crippled." Even with the 4,500 Union troops believed by the Rebels to be at Hatteras, Forrest was satisfied the Federals could be "easily whipped," and right away, and saw the newly acquired Confederate steamer *Curlew*, not yet fitted out, as a big part of the best solution. Forrest planned for the *Curlew* to be armed with a thirty-two-pounder rifled cannon on the bow and two smaller guns at the stern in the event of a retreat.[238]

A new encampment for the Third Georgia at Roanoke Island, Camp Georgia, was laid off, and clearing commenced "in the roughest kind of forest," on September 3. The new camp was located halfway between Pork Point Battery and Weir's Point, where yet another battery was planned. A makeshift wharf was constructed, making easier work of unloading supply boats.[239] The original encampment, Camp Rescue, had been "an excellent locality," but it was four miles from the Pork Point battery, which was "going bravely forward."[240]

The Pork Point Battery, after only thirty hours of work, was ready for its platforms by Tuesday night. The work was "soldiering in earnest." The men were literally wearing out their shoes and boots "walking back and forth four miles…constantly loading and unloading boats, wading to their waists in water, (as there is no wharf) and carrying great burdens on their shoulders, besides doing guard duty, and clearing up a new camp." Over one hundred free Negroes were quickly impressed, additional axes and shovels procured and all put to work the following day.[241]

One of the companies of the Seventh North Carolina Volunteers, Company L, under command of Captain John Bartlett Fearing, was, as its name suggests, from Pasquotank County. The people of Elizabeth City, in Pasquotank County, were particularly warm toward the soldiers on Roanoke Island and not just their own boys, the State Guards. Third Georgia adjutant Turner wrote on September 4, "The citizens of Elizabeth City sent us down, last night, a quantity of cooked provisions, and say they will send any thing [*sic*] we need, if we will let them know what it is. This supply came in the nick of time. Our boys can hardly find leisure to cook."[242] However, despite this goodwill from the people of Pasquotank County, Colonel Wright found that the North Carolina soldiers were "in a state of disorganization, and but little can be expected from them."[243]

On September 4, the Second Battalion of the Third Georgia, including Private Marion Moss's Company H, moved their tents from Camp Rescue to the new Camp Georgia nearby: "As it rained powerful hard, we had a bad time putting them up."[244] On September 5, the first gun was mounted on Pork Point Battery, and some of the Third Georgia men returned from Fort Oregon.[245] The rest of the Third Georgia Regiment on Roanoke Island marched to join their comrades at Camp Georgia.[246] Seven guns were in place on Pork Point by the evening of September 6.[247]

Work commenced on the second battery at Weir's Point on September 7. Word was floating through the Third Georgia camp that after the completion of this battery, the regiment would again be ordered to Portsmouth or even back south to Savannah, Georgia. Tired of the incessant construction, the Georgians' spirits were buoyed by these constant rumors.[248]

Meanwhile, eleven Third Georgia troops, along with Major Lee and Commander Hunter, steamed to Bodie Island to destroy the lighthouse and what was left of Fort Oregon. Private Marion Moss was one of those eleven and wrote in detail how he, with Private George Levy, destroyed the Bodie Island Lighthouse:

We fired the wood and the tar barrels created a terrible black smoke. The light house was or had 146 steps to the lamp. The glass was 1 inch thick and clear as crystal. Me and GEORGE LEVY pecked a hole into the outside wall with a pick and there was a vacancy between the outside and inside walls. We put about 25 pounds of powder in that vacancy and saturated some paper with gun powder and dried it in the sunshine and rolled up the paper in a long tube. I struck fire to it. The rest had got out of the way. I ran and got behind a bank of sand, and it blew up and fell full length on the ground. We then left the island to return to Roanoke Island. We captured a schooner on our way. The light house is said to have cost the government $300,000.[249]

On the morning of September 8, Colonel Rans Wright took a detachment of the Third Georgia, including the regimental band, across the Croatan Sound to search for a point suitable for another battery. Having found their site at Redstone Point, the party made their landing nearby, while the band played "Dixie." Musician Alva Spencer imagined that it was "perhaps the first time it was ever played there. Some of the inhabitants hearing the music were so much frightened, that they even left their houses."[250] Thirty men from Private Marion Moss's Company H were still working on this battery ten days later.[251]

Third Georgia's Company D, the Madison Home Guards, under the command of Lieutenant Colonel James S. Reid, originally constructed a sand battery in the marshes at Redstone Point. However, that effort was scrapped and "some old barges were fixed in the mud, and some guns placed on them, with Seventh North Carolina men placed in command."[252] This battery would later be named Fort Forrest.

Commander Hunter still commanded the "expedition for defense of the inlets North Carolina" on September 10. Hunter penned a letter that day to Brigadier General Benjamin Huger, openly accusing the troops from North Carolina's eastern counties of disloyalty. The letter was indicative of the depths to which the mutual mistrust had plunged between the commander and the North Carolina men, particularly from the Seventh. Hunter wrote, "I will confine myself to one remark. It is this: From all I have seen and heard since taking possession of this island, I am free to declare that I regard the maintenance of this position possible only so long as it is defended by troops from another State, or from a more loyal part of North Carolina."[253] The three companies forming the remnant of the Seventh Regiment were mostly from Currituck, Perquimans and Pasquotank Counties.[254] One navy flag officer would later come to an equally pessimistic conclusion, saying, "My opinion is that North Carolina volunteers will not stand their guns. Men so devoid of energy are incapable of determined and long-continued resistance."[255]

The work on Pork Point Battery was complete September 11, and Colonel Wright informed Brigadier General Huger of the good news, stating, "The battery at Pork Point is now ready to give the Hessians a warm reception." Wright was getting along in construction of defenses but felt "crippled for want of men" for a proper defense of his position on Roanoke Island. Wright told Brigadier General Huger, "I need not call your attention to the fact that the force on this island is entirely inadequate…The North Carolina companies here are completely disorganized and demoralized. I can hope nothing from them."[256]

Wright began forming a "light" or "flying" artillery company, and by September 11, two howitzers, a twelve-pounder and a twenty-four-pounder were received for that purpose from Gosport. He had also received two wagons and four mules. Wright pulled the axles and front wheels of the wagons to create limbers for the two guns. "I shall get a pretty good battery of light artillery fixed up during the day," Wright informed Huger. The colonel hitched the mules to the two guns and pulled them another five miles south to protect the batteries from a rear attack. The town of Edenton, North Carolina, offered to provide horses for artillery purposes, but Wright decided to let Brigadier General Huger make that decision.[257]

Colonel Wright later indicated, on September 22, that the Weir's Point battery was "nearly finished."[258] Mounting twelve guns, this battery was later named Fort Huger. Hearts sank, though, when a dispatch arrived that day from Portsmouth ordering the Third Georgia to remain at Roanoke Island through winter. Private Alva Spencer wrote, "I heard a great many remark that they had much rather be confined in the Georgia Penitentiary the same length of time, than on this island."[259] A few more days passed, and the weary Georgians were again speculating about returning to Portsmouth within two weeks, as soon as the batteries they were working on were completed. Return addresses on outgoing mail were presumptively changed from "Camp Rescue" to "Portsmouth, Va., Care."[260]

A portion of the Third Georgia was detached on September 17 to work on the guns at Pork Point Battery, which later was renamed Fort Bartow. A light artillery company formed that day consisting of forty-five Third Georgia men under the command of Lieutenant John R. Sturgis of the Burke Guards.[261] A new battery was started on September 20 for the Flying

Flag Officer William F. Lynch, Confederate States Navy, Naval Defenses of Virginia and North Carolina. *U.S. Naval Historical Center.*

Artillery.[262] Located about six miles south of the Weir's Point battery, the work was constructed "at the causeway, across the marsh, on the center of the Island," and was completed on September 22.[263] The battery, a Third Georgia historian later explained, was at an "entrenchment made at Supplie's Hill, one and a half miles above Ashby's landing."[264]

William F. Lynch, a Confederate navy captain at the time, was given orders on or about September 4 for his "sudden detachment" from the Bureau of Ordnance to succeed the captured Flag Officer Samuel Barron as flag officer and commander of naval defenses of Virginia and North Carolina.[265] Lynch's stretch as chief of office of orders and detail at Richmond also abruptly ended on September 4.[266]

A native of Norfolk, Virginia, William Francis Lynch entered U.S. Navy service as a midshipman at the age of seventeen in 1819.[267] Beginning his 1851 semi-autobiographical account, *Naval Life*, Lynch described his entrance into the navy:

> *A motherless child, with a father who, though not devoid of affection, was engrossed by the care of his property, I esteemed myself fortunate that at the age of sixteen, with the love of adventure enkindled by the very perils arrayed to deter me, I abandoned my studies, and embraced the roving, stirring, homeless, comfortless, but attractive life of a sailor.*[268]

In his earliest years at sea, from 1823 to 1825, then Midshipman Lynch served aboard vessels in U.S. Navy commodore David Porter's West Indies Squadron.[269] This expedition, on a mission for the suppression of piracy in the West Indies, had a fleet of sixteen small, shallow-draft vessels that were able to hide in shallow inlets and coves to chase and capture pirate crews. Porter's fleet gained a reputation for being aggressive, persistent and feared by its enemies. Porter called his fleet of small vessels the "Mosquito Fleet" after the *Mosquito*, one of the lead cutters in this group. Commodore David Porter's expedition, particularly with the scrappy "Mosquito Fleet," gained a reputation from its fearsome naval service in the early 1820s. Porter's squadron effectively eliminated piracy and saved American merchants from the losses they had suffered for many years.

Lynch had become famous for a narrative of his controversial expedition to the Dead Sea, which commenced at the close of the Mexican War. Lynch's "Expedition to the Dead Sea and the River Jordan" left the United States in November 1847.[270] After an overland journey through Palestine, Lynch explored the Dead Sea and conducted what would appear as a federally funded pilgrimage to the great cities and sites of the Holy Land including Jerusalem and Bethlehem, "'the city of David,' and the birthplace of the Redeemer."[271] Lynch's expedition returned to the United States early in December 1848. His narrative Washington's *Daily National Intelligencer* declared "a lasting memorial of a great national enterprise skillfully consummated."[272]

Lynch had been serving a number of posts in the Confederate navy during the early months of the Civil War, after resigning from the United States Navy in April. Most recently, he had taken on the position of chief of the Bureau of Ordnance in Richmond. Lynch had been acting as bureau chief of ordnance,[273] while at the same time serving as bureau chief of orders and detail in Richmond,[274] the latter post assumed in recent weeks, on August 23, 1861.[275]

The day Lynch received orders to take command, in the absence of Flag Officer Barron, instead of proceeding directly to either Roanoke Island or Norfolk, he was off to New Bern. His business was to consult with General Richard C. Gatlin and North Carolina governor Henry T. Clark about an expected Union attack on Fort Macon.[276]

As a new flag officer, Lynch considered Roanoke Island "the back door to Norfolk," a highly strategic position for the Confederacy to protect at all costs. However, on taking command, Lynch believed the island's proximity to "high military command" provided an acceptable level of security, strengthened with a recent deployment of troops and guns. His first priority before cruising to Roanoke Island was to get to Fort Macon where the "capacity for defense was questionable." There was an anticipated attack on the inexperienced garrison there. Fort Macon's remote location from Norfolk made it highly vulnerable to attack by the Union navy.[277] In the meantime, Commander Thomas T. Hunter remained in command of the defense of North Carolina's inlets while Flag Officer Lynch's arrival was delayed.

Flag Officer Forrest did not want to wait for Lynch to take command at Roanoke Island, which wouldn't be for another ten days. Forrest was bent on reclaiming Hatteras for the Confederacy. On September 5, Forrest ordered Commander Arthur Sinclair Jr., who was at New Bern when Lynch arrived there, to Roanoke Island to cooperate with Commander Hunter in "dispossessing the enemy of the position he now occupies." Sinclair was to deliver the armed barge *Superior* with four guns, take two rifled guns from the gunboat *Harmony* and mount them on the CSS *Empire*. Forrest wrote, "With this force I am of the opinion you can drive the enemy from [Hatteras] island." Forrest continued by revealing he had learned that the Union steamers were, as he put it, "in a crippled condition, and if brought soon to action can not long hold out."[278]

Flag Officer Lynch finally left New Bern on September 12 and sailed for Roanoke Island as the new commander of naval defenses of Virginia and North Carolina,[279] relieving Hunter of the command he had held since the crisis began two weeks earlier. Lynch continued outfitting the gunboat squadron launched by Commander Hunter under the close direction of Flag Officer French Forrest.

Forrest received word from Lynch on September 23 that the CSS *Curlew* was about ready for gunboat service. Lynch, under Forrest's direction, mounted on the *Curlew* one of four rifled guns already available at Roanoke Island. Two additional thirty-two-pounders were added soon thereafter.[280]

It is important to this study to note that at this point, the Confederate naval squadron of which Flag Officer Lynch took command was not referred to as the "Mosquito Fleet" and that it is inaccurate to do so. The term "Mosquito Fleet," the name most commonly used today for Lynch's squadron of light-draft steamers did not appear until as late as February 1862 during the Battle of Roanoke Island. It was used first, it seems, by a newspaper correspondent in a report from Norfolk published later in the February 11, 1862 issue of the *New York Times*.[281] The following day, February 12, the *New York Times* published a February 10 story from Fort Monroe with a front-page headline announcing, "Commodore Lynch's Mosquito

Fleet Demolished."[282] This was the newspaper coverage Brigadier General Henry A. Wise of Virginia was most likely referring to in his official report of the Battle of Roanoke Island. In the report, addressed to Brigadier General Benjamin Huger and dated February 17, 1862, Wise reported on Lynch and "the fleet which got the name Mosquito Fleet."[283] Use of the term "Mosquito Fleet" in reference to the light-draft squadron fitted out by Commander Hunter in September 1861 under the direction of Flag Officer French Forrest is simply anachronistic. Even after Lynch took command of the squadron in late September, no record was found contemporary to the 1861 engagements, or even immediately prior to the Battle of Roanoke Island, in which it was called a "mosquito fleet." Flag Officer Lynch, in his reports typically referred to the fleet as simply his "squadron."[284]

The Eighth North Carolina Volunteers commanded by Colonel Henry M. Shaw "took up the line of march" from camp near Warrington, North Carolina, on September 18, for Roanoke Island.[285]

Colonel Henry Marchmore Shaw, forty-one years of age, was the son of a Rhode Island businessman turned Baptist preacher. Shaw's parents were both of Scotch-Irish descent. Young Shaw came to Indiantown, Currituck County, North Carolina, at the age of nineteen to practice medicine, having already earned his MD and two certificates of surgery at the University of Pennsylvania in 1838.[286] "Colonel Shaw won the hearts of all who knew him, not only as their physician but their friend and counselor"[287] and was elected to the North Carolina State Senate in 1851 as a Democrat. In 1853, Shaw won a seat in the U.S. House of Representatives, was defeated in 1855, but regained his seat in 1857.[288] He served his term through March 3, 1859, having been unsuccessful in a reelection bid in the Thirty-sixth Congressional race.[289]

At the outbreak of the Civil War, Dr. Henry Shaw was not at all ambivalent about whether to side with the Union of his birth or the South of his adulthood. Shaw was elected to represent Currituck County at the North Carolina Secession Convention, which was scheduled to meet on May 20, 1861 in Raleigh. Shaw, however, knowing the convention would soon unanimously vote for North Carolina's secession from the Union, resigned from the convention, casting his vote in favor of secession instead by joining the Confederate army.[290]

Shaw was commissioned colonel of what was originally the Eighth North Carolina State Troops on May 8. In September 1861, he "entered the Confederate Military Service at Camp Macon, near Warrenton and was given command of the 8th Regiment of Volunteers, one company consisting mainly of men from Currituck, Camden, Pasquotank and Perquimans Counties."[291]

Eighth North Carolina drummer, Private H.T.J. Ludwig, Company H, reminiscent of the march for Roanoke Island, recalled the 158 men of his company

> struck camp and started on the road to the fortifications of Roanoke Island…the trip on the canal and the sound on the way from Camp Macon was delightful, it being the time of the full moon and the weather being fine. We arrived at Roanoke Island on the twenty-first of September. The first duty after landing was to arrange camp. Dig wells, etc. This work took several days.[292]

Establishment of the Eighth North Carolina's new "Camp Raleigh," continued through Monday, September 30.[293] Ludwig's Company H, the Cabarrus Phalanx, was the largest company in the regiment of 650 men.[294]

The arrival of the 650 men of the Eighth North Carolina particularly brightened the picture for Third Georgia Private Alva Spencer, who wrote, "It was then thought to be certain that we would return to Portsmouth soon."[295] Private Spencer was not the only Georgian hopeful following Colonel Shaw's arrival. Colonel Wright wrote Brigadier General Huger the day after Shaw's arrival, revealing, "I had indulged the hope that I should be relieved by him."[296]

The Pork Point Battery was alive with artillery target practice on September 25,[297] and Sturgis's Light Artillery Company fired their guns for the first time at a buoy placed three miles away in the Croatan Channel. The Georgians had never fired an artillery piece, so a blank cartridge was fired first from each gun followed by more advanced practice: "Next they fired shot and shell at the buoy, and some came very near it particularly the fine 32 pound rifled gun."[298] The artillery practice in the Croatan was soon followed by a general inspection of arms at Roanoke Island on September 29.[299]

On Tuesday morning, October 1, Colonel Wright and Flag Officer Lynch received intelligence from a Roanoke Islander who had gone in the direction of Hatteras searching for his runaway slaves. An enemy gunboat was ashore about twenty-five miles south.[300] It seems Wright was told "the Yankees were about landing men near Chicamacomico" as well, and he and Lynch immediately prepared to leave Roanoke Island to confront the Federal presence in the sound.[301]

Chapter Seven

"What Madness Rules the Hour!"

On the 1ˢᵗ day of October, 1861, receiving information that a Federal steamer had been seen just south of the Island, Colonel Wright at once determined to intercept and capture her; displaying at the very commencement that acuteness of forethought, wisdom in contriving and decision in acting which rendered his subsequent career so brilliant.[302]

Flag Officer Lynch had had command of his small squadron of light-draft vessels for little more than two weeks. On October 1, Lynch's expedition into the Pamlico consisted of only three of these vessels: the CSS *Raleigh*, the CSS *Curlew* and the CSS *Junaluska*. The only one of the three steamers armed prior to September 30, though, was the *Raleigh*, which boasted two smoothbore six-pounder naval howitzers.[303]

The CSS *Raleigh* was originally built as a steam tug for the Chesapeake and Albemarle Canal. The small sixty-five-ton, iron-hulled, screw-steamer was taken over by the State of North Carolina in May 1861 and more recently by the Confederate States Navy.[304]

Lynch, like Flag Officer French Forrest, wanted each steamer of the squadron outfitted as a gunboat, but the *Curlew* and *Junaluska* were yet unarmed. A long thirty-two-pounder navy gun was removed from its mount at Pork Point Battery, where it had been placed *en barbette* just days previous. The gun had been rifled and reinforced at the Gosport Navy Yard at Portsmouth. In the darkness of night on September 30, Colonel Rans Wright had it removed from the fort and mounted on the bow of the *Curlew*

"Capture of the United States Gun-Boat 'Fanny,' at Chickamacomico, North Carolina, by Three Rebel Tug-Boats." *Harper's Weekly*, November 19, 1861. *Outer Banks History Center.*

on a pivot. The *Curlew* also received a smoothbore twelve-pounder that had been, up to that point, mounted in a field carriage. The old gun, removed from its original carriage, was mounted on the *Curlew*'s stern. The *Junaluska*, then, was fitted with a single field cannon, a six pounder.[305]

Third Georgia Private Alva Spencer made an entry into his diary while Wright was preparing Lynch's fleet for the expedition. Spencer wrote that Lieutenant John Sturgis's "flying artillery were also ordered to strike their tents, and bring their guns to this place. They have since arrived, and are now putting their guns aboard a boat."[306]

Flag Officer Lynch and Colonel Wright agreed earlier to make an attempt to destroy the Cape Hatteras Lighthouse and were simply waiting for the right conditions to present themselves. Lynch working in concert with Colonel Wright sent "an emissary" from Roanoke Island to Hatteras to "glean intelligence as to the force of the enemy in that vicinity." While the officers awaited the return of their spy, intelligence came "early in the forenoon" that one of the Union steamers was at Chicamacomico. Lynch reported he "determined to go after her." Lynch, in later reports, would indicate that the intelligence came to him personally, that the spy went out at his initiative and that he launched a speedy response to the Federal presence in the Pamlico waters. Wright claimed the same in his reports, that the informant was his, that the information came back to him personally and that the operation was launched at his initiative. Regardless of the truth behind the reports, it is certain that the army and navy commanders worked surprisingly in concert with and in full appreciation of the other's leadership during these combined operations.

Lynch and Wright's source had evidently seen the *General Putnam*, which had been alone at the north end of the Pamlico since the predawn hours of Sunday morning after it had disembarked the Twentieth Indiana at Live Oak and taken on the *Fanny*'s Sawyer gun. Colonel Wright, unlike Lynch, did not want to go after the Federal steamer without also using the opportunity to make a combined assault with Lynch's squadron and at least destroy the Hatteras Lighthouse. Lynch said of Wright, though, that he "is a man after my own heart in these matters." Lynch "could not, in courtesy, refuse to wait for the embarkation of the troops, although two precious hours were thereby lost."[307]

By 2:30 p.m., Flag Officer Lynch and Colonel Wright, with a total combined force of about two hundred, boarded Lynch's flagship, the CSS *Curlew*, commanded by Commander Hunter, and pushed away from Roanoke Island. The CSS *Raleigh* was under the command of Lieutenant Commander Joseph W. Alexander and the CSS *Junaluska* under Midshipman William H. Vernon. Midshipman James M. Gardner was also assisting aboard the flagship *Curlew*. These were the only naval officers Lynch had with his squadron on October 1. The CSS *Cotton Plant* under Midshipman Samuel S. Gregory and another floating battery commanded by Midshipman James Tayloe were left behind at Roanoke Island that afternoon.[308]

Lynch's crew on the *Curlew* was small but "worked with great alacrity." The flagship steamer, Lynch reported, was "managed and fought by a crew of eight men, assisted by ten of the Georgia volunteers…sailors and soldiers toiled vigourously [*sic*] together."[309] One of the large pieces was fought by a five-man crew from Company D and included: Corporal James A. Wilson, and Privates L.C. Randall, Augustus J. Reese, Columbus C. Taylor and Charles W. Richter.[310]

The guns on all three Rebel steamers were crewed by Third Georgia troops recently trained on them but with only minimal practice actually firing them. Colonel Wright also took with him, in addition to his gun crews, 150 men, three companies of Georgians—Company C, Company E and Company K— each man armed with an Enfield rifle, and moved down the sound to attack the enemy.[311] The Rebel squadron was underway at 2:30 p.m., and in just a few hours, the object of the expedition was spotted.[312]

As the Union gunboat *Fanny* approached Live Oak, still five miles off, it met the *General Putnam* steaming south. On meeting the *Fanny*, the *General Putnam* turned about and convoyed it to a point three miles off the beach at Live Oak.[313] Hotchkiss "reported the Sound as clear."[314] The *Fanny* anchored in six feet of water,[315] "the wind mill on the Northern End of Chicamacomac [*sic*] bearing ENE Distant 3 miles,"[316] marking the location of the camp. The Sawyer rifle, borrowed earlier by the *Putnam*, was there returned to the *Fanny*. The *General Putnam*'s captain, Acting Master Hotchkiss, ignoring Commander Stephen Rowan's specific orders to remain, left his station and started a return to the inlet. Hotchkiss surprisingly later admitted he did not start his return until after spotting a Confederate steamer off to the west.[317] The Twentieth saw the two Union steamers approaching from the southwest. Colonel Brown then observed the *Putnam* turn back to the southwest and toward the inlet after the *Fanny* was already at anchor.[318]

The *General Putnam* originally had been armed with one thirty-two-pounder cannon and a twenty-pounder Parrott rifle. Commander Rowan later grilled Hotchkiss about abandoning his post. Hotchkiss informed Rowan that he came down the sound to get coal as he was low on fuel. Rowan was steamed that Hotchkiss did not simply get coal from the *Fanny*. Rowan expected the *General Putnam* would be fully prepared to "give countenance and support" in the event of a Rebel attack. The Twentieth Indiana troops at Camp Live Oak could have gathered enough fuel for the *General Putnam* to allow it to stay for a few additional hours. Rail fences could have been used if necessary. The *General Putnam* made it back to the bulkhead in the inlet before sundown where it was secure for the evening.[319] Not so for the U.S. gunboat *Fanny*.

Commander Rowan already knew the weaknesses with the command and crews of the Union gunboats in the Pamlico Sound. He was especially aware of the tactical weaknesses of Acting Masters William Hotchkiss and Jared Elliott. The day before the *Fanny* returned to Live Oak, Commander Rowan reminded Captain Chauncey that the tugs *Ceres* and *General Putnam* were commanded by "acting masters from civil life, who are ignorant of the necessary preparations for defense, and ought not to be sent away without a [regular navy] lieutenant." Rowan wanted to take one of Chauncey's lieutenants and put him in command "afloat in the inlet and send him with both tugs to blockade."[320] However, on September 30, the *General Putnam* was already at the north end of the sound and definitely in need of a regular navy lieutenant to command in case of a turn of events such as occurred the afternoon of Tuesday, October 1.[321]

Regular navy lieutenant Peirce Crosby had been the commander of the army quartermaster transport steamer *Fanny* since August and continued in that role until several days after the Union capture of Forts Hatteras and Clark. On September 24, however, Navy Secretary Welles ordered Crosby to proceed to New York for the command of the USS *Pembina*. Welles, congratulating Crosby for his service aboard the *Fanny* during the Butler Expedition, added,

"In assigning you this command, the Department is not unmindful of your recent active and efficient services whilst attached to the Atlantic Blockading Squadron."[322] Crosby proceeded to New York immediately after receiving Welles's orders, taking command of the *Pembina* on October 1.[323]

Up until October 1, the Naval Brigade, also known as the Union Coast Guard, under Captain William Nixon, crewed the guns on the *Fanny*, just as it had in the mid-September bombardment of Fort Ocracoke. Joining in the Butler Expedition of August 28 and 29, these men were experienced seamen and "good fighters."[324] General Wool, however, sent an order arriving at the inlet along with the Twentieth Indiana, commanding Colonel Rush Hawkins to return "all of the men of the Union Coast Guard within your reach, by the Steamer Spaulding when she returns…this will not be omitted."[325] Some 108 men and three officers,[326] the "remnant of the Naval Brigade" still at Hatteras, were returned to Fort Monroe with the S*paulding* on its return the morning of October 1.[327] The unexpected and immediate recall of the Naval Brigade proved to be an additional problem for Commander Rowan, who was on his way out, and for Hawkins who had to get supplies to the Twentieth at Live Oak without delay.

The Naval Brigade detachment, part of an infantry regiment not an actual naval unit, had been under Hawkins's command, not Rowan's, since August 30. Finding effective replacements for the Naval Brigade gun crews with only a couple days' notice required Colonel Hawkins to look to Ninth New York men trained to fight the USS *Minnesota*'s two howitzers left behind at Fort Clark. Hawkins called on men who were among the three Zouave companies which made the assault on Hatteras on August 28. A number of them had already been detailed for artillery duty, some actually preferring it to drilling as an infantry soldier.[328] Two crews of Ninth New York men whom Rush Hawkins trained under command of Sergeant Major Francis Milford Peacock were assigned to the *Fanny*.

The facts concerning Sergeant Major Francis Milford Peacock before October 1861, who he was and from whence he came, are relatively few. Peacock was twenty-nine and had enlisted for two years service as a private with the Ninth New York's Company K on May 25. Only one-month later, on June 25, Peacock was appointed sergeant major.[329] Peacock was a man of the sea, and was a naturally persuasive leader. One navy officer who spent significant time with him later wrote, "He was a rollicky, bull-headed sailor, spoke several languages, had the gift of story-telling to perfection."[330]

Peacock definitely had the spirit of a soldier of fortune. Hawkins Zouaves historian J.H.E. Whitney wrote, "He enlisted from motives purely mercenary…Upon one occasion he told us that he was fighting for the Federal Government simply because on our side he could get a few dollars per month more than the Confederates would give."[331] Peacock claimed his father, a native of Albany, New York, was a sailor who eventually established a commercial shipping business in Macao, China, where Peacock was born. Later, Peacock claimed to have "commanded a Siamese war cruiser, and in 1856 he accompanied the Siamese embassy to England."[332]

Peacock related to Union officers later how he came to be a Zouave:

His father was connected with the coolie trade, and early in February, 1861, shipped a cargo of his human freight to Havana in charge of his son. Before his departure, his father instructed him to enlist in the United States Army if he ascertained on his arrival in Cuba that war had broken out. But eight days before he sailed his father died, leaving him a large inheritance. He, nevertheless, started on his voyage, and arrived in Havana after a passage of nearly four months. Having disposed of his cargo and arranged his business he came to New York with full knowledge that war had broken out, and enlisted in Colonel Bartlett's Naval Brigade, under a promise of a commission. The brigade failed in completing its organization, and on the 26th [sic] of May he again enlisted in "Hawkins's Zouaves," and went upon the expedition under Commodore Stringham, who captured Fort Hatteras…He was both a Yankee and a Chinaman, and a pretty good type of both, whenever he chose to represent the different nationalities…He came to aid the Republic in the hour of her need, and will be immortalized for his many deeds of noble daring.[333]

Sergeant Major Peacock communicated a profound respect for Colonel Rush Hawkins. One could easily conclude, from the language of private letters written later to Hawkins, that Peacock and Hawkins shared a friendship and mutual respect, which even the vilest of circumstances would hardly shake.[334] When Hawkins needed a capable soldier to lead two gun crews aboard the *Fanny* in the absence of the Naval Brigade on October 1, 1861, Francis Milford Peacock was his choice.

The two guns were crewed by eleven men, including nine Zouave privates and two corporals. The privates included John S. Rowan, John R. Havens, William H. Cunningham, Joseph Van Kirk Page and Daniel Doherty of Company C, and William H. Edsall, John Carson and James Beith of Company G. One additional crewmember was Private Frank E. Trotter of Company H. Each of these men, mostly from New York City and neighboring New Jersey, appeared to have had extensive experience aboard ships prior

Above: "Zouaves, 9th N.Y. Volunteer Infantry, ca. 1860–ca.1865." Hawkins Zouaves. Photo by Matthew Brady. *National Archives.*

Right: Private William H. Cunningham, Ninth New York (Hawkins Zouaves), Company C. Cunningham was captured aboard the *Fanny*, a member of one of the two Zouave gun crews under Sergeant Major Francis M. Peacock on October 1, 1861. This rare 1917 photo is from "W.H. Cunningham Honored; Oldest Post Office Clerk," *Brooklyn Daily Eagle*, March 2, 1917. *Danny Conroy Collection*

Private Charles F. Johnson, Ninth New York (Hawkins Zouaves). Self-portrait. *Plate II from The Long Roll.*

to the war. A handful included immigrants from the British Isles. Corporal Joel E. Tuttle, Company C, and Corporal Gardner Everard, Company G (a recent immigrant from England), were the gunners of each crew, responsible for making sure the piece was fired correctly and safely as well as accurately.[335]

Private James Beith, a Scottish immigrant, was a messmate of Hawkins Zouaves diarist Private Charles F. Johnson. Johnson, an eighteen-year-old Swedish immigrant to Minnesota, recalled Beith as "a good enough fellow, but lazy. He could never be made to drill as an infantry soldier, and actually compelled his superior to detail him for artillery duty whenever it was required, it being impossible to do anything else with him—hence his position as gunner on board the 'Fanny.'"[336]

Having arrived off Camp Live Oak at Chicamacomico in the afternoon around 1:30 p.m., the men on the *Fanny* sat and waited for communication from shore, which came two hours later.[337] The tents of the encampment clearly in view, Commissary Captain John Clark could also see a "dozen boats lying idle on the shore" and wondered why they were not being employed "to remove the government troops and stores."[338] Colonel Brown, however, already understood the logistical problems associated with a nighttime transfer of men and equipment through the shoal water to the beach at Live Oak. He was making preparations for a more efficient landing than took place a few nights earlier at Live Oak. Brown reported later that he put Major Benjamin H. Smith in charge of procuring *what small boats he could and with our launch board the vessels soon as possible after anchoring and assist in...landing the freight intended for our camp. Major Smith took with him a good and reliable pilot to offer to bring the vessels to an anchorage nigher shore. Major Smith with these small boats left the shore a considerable time before the Fanny came to anchor, boarded her soon after her anchor was cast, offered the pilot assistance which was declined by the Captain of the Fanny, then loaded and left for the shore.*[339]

Major Smith was "annoyed on nearing the *Fanny* at absence of flag or signal from her" but still "supposed her to be friendly,"[340] so he rowed out with Twentieth Indiana's commissary sergeant John "Jack" Evans and Adjutant Israel N. Stiles in a small fisherman's skiff. These officers began offloading supplies to prepare supper that evening for the officers.[341]

Meanwhile, a launch was also brought out under command of Captain Oliver H. Bailey, of Company C.[342] A number of boys were onboard with punting poles attempting to quickly cover the three miles out to where the *Fanny* was anchored.[343] They took on the first load of equipment and tents,[344] along with a couple of the sick men who had been convalescing back on the *Spaulding*, while Surgeon Everts established the camp hospital.

One very young, rather tall and lanky Hoosier watching with interest was Hiram Augustus Unruh, of Bailey's Company C. He disliked the name Hiram and so enlisted as "Henry" A. Unruh, lying about his age as well.[345] This six-foot private was still a month short of a sixteenth birthday. At the breakout of the war, Unruh had been enrolled at Valparaiso Male and Female College, one of the nation's first co-educational schools, but quit at fifteen to enlist in the Twentieth Indiana and go to war.[346]

The three officers on the skiff finished loading and quickly

Adjutant Israel N. Stiles, Twentieth Indiana. *Meserve Collection, New York State Library.*

shoved off, ahead of Bailey's loaded launch. The launch soon got away from the *Fanny* as well and headed back to shore with ten men on board.[347] Commissary Captain Clark complained that the boat was "loaded to the gunwale—leaving no seats for the rowers." Clark was not pleased with the chaotic process and reported, "The launch was freighted pell-mell, with provisions, ammunition, hospital stretchers, trunks and forage."[348]

Heavily laden with ammunition, tents and other supplies, Captain Bailey's launch was still a mile out by the time the officers had rowed onto shore.[349] German-immigrant-turned-privateer Charles H. White made it off the *Fanny* and helped punt the flatboat to shore.[350] Commissary Captain Clark also got off the *Fanny* and was on the launch trailing behind the officers' skiff, having personally accompanied the commissary stores from Fort Monroe aboard the *Spaulding*.[351] Clark, former editor of the *Boston Courier*,[352] was about to become a very lucky man that afternoon.[353] Private Lucius L. Bennett, who was showing signs of measles, was also taken off the *Fanny* and transported in the launch to Live Oak to be placed in the newly established hospital there.[354]

Having shoved off from the gunboat twenty minutes earlier,[355] the launch was halfway to shore at 4:00 p.m.,[356] and things started getting exciting. The Hoosiers at Live Oak "saw in the Northwestern direction three great lines of black smoke. They grew blacker."[357] Then, a steamer appeared on the horizon to the west. It was "secesh." Soon, two more Confederate steamers were spotted, and all three vessels were moving directly toward the *Fanny*, which was then sitting alone and vulnerable, the *General Putnam* long since out of sight.[358]

The Union soldiers saw the first steamer begin the fire and the two trailing steamers get into position for some of the same.[359] The very appearance of the Rebel steamers moving rapidly in the direction of the *Fanny* "threw [the Hoosiers] into a state of trepidation." Each steamer was visible from the shore. The Twentieth saw first "a side wheel boat of good size," which was the CSS *Curlew*, and then a propeller steamer, the CSS *Raleigh*, as well as what it misidentified as a stern-wheeler farthest from view, the CSS *Junaluska*, which in fact was also a screw steamer.[360]

The *Curlew*, the large side-wheeler, began the fire, followed by the *Raleigh* when in position.. The *Junaluska* was unable to get in range.[361] The *Fanny* could be seen moving off from its original anchorage but soon became grounded again in the shoal water. At Live Oak the report of the guns was not heard because the wind was blowing from the east, carrying the sound away. Nevertheless, the beach was full of men watching the action as smoke

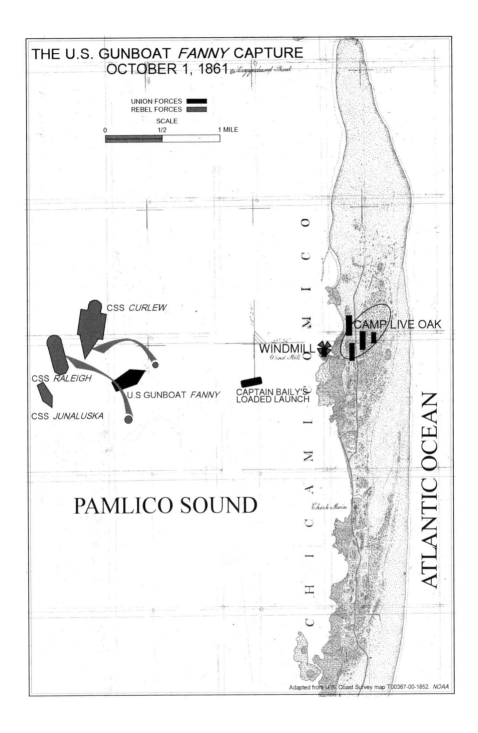

belched from the Rebel guns and the shells splashed in the water near the Union gunboat. All the while, the boys on Bailey's launch "punted like old salts," quickly and safely bringing their load to shore.[362]

The side-wheel steamer *Curlew* had been operating privately in North Carolina's coastal waters since soon after its construction and purchase in 1856 from Harlan & Hollingsworth Iron Shipbuilding Company in Wilmington, Delaware. The 236-ton *Curlew* was 135 feet long and 23 feet wide. As large as it was, *Curlew*'s draft was an amazingly shallow 5 feet. Its paddle wheels were 18 feet in diameter and 8 feet wide, allowing *Curlew* to cruise at twelve knots.[363]

The *Fanny*, its retreat blocked by the enemy steamers, fired nine shots without effect from the nine-pounder rifled Sawyer gun retrieved from the *General Putnam* earlier. Civilian Captain Morrison, onboard the ship, later reported in error that one shell from the *Fanny* hit the bow of one of the three Rebel gunboats. Morrison's civilian first mate, George Ridgely, and a few other soldiers commenced heaving cases of ammunition overboard. Thirty or forty cases, of a thousand cartridges each, and a barrel or two of bacon all made it into the shallow waters of the Pamlico before Quartermaster Hart stopped the party. Sergeant Major Peacock refused to drop the artillery pieces overboard, believing it would make it worse for them once they were captured. The Sawyer gun, known to have been "a favorite," would surely not be tossed in. Peacock later stated that "the number of men on deck," and "a force far Superior to that under my command," was what later compelled him to surrender.[364]

A flag of surrender not yet raised, Quartermaster Hart ordered the cable slipped.[365] October 1 was coincidentally the quartermaster's forty-seventh birthday. Typically, "a man of remarkable cheerfulness,"[366] Hart—of Attica, Fountain County, Indiana—was a most

Quartermaster Isaac W. Hart, Twentieth Indiana. *Craig Dunn Collection.*

"Capture of the Propeller 'Fanny' in Pamlico Sound, on the 1st of October, by Three Confederate Steamers, while Conveying Men and Stores to the 20th Indiana Regiment, Encamped at Chicamacomico, 40 Miles from Hatteras Inlet—from a Sketch by an Officer of the Indiana Regiment." Hand-colored engraving original to Frank Leslie's *Illustrated News*, October 26, 1861. The officer who drew the original sketch was Twentieth Indiana surgeon Orpheus Everts. *Outer Banks History Center.*

likeable man who had become an equally likeable officer. Hart's twin brother, James, was a lawyer, as was his older brother, Ralph, both with reputations as eloquent orators.[367] The quartermaster, too, was a powerful speaker and could easily draw a crowd, being known for his "brief and animated speeches always made pungent by some original and well-pointed anecdote...He was a kind husband, a genial gentleman, and a remarkably companionable man; and more than all, a Christian."[368] "Old Hart," as he was known, "nearly always in fine spirits," would be remembered by fellow soldiers as "being not only a beautiful singer, but also a capital poet," composing a number of songs during the war.[369] A line of one of Hart's better remembered songs, "The Prisoners' Song," went, "Roll on, roll on, sweet moments roll on."[370]

During the engagement, the *Fanny* continued to drift farther and farther away from its original position and finally ran aground five miles off Live Oak. Then, the flag went up. Hart, according to Morrison, was the first to recommend surrender.[371] The six-member civilian crew of the *Fanny* made its escape in one of the two launches onboard,[372] and the Rebels appeared to make no attempt to capture the fleeing crew as it rowed off.[373] It was later the uninformed opinion of some in the public that had Morrison "stood by his post, and followed the directions of the pilot, no loss would have occurred."[374]

Lieutenant Thomas H. Logan was nearby in a small fishing boat as the situation grew progressively more desperate. Two of Logan's own men from Company F were aboard the *Fanny*: Privates Comingore and Wilkinson. It was Logan's intent to set the *Fanny* on fire and with that objective, offered all the money he had (sixty dollars) to the poor island men who rowed him out on the sound. The plan was too risky, and the men refused, as poor as they were, not willing to gamble their lives or freedom for Logan's cash offer.[375]

Private Marion Moss of the Third Georgia, Company H, recorded second-hand that "the Yanks went below after raising the white flag and were helping themselves to liquors and champagne. Baskets were broken open and they were having a good time when our men boarded her."[376] The "state of trepidation" among the men on board the *Fanny*, sparked by the first reports of Rebel artillery, was not allayed, however, after the men were actually in enemy hands.[377] Peacock commended his Zouave gun crews, and Corporal Tuttle in particular, who "acted bravely and exhibited throughout the utmost coolness and bravery." Peacock also noted that he would remember Quartermaster Hart's "coolness and the manner in which he controlled the men under his command from the Indiana Regiment."[378]

Back at Camp Rescue on Roanoke Island, the Rebels could hear the heavy firing, knowing that at least some, if not all, was from Lynch's little squadron. Private Spencer noted, "There were, according to my counting, about twenty guns."[379] Third Georgia historians recorded twenty-nine shots fired from Rebel guns.[380] Twentieth Indiana lieutenant Gilbreath, who witnessed the engagement from Live Oak, later noted, "After a short resistance of 35-minutes, the '*Fanny*' was overpowered, and within four hours of her coming to anchor she was a captive, and on her way to Roanoke Island."[381]

John C. Langhorne was the first Confederate to set foot on the deck of the surrendered *Fanny*.[382] Langhorne took the stars and stripes down and ran up Confederate colors, "amid deafining [sic] shouts of the victors." Langhorne, formerly the local editor of the Norfolk *Day Book*, was on this day captain's clerk aboard the CSS *Raleigh*.[383]

The significance of the capture of the *Fanny* was defined by Colonel Claiborne Snead of the Third Georgia when he later wrote, "This was the first naval success in North Carolina, the first capture made by our arms of an armed vessel; and more than all, it was a naval victory achieved by infantry marines."[384] The Confederates considered the *Fanny* a special prize, particularly because it had been General Benjamin Butler's "flag-ship."[385] Back on Roanoke Island, Private Spencer wrote, "The whole camp was alive with joy on account of our glorious victory. Some were so much elated that they had to go and get 'tight.' And what was worse than all, some of the staff officers were among the number that were guilty of the above act."[386]

Witnessing the engagement, which ended in the capture of the *Fanny*, their comrades and their equipment, brought forth a full array of emotions among the men of the Twentieth. Excitement gave way to devastation, devastation to anger, and the anger to fear as is evidenced in one soldier's account that made it to the front page of the *New York Times*:

> *It was an exciting scene, a mortifying one, for there were we…ready and eager to take part in the battle, yet not a gunboat, not a piece of artillery, nothing but a dozen fishing skiffs, to cope with these steamers. We had to stand like children and see our boat, our provisions, and our men, captured before our eyes….It is enough to make one's blood boil. It is the old story that has been told in Missouri, at Springfield and at Lexington, the game of four to one. We saw all this, and wonder next what our fate will be. A puff of smoke, a tongue of flame, and the Fanny was gone, and we felt that our doom was sealed…in the heart of the enemy's country, no supplies, no reinforcements! What madness rules the hour!*[387]

Forty-two prisoners in all were taken from aboard the *Fanny*. At the end of the day, Twentieth Indiana sergeant Thomas White Stephens of Captain Alfred Reed's Company K wrote simply, "We saw the fight but could not help. No artillery." Sergeant Stephens documented the taking of the *Fanny*, specifically noting the capture of his five Company K comrades: Noah Kelly, Calvin Keefer, Michael Casper, James B. Smith and Van Buren Hinds.[388] Van Hinds, twenty-two, of Remington, Indiana, as so many others of the Twentieth, had come from generations of men who had given themselves in each of the great wars of the nation. His father served during the Mexican War, his grandfather in the War of 1812, and his great-grandfather was a fifer in the Revolutionary War.[389] Van, now a captive, would give a little bit more. Private Henry F. O'Blenis, twenty-five, of Company C, looked on helplessly from the safety of camp as his older brother, Abel, twenty-eight, also of Company C, was taken away.

The sutler's clerk, Hugh Watson, was one of four civilians captured. The sutler, Speakman (his first name unknown), though some reports listed him captured aboard the *Fanny* as well,[390] was actually watching the spectacle

from shore. Speakman lost everything aboard the tug, "his goods, his money, and his partner in business."[391] Watson, unfortunately, also had "the funds of the concern with him,"[392] which were now in Confederate hands.

Commissary Captain Clark was convinced that "this vast loss of property could…have been avoided, had the commandant on shore dispatched the sail boats under his control, when the '*Fanny*' first arrived. Had he done this, every soldier on board, and all the provisions and government property could have been on shore…the hour at which the action began." Clark left Live Oak that evening at eight o'clock on a sailboat for the inlet. He claims to have heard and seen the flash of cannon fire off Chicamacomico soon after departure and again during his journey. He interpreted the firing as a Rebel victory celebration. He arrived back at Hatteras before sunrise the next day,[393] at about the same time as the six civilian crew members.

The northern papers reported the *Fanny*, "having been condemned," to have been a poor prize apart from its stores. Reports circulated that "she was under orders to proceed to Philadelphia for a new boiler, and was to have left the day she was taken. Her worn-out boiler will shortly prove to be a bomb-shell of greater magnitude to the enemy than they have yet received."[394] There are no other official records indicating the *Fanny* had problems with its boiler or that it was in any way crippled. The records do show that in August prior to the Butler Expedition, anticipating the rolling ocean waves, Lieutenant Peirce Crosby had the boiler chained down to prevent damage on the ocean waves. Another repair was made to the *Fanny*'s rudder just prior to the Ocracoke expedition of mid-September. However, there is no indication that the *Fanny* was anything less than a fine little tug, troop transport and gunboat.

Thinking it to be unsafe for the squadron to return to Roanoke Island at night and risk friendly fire from Pork Point battery, Lynch "anchored off the scene of the conflict for the night." The next morning early, the expedition

Opposite, top: "Capture of the Steamer 'Fanny' by Three Confederate Steamers Off Chicamicomico, N.C." This Thomas Nash engraving is from an unknown illustrated newspaper. It depicts Twentieth Indiana officers arriving at Live Oak in a small fishing boat, having been aboard the *Fanny* just before her capture. This was most likely from an original drawing by Twentieth Indiana surgeon Orpheus Everts. *Outer Banks History Center*.

Opposite, bottom: Civil War identification disc, or "dog tag," of Private Henry F. O'Blenis, Twentieth Indiana, Company C, younger brother of Private Abel O'Blenis, of the same company. Abel O'Blenis was captured aboard the gunboat *Fanny*, while Henry watched from shore. ID tags such as this were often available through the sutler's store that moved about with the regiment. The Twentieth Indiana's sutler, Speakman, had all of his goods and his clerk, Hugh Watson, captured on the *Fanny*. *Joseph W. Stahl Collection*.

returned to Roanoke Island. The captured *Fanny* was brought in with Union colors hoisted, the commander not thinking that the battery was unaware of the capture. The battery at Pork Point "threw a shot across her bows, to which the steamer paid no attention…then threw another shot much nearer…when the obnoxious colors were hauled down and the Confederate flag was thrown to the breeze."[395]

Flag Officer Lynch, of course, was quite pleased with the new addition to his growing Rebel squadron. Directly after the capture, he reported to Secretary Stephen R. Mallory that the CSS *Fanny* was "a much larger and finer steamer than the *Raleigh*, and will prove a valuable acquisition to our squadron. Her hull is iron, cased with wood, and her engine and boilers are reported as in excellent order."[396]

News of the capture of the *Fanny* quickly broke to the Zouaves at Camp Wool and Fort Clark. Welcoming the break in monotonous drilling, Private Johnson quipped, "Well, we have been quiet so long, what if we should have a little excitement, say I."[397] News was getting out "that the capture of the steamer was effected through the treachery of the commander."[398] The commander pointed to was the civilian captain, Morrison. However, scrutiny of the Twentieth Indiana's quartermaster, Lieutenant Hart, and Hawkins Zouaves sergeant major Peacock was minimal at best. Evidence would emerge many months later that would give sufficient cause to take eyes off Morrison and lay at least some of the blame at the feet of each of these two men.

Chapter Eight

"Over a Thousand New Blue Winter Overcoats"

T hird Georgia colonel Rans Wright wasted no time getting off his official report of the capture of the Federal steamer *Fanny*. He wrote a brief account of the singular success as soon as he returned the following day, knowing Brigadier General Huger would want to hear immediately of the quartermaster and commissary stores taken and Federal ammunition surrendered. Wright noted he was enjoying cooperation with Flag Officer Lynch. Contrary to how Union papers were reporting the intensity of the fight from the *Fanny*, Rans Wright praised the crew of the Union gunboat for having "made a gallant resistance, but the superior weight of our guns gave us the advantage…after an engagement of thirty-five minutes the *Fanny* surrendered." The Georgian colonel was convinced that with more fuel their expedition would have been extended. Fuel in short supply, however, the Georgians with their navy comrades returned to Roanoke Island, and every able body immediately began cutting wood to fuel a return to Camp Live Oak and Hatteras Lighthouse. [399] Wright reported that 791 Third Georgia men were ready for duty. [400]

The primary objective of a return expedition to Hatteras, Wright pointed out, was to "capture the Federals who are encamped at Chicamacomico." Secondarily, he intended to at least move south far enough to "demolish the light at Hatteras." "Look for something stirring in a few days," Wright signaled Huger. In the meantime, Wright would not bring the *Fanny* prisoners up to Norfolk due to scarcity of fuel. [401] To gather enough wood for the steamers, the Rebels even appropriated a farmer's rail fence from around his fields and cut it up. [402]

Wright lost no time in staking out a claim on one significant portion of the captured quartermaster stores—specifically, over one thousand new blue winter overcoats, which would contribute "greatly to their comfort during the ensuing winter."[403] The October air was already turning cooler, and the acquisition of the coats could not have been timelier. Wright conveniently downplayed the quantity by not giving the specific number of coats in his report, mentioning them in passing: "Among the captured stores are a number of coats (over), which my men need very much. May I not distribute them among my men?"[404] Reports had already reached Elizabeth City by October 5, though, stating Wright had captured 1,050 overcoats, 1,200 pair of blankets and two large cases of brogan shoes.[405]

The *Fanny* had been carrying "enough sutler's stores to set up quite a large establishment in North Carolina."[406] Among the sutler's inventory were "cheese, jellies, cakes, wines, brandy, cigars" and more.[407] The commissary stores onboard included sixty barrels of flour and nine thousand pounds of beef.[408] Third Georgia quartermaster Alexander Phillips was relieved, and Commissary H.S. Hughes was equally pleased with the captured Federal goods. The *New York Herald* reported early on that a large and valuable quantity of medical supplies was aboard the *Fanny*. However, that information came through a Federal officer who "merely guessed…at the quantity." The reporter later corrected his earlier report, stating that the amount of medical supplies was "by no means large or very valuable."[409] Early southern reports told of an unconfirmed $30,000 in specie having been taken as well.[410] It was reported that saddles, seventy-three thousand cartridges and twenty-five thousand percussion caps were also captured aboard the *Fanny*.[411] Values were placed on the captured goods of $70,000 to $80,000 and even as high as $100,000 or more.[412]

Mixed rumors of what occurred in the Pamlico Sound on October 1 quickly flowed north into Norfolk. Mixed and errant reports made their way into the papers, both Northern and Southern. One Norfolk paper, by Friday, October 4, revealed, "It had been reported here that the Yankees had attempted to land at Roanoke Island in flat-boats, for the purpose of obtaining provisions, but were driven off by the Confederate troops. The rumor requires confirmation." The twisted rumor was pleasantly straightened out that evening during a "grand musical soiree" to benefit the Ladies' Soldiers' Aid Society in Norfolk. The capture of the transport *Fanny* was announced "at the Opera House, during the performances by the Amateur Minstrels, causing tumultuous cheering and great excitement in the large audience."[413]

The next morning, October 5, Brigadier General Huger wrote Adjutant and Inspector General Samuel Cooper informing him of the capture of the

"Lincoln steamer *Fanny*," along with the prisoners and quartermasters stores. Huger believed there were fifty prisoners taken, of which two were officers, and inquired of Cooper, the highest-ranking officer in the Confederate army, "What disposition shall I make of the prisoners?"[414] Cooper, in Richmond, was crowding every available tobacco warehouse with prisoners taken at Ball's Bluff and First Manassas. Richmond simply did not have room for fifty more. On October 6, Cooper wrote back, stating, "If you have any means of providing for the prisoners taken by [Flag Officer] Lynch, you are advised to do so. We are too much crowded here already."[415]

After acting Secretary of War Judah P. Benjamin received Huger's announcement of the capture of the *Fanny*, War Bureau chief Albert T. Bledsoe informed Huger that the situation had changed. In Bledsoe's October 8 response, Huger was directed by Secretary Benjamin to transfer the *Fanny* prisoners to Richmond if they could not be kept "conveniently in Norfolk."[416]

Meanwhile, Flag Officer William Lynch wasted no time in transforming the new addition to his squadron, the CSS *Fanny*, fitting it out as the man-of-war he envisioned. Lynch removed the six-pounder James rifle and replaced it with a thirty-two-pounder rifled cannon. The favorite nine-pounder Sawyer rifle remained aboard the Rebel gunboat. The Confederate officer transferred to the command of the CSS *Fanny* was the 1860 Naval Academy graduate Midshipman James Langhorne Tayloe.[417]

The Union prisoners from the gunboat *Fanny* were confined on a schooner at Roanoke Island until October 8.[418] The schooner *M.C. Sumner*, under Captain James Cartwright, which had been chartered since September 3, had also been used in the construction of the Pork Point Battery and in conveying stores from the abandoned Fort Oregon. The Sumner would also be used to transport troops to Chicamacomico on October 4.[419] The Norfolk *Day Book* reported that Negroes were captured aboard the *Fanny*. Without numbering them, it was stated that some of them were "said to have been stolen by Picayune Butler from citizens of the ill-fated town of Hampton, and will no doubt be restored to their rightful owners."[420] In reality, there was only one black captured aboard the *Fanny*. That was J.H. Edwards of Dulaney Valley, Maryland, near Cockeysville, who had attached himself to the regiment when it was guarding the Northern Central Railroad.

Chapter Nine

"The Command Will Remain and See What Will Turn Up"

Word reached Colonel Rush Hawkins of the *Fanny* capture early on the morning of October 2, and the colonel called on Commander Stephen Rowan for a force to relieve the Twentieth. That morning from Live Oak, Colonel Brown sent a dispatch to Hawkins by the hand of First Lieutenant George W. Meikel of Company H. Company H had a corporal and six privates taken aboard the *Fanny*. Brown communicated:

> *By the loss of the* Fanny *yesterday…I find my command in a destitute and suffering condition. But two of my companies have any tents or camp equipage, and these two are only partly supplied. We have provision short for one day—and no possibility of procuring any from the inhabitants around us. The overcoats for the regiment were also lost as we supposed…I shall remain with the rest of the regiment as long as we can subsist unless otherwise ordered.*

Brown also informed Hawkins that he was sending to him all the men on the sick list. Brown wrote, "We are totally unable to care for them here as they should be, hoping you will care for them to the best of your circumstances."[421] To the Twentieth, Brown issued General Order Number 11, from "regtl headqrs at Camp Live Oak, Hatteras Island," which directed that "having been freed from such incumbrances [*sic*] as the sick and the baggage of the reg't, which will be sent to Fort Hatteras, the command will remain and see what will turn up."[422]

Navy commander Rowan was still inside Hatteras Inlet, waiting to get the *Pawnee* across the bar and north to Washington. Rowan informed Hawkins that he had already transferred command of the inlet to Lieutenant Commander Reed Werden, of the USS *Stars and Stripes*. The *Stars and Stripes*, along with the USS *Monticello*, had arrived at Hatteras the day previous, before the *Fanny* had left the inlet for Chicamacomico. Rowan, though not in command, expressed to Hawkins the "propriety" of an expedition commanded by officers of the USS *Susquehanna* and including a couple of its launches. Hawkins and Werden, armed with a letter from Rowan, were sent to consult with the *Susquehanna* captain, James Lawrence Lardner. Rowan in the meantime commenced getting the *Ceres* and *General Putnam* "coaled, watered, and provisioned."[423]

Commander Lardner had been ordered to Hatteras to take command of the USS *Susquehanna* and relieve Captain Chauncey. Lardner was to maintain the blockade and provide "assistance to our people at Forts Hatteras and Clark."[424]

Colonel Hawkins and Commander Werden returned from their consultation, having acquired "two competent officers and an armed launch and twenty-five well-trained men. The tugs were loaded that night and the expedition left early the next morning."[425] The armed expedition left the inlet Thursday morning, October 3, under command of Lieutenant J.P. Bankhead, one of those "competent officers" from the *Susquehanna*. The Bankhead expedition consisted of the *General Putnam* and the *Ceres*,[426] towing the *Susquehanna's* launch, which was armed with a boat howitzer[427] and loaded with the twenty-five men.[428] These two gunboats were dispatched, as Northern papers would reveal, "in hope of overtaking and recovering the *Fanny* and capturing the [Confederate] tugs."[429]

Bankhead's expedition steamed to Chicamacomico[430] and arrived at two o'clock in the afternoon on October 3,[431] successfully landing the remaining stores and tents left at the inlet,[432] as well as provisions for a week.[433] The provisions were a welcomed sight to the hungry Indianians. Rations having been in very short supply for a couple days, the men were living off whatever they could find to eat and had been foraging constantly for oysters in the sound. Lieutenant Gilbreath of Company I recalled many years later, "For two days we had little to eat. I remember that the watery oysters we found on the sound side, and the sweet potatoe [*sic*] pies we got from the people living on the Island, tasted very good. I have not wanted any of either since, however."[434]

Along with the *General Putnam* and *Ceres* that afternoon, Brown sent all those Indiana men on the regimental sick list into Hawkins's care, as he earlier indicated. Alarmingly, a Rebel steamer showed itself at that time, and the *Ceres* and *General Putnam* "gave her chase, and were not seen again" by the Hoosiers at Live Oak:[435] "Hastily landing [the supplies], they steamed to the NW, not again to return whilst we remained at Chicamacomico."[436] Some Northern newspapers reported that the Union gunboats saw nothing of the Rebels and returned to the inlet that very evening.[437] In any case, Hawkins sent Ninth New York captain Edward Jardine, Company G, on horseback up to Chicamacomico that evening, and Jardine spent the night at Live Oak keeping an eye on the situation, watching for any indications of a return of the Rebel fleet.[438] In the absence of the regiment's major, Edgar Kimball, who was at Newport News with companies B and K, thirty-one-year-old Captain Jardine was Hawkins's right hand. Jardine also had won a senior position among the other captains by drawing lots during the early weeks of the regiment's formation.[439] Brown was not informed at the time, but Jardine had also brought with him Hawkins's orders for the Twentieth's full retreat from Live Oak, only to be given in the face of an imminent threat of an attack.

Colonel Brown still was without the promised artillery after Bankhead's departure and Captain Jardine's arrival at Live Oak. In Hawkins's defense, it was reported that the capture of the *Fanny* actually delayed the delivery of the promised artillery, with the "attention" of the gunboats *Ceres* and *General Putnam* being called elsewhere.[440] Besides, the only two trained gun crews had been captured aboard the *Fanny*, along with Sergeant Major Peacock, and the Naval Brigade had already been ordered off Hatteras.

Before the USS *Pawnee* and Commodore Rowan finally left Hatteras Inlet on Thursday afternoon, October 3, accusations were tossed about that the two Union tugs, *Ceres* and *General Putnam*, had already "abandoned their position and were on their way back to Hatteras Inlet."[441] The orders for Lieutenant Bankhead's gunboat expedition are not clear today. If the orders were simply to take provisions to Live Oak, then the task was completed. If the orders included remaining at the north of Pamlico Sound to prevent a second attack on the Indiana encampment, then that mission was abandoned. Carrying a number of the Twentieth's sick men aboard was another reason for returning quickly to the inlet and not pursuing the enemy if detected.

One thing was certain: the Rebels on Roanoke Island were not satisfied with only capturing the *Fanny*, the Twentieth's winter coats and forty-two Lincolnites. Southern secessionist visitors at Fort Monroe under a flag of truce immediately after the surrender of the *Fanny* openly revealed that the Rebels on Roanoke had plans to "bag Colonel Brown and his command" by Saturday, October 4.[442]

Chapter Ten

"Stern and Savage War Was Upon Us"

W ashington's *Daily National Intelligencer* of October 10 described the
events of October 4 and 5, 1861, on North Carolina's Outer Banks
as "A Brush in North Carolina."[443] Most often, however, both Northern
and Southern newspapers consistently referred to the "brush" as the "Affair
at Chicamacomico" and the "Chicamacomico Affair." Today's popular
reference, the "Chicamacomico Races," was not a familiar phrase to the
American public and readers of Southern and Northern newspapers printed
immediately after the events. It was not long, however, before those who
actually were there in the middle of it all began to, at least privately, call it
a "race."

Colonel Brown wrote on November 4 to a friend back in Indiana: "You
have heard of our run, we passed over the sand in good time…Nigh 50 miles
from help and that from experience doubtful, our rebel friends in possession of
the sound. The race commenced."[444] This may be the earliest known reference
to the Chicamacomico Affair as a "race." However, it was most certainly the
men of the Third Georgia Regiment who first privately called the retreat from
Live Oak the "Chicamacomico Races." And rightfully so, as it was only the
Third Georgia Regiment that ran the full twenty-plus miles in both directions,
dragging its artillery with it through the sand of Hatteras Banks.

Third Georgia adjutant William Turner probably was the first to use
today's popular term in a publication. That publication was the July 19,
1864 installment of his memoirs "The First Twelve Months of the 3rd
Georgia Regiment," which appeared in the Turnwold, Georgia newspaper,
the *Countryman*. Turner detailed there his "account of the Chickamicomico
[*sic*] Races."[445] A decade later, Third Georgia colonel Claiborne Snead, in

The *New York Herald*, October 13, 1861. Front-page map depicts "The Affair at Chicamacomico." *Oxford Collection.*

his keynote address at the 1874 reunion of the Third Georgia Regiment at Union Point, Georgia, described the "chase which has been properly styled the Chicamacomico races."[446] The term the "Chicamacomico Affair" will be used throughout this narrative, however, as it best represents what the Union and Confederate governments, the newspapers of the day, the Union and Confederate soldiers involved and the general public called these events at the time.

Late on Wednesday, October 2, after the *Fanny* was taken, Colonel Rans Wright of the Third Georgia gave orders to march and take four days' rations.[447] Wright ordered the Eighth North Carolina to join the Georgians for what would be "a jolly crowd and a jolly time…all in high spirits to meet the Twentieth Indiana Regiment on the Island at Chickamacomico." Private Marion Moss and Private Hal Lee were left back at camp with the many watches and pocket books the men had left in their care in case of death or capture. Moss and Lee were also left with a trunk and instructions to take everything to Nags Head and on to Norfolk in case the assault failed and the men were captured en masse.[448]

Earlier in September, the Confederates had captured a large iron barge that had previously drifted into the sound.[449] The iron boat was designed to be used in the Atlantic surf to land Federal troops during the Butler Invasion. On September 11, the landing craft drifted away from its anchorage inside the sound near Fort Clark. Colonel Hawkins of the Ninth New York informed Union navy commander Rowan of the problem only after the barge was nearly out of sight. Both navy tugs, *Ceres* and *General Putnam*, were away towing prizes out into the Atlantic, leaving no immediate help available for retrieval. The army tug *Fanny* was later sent in search of the barge but to no avail. This loss of a very practical vessel, and particularly Hawkins's delayed response to the problem, irked Commander Rowan enough that he wrote Commodore Stringham about it the following day.[450] The barge was large enough to carry one hundred Federal troops, but soon it would be carrying Georgia soldiers set to attack the Federals at Live Oak.[451]

Colonel Rans Wright left Camp Georgia at midnight Thursday and arrived off Chicamacomico on Friday morning, October 4.[452] One Third Georgia historian recalled, "The heavy breathing of [the steamer] engines, and the noise from propeller and paddle wheels quickly told that each vessel was in motion. But the sound sleep of the soldiers, stretched upon their decks, was not broken; nor were their sweet dreams of home and of loved ones disturbed."[453]

A colonel, said to be Solomon Cherry, of Norfolk, not clearly connected with any of the regiments then at Roanoke Island, was detailed ahead of the Rebel flotilla in a small boat to take soundings. Cherry "got within musket shot of the pickets from Hatteras, who ran off, apparently much alarmed at his approach. Having no gun in his boat, he was unable to shoot at the scamps as they made their way up from the shore."[454] Flag Officer Lynch's little gunboat squadron on this day included the CSS *Curlew*—again the flagship—the captured and newly-named CSS *Fanny*, the CSS *Raleigh*, the CSS *Junaluska*, the CSS *Empire* and the CSS *Cotton Plant*.[455]

Signals detected from various points around the sound indicated to the Federal forces that the Rebels were aware of the departure of Bankhead's gunboat expedition from Live Oak. (The Confederates had, in fact, observed the gunboats as they brought provisions to Live Oak.) Colonel Brown and his Indiana men, along with Ninth New York captain Edward Jardine, therefore, were vigilant through the night on Thursday, October 3, though no alarm was sounded.[456]

About sunrise at Live Oak, Colonel Brown observed two smoke trails from steamers passing south on the west side of the sound. "They were soon out of sight and in less than an hour were seen returning accompanied by seven

Boarding trumpet of the CSS *Curlew*. *Walter White and the Museum of the Albemarle*.

other steam and sail vessels." As the steamers approached, closing in from the southwest, no colors were showing and the vessels' movements "gave rise to suspicion that they were rebel steamers."[457]

By 8:00 a.m., more of the Twentieth Indiana officers and men were on the beach looking west out over the sound, watching the approach of the unidentified steamers. Since there had been "evidence of a fight on the Sound" the day before, after the *Ceres* and *General Putnam* steamed off in hot pursuit of a Rebel gunboat, some of the Hoosiers assumed the steamers were Federal, towing several Rebel prizes.[458] Private Joshua Lewis of Company H was on guard that morning from 7:00 to 9:00 a.m. along the water's edge on the sound side of the island. Not able to call the steamers friendly at this point, the Twentieth's officers, as Private Lewis later recalled, "were uncertain as to the proper course to take, for we had no weapons save the old muskets that kicked almost as hard as they shot."[459]

Soon after 8:00 a.m., however, the boys at Live Oak were certain the incoming squadron was indeed Confederate, and the fleet's movements made its intentions clear. The Indiana Twentieth heard the long roll, formed into companies and readied to receive a Rebel landing party. The Rebel squadron then curiously "changed its course heading direct for the shore some 4 to 5 miles below camp and came to anchor two miles from land."[460]

The situation developed rapidly. One Rebel steamer was seen breaking away to the north toward Live Oak while another steamed yet farther south. Brown could see with the glasses that the steamers and their towed barges and launches were filled with troops, the number of which Brown thought conservatively "could <u>not</u> be less than two thousand." Estimates by Brown's officers were even higher, though. While the Federals were gauging the size of the Rebel forces, "several shots were fired which were supposed to be signals." It appeared to Brown, initially, that only two landings were going to be made, one north at Live Oak and another at a landing a few miles south of the encampment, due east of the Rebel squadron's current position. Brown expected this second landing would include the largest part of their forces.[461]

The Rebel fleet launched its initial artillery attack at 9:00 a.m.[462] The steamer seen moving north toward the camp took a position one-half to three-quarters of a mile from shore, directly west of Live Oak, and soon began throwing artillery into the camp. Brown could see the enemy "was evidently at this time <u>master</u> of the upper end of the sound."[463]

One Hoosier later wrote to his hometown newspaper in Logansport, Indiana, "The fleet of the enemy gradually drew up in line of battle, and first a shot plowing up the sand, and then a shell bursting in air directly over the camp, told us that stern and savage war was upon us."[464] The colonel initially moved the regiment to the left of Camp Live Oak into a grove of trees on a hill. It was not long before the Rebel artillery had a fix on the camp. The tents were on fire from the shelling,[465] and the Banker house Surgeon Orpheus Everts used as a hospital was destroyed.[466]

The loss of able-bodied men captured with the *Fanny*, the three companies left behind at Fort Monroe, sick men sent back to Hatteras with the Bankhead expedition and a number of men on the sick list at Live Oak since the previous Wednesday left the regiment as a weakened force of about five hundred effective men at Live Oak.[467] The Hoosiers were ready for a fight, though. "Cool and merry," they began shouting when shells would come up short. They taunted the Rebels with, "Put in more powder!" and, "No lives lost yet!"[468] Colonel Brown wrote later the "will of the officers and men was Battle. They wanted to take pay for their over Coats lost on the *Fanny*."[469] The regiment still on the hill south of camp, Colonel Brown sent sharpshooters into the trees.[470]

Brown then marched six companies of his command farther south. They stopped at a point along the sound that was "about mid way between the fleet and our camp where [the regiment] waited a short time for further developments." (Since the day before, Company F had been guarding the landing four or five miles south that was now directly opposite the Rebel fleet and so was already in position in case of attack.)[471]

The Rebel fire began with two twelve-pounder brass howitzers from the flying artillery company aboard the light-draft stern-wheeler *Cotton Plant* loaded with forty men, its guns commanded by Third Georgia lieutenant John R. Sturgis.[472] The *Curlew* was unable to come any closer to the shore.[473]

The eighty-five-ton CSS *Cotton Plant* was 107 feet in length and over 18 feet wide but had a draft of only 4 feet and 6 inches.[474] The *Cotton Plant*, therefore, came up alongside the *Curlew*, and Colonel Wright, Major Lee and the men boarded the lighter-draft vessel, along with Commander Hunter of the flagship *Curlew*. Hunter then took command of the *Cotton Plant* from Midshipman Samuel S. Gregory. Third Georgia lieutenant colonel James Reid previously had been ordered to stay with the *Curlew* and the remaining men of the Third Georgia.[475]

Adjutant Turner, not hearing Wright's order for Reid to stay back, boarded the *Cotton Plant* to take his expected place with Colonel Wright at the head of the regiment, but the colonel ordered his adjutant back to the *Curlew*. Turner, visibly unhappy with the order, "turned to obey, with intense chagrin expressed on his countenance." Before shoving off, though, Wright told the adjutant, "I would like to have you with me, but you must remain, and assist in landing the other troops. Watch my boat, and when I raise and lower the flag three times, the other troops must commence landing."[476]

The *Cotton Plant* advanced to within a mile of shore, directly opposite Live Oak. Midyett's windmill and the few tents of the camp were clearly visible and several rounds were fired directly into the camp.[477] From the Georgians' vantage point, that direct fire was what started the retreat of the Twentieth Indiana from their camp.[478] They were not wrong.

Ninth New York Captain Edward Jardine had come up "on the ground" to Live Oak from Fort Clark on the previous night. Jardine also carried Hawkins's orders for Brown to retreat if it became necessary. Jardine, however, was to deliver the orders to the Indiana colonel only when, in Jardine's opinion, it became necessary.[479] Colonel Hawkins, though, remained at Fort Clark while keeping a pulse on the ever-changing situation south of Loggerhead Inlet.

Why a retreat order was not immediately given, on October 2 or 3, is not clear. Hawkins's intense concern for the safety of the loyal Hatteras citizens at Chicamacomico had always been paramount—even above the lives of his own men—and he certainly did not want to call for a premature retreat and further jeopardize the natives' already fragile existence at the north of Hatteras Island. Also, by the time Jardine made it to Live Oak by horse with retreat orders on the evening of October 3, a retreat in the dark, including the fifty families of Chicamacomico, was not practical, particularly with the high tide not affording them a hard packed surface along the Atlantic beach on which to flee.

The navy officers at the inlet were quickly aware the Twentieth Indiana was deployed in a dangerous position, and that following the capture of the *Fanny*, the naval force at the inlet was not in a place to supply the Indiana Regiment adequately or provide sufficient firepower from within the sound to cover a safe retreat. U.S. Navy commander Henry S. Stellwagen, who had arrived at Hatteras Inlet on October 1 (on a navy mission to sink hulks in and thus block the various inlets of the Pamlico), became immediately aware of the critical status of the Hoosiers at Live Oak and of the need for Brown to immediately retreat. Stellwagen informed Flag Officer Goldsborough, "It is the impression here that our troops [the Twentieth Indiana] will have to fall back, as we can not expect to use the sound with present force of steam tugs to send them supplies. This is very serious; two or three more light-draft vessels would have prevented [the *Fanny* capture]."[480]

Captain Jardine held Hawkins's retreat order, which he had brought with him the night before, until moments after 9:00 a.m. on the fourth, at the commencement of the Rebel artillery barrage at Live Oak.[481] Very early that morning, Jardine found a vantage point in the wooden windmill adjacent to the camp from which he could observe through his spyglass the approach of Rebel steamers.[482] It was

Captain Edward Jardine, Ninth New York (Hawkins Zouaves). Company G. *Dennis C. Schurr Collection.*

soon obvious that a Rebel landing "rendered escape imperative, where the island was narrow and offered every facility for a flanking fire from the guns." Jardine, therefore, promptly stepped out of the windmill to issue Hawkins's retreat orders to Brown and to carry word south to Hawkins of the perilous conditions at Live Oak.[483] Jardine's timing was perfect. Midyett's windmill was hit and shattered "at first fire."[484]

Captain Jardine, "in hot haste" from Live Oak, immediately after delivering the retreat order to Brown, covered nearly forty miles and arrived at Fort Clark that afternoon, about four o'clock, "with intelligence that the Twentieth was attacked and surrounded at [Live Oak] and its retreat cut off."[485] In his haste to reach Colonel Hawkins with a report, Jardine "rode down three horses on the way."[486] Hawkins, having received this critical status report on the assault on Live Oak and the flight of the Twentieth along with the islanders, gave orders to Jardine to return north immediately and "render what assistance he could pending the arrival of reinforcements."[487] By 5:00 p.m., a detachment of the Ninth from Fort Clark was on the move north along the ocean beach.[488]

Brown's retreat orders from Colonel Hawkins, dated October 2, were to "immediately remove with [his] command to Hatteras Light House." The Indiana colonel began the evacuation of Live Oak immediately and expeditiously along with the entire civilian population of Chicamacomico south of camp: "Orders were accordingly given for the command to form farther down the Island."[489] The bulk of the regiment had already left the camp, though without expectations of a full retreat, to take up a temporary defensive position a few miles down the island.

Third Georgia adjutant Turner witnessed the *Cotton Plant*'s landing through the flag officer's glass while kneeling on the deck of the *Curlew*, watching intently for Wright's signal from his landing party, a thrice-raised flag. "It seemed an age," Turner later recalled. Both of Sturgis's field howitzers on the *Cotton Plant* continued "throwing shot and shell," covering the advance as the first wave of Georgians jumped into the water about a half a mile from shore where the vessel had anchored. Wright's signal to the *Curlew* was given as the *Cotton Plant* dropped anchor just off Live Oak.[490] When Wright saw the Indiana men retreating, he moved his three companies and their guns from the *Cotton Plant* to a flatboat to make a landing, along with one of the two howitzers.[491] The bombardment of Live Oak continued for an hour.[492]

Three Third Georgia companies, consisting of 210 men, were landed immediately from the flatboat: Company E under Captain Joel R. Griffin, Company B under Captain R.B. Nesbit and Company N under Captain John F. Jones.[493] This first wave of Georgians landed about three miles up from Live Oak on the south bank of Loggerhead Inlet, the northernmost post of the Twentieth Indiana pickets. The Indiana men could see that another landing was being prepared in the sound immediately to the west of Live Oak while yet a third wave of men was moving to land farther down the island.[494]

The remaining Georgians who had not yet landed, along with the Currituck Atlantic Rifles of the Seventh North Carolina, were aboard the *Cotton Plant* and its flatboats. The Eighth North Carolina Regiment was behind a few miles,[495] aboard the steamer *Empire* and its towed barges. The *Empire* initially sat three and a half miles offshore with the rest of the fleet firing with its rifled cannon "to drive the game from cover."[496]

Colonel Wright took only one of the field howitzers on shore with him during the first landing and left the other—commanded by Captain Nathaniel A. Carswell, Company I, Wilkinson County—on the *Cotton Plant* to cover the landing of the remaining Georgians and the Currituck Atlantic Rifles.[497]

Wright, making shore at Loggerhead, signaled Turner for the rest of the Third Georgia to commence its landing under the protection of Carswell's second gun. The Currituck Atlantic Rifles, sixty to seventy men, landed together with this second wave of the Third Georgia, "and joined in the pursuit with great bravery," the other two companies of the Seventh remaining back at Roanoke Island. The second howitzer was then brought onshore and the men dragged both heavy brass guns and limbers through the deep sand since the mules had been left behind at Roanoke Island.[498]

This second wave loaded onto "an immense, heavy, old flat, and commenced a tedious approach to the land. No snail ever went slower." The second wave made it to the beach after what seemed to some to be about two hours. The first wave of the assault, having landed farther north at Loggerhead Inlet, had already entered and occupied Camp Live Oak before the second wave made it to shore. Among the trees, the hidden camp had been abandoned, and the first wave was having "all the fun to themselves." Prisoners were taken of those who had not left camp yet, consisting of some of the pickets, the sick and the cooks. The Twentieth Indiana had "fled leaving everything behind except arms and accoutrements." Everything at Camp Live Oak was left "strewn around promiscuously…breakfast on the fire." Third Georgia Private George N. Dexter recalled Colonel Brown's breakfast "was spread and waiting to be eaten. It consisted of coffee, milk, butter, biscuit, fried fish, chicken, duck and canned fruit. I called in Surgeon [James Erwin] Godfrey and [quartermaster] Captain Phillips, and we enjoyed the breakfast. I can say, that for one time during the war I had a good square meal."[499]

Twentieth Indiana private Abraham Van Horn, Company H, was one of those first captured by the Third Georgia. Twenty-seven-year-old Van Horn "was standing picket at the time [of capture] and fought until taken." Van Horn grew up tough. On New Year's Day in 1850, Van Horn's mother died giving birth to the youngest of his six sisters. However, that spring, fourteen and the only son, Abraham and his father led their family to California from Hickory Creek, Kankakee County, Illinois, to strike it rich in the gold rush. Disappointed, as so many were, Abraham returned east, and joined with Colonel Brown's regiment to distinguish himself in the suppression of the rebellion.[500]

Another Hoosier captured early in the affair was Private Charles M. Gross of Company G, from Tippecanoe, Indiana, who was "detached on hospital service when captured." The men of Company G were at Fort Monroe under Captain Herron waiting to join their Indiana comrades in a few days. Though two civilian cooks from Company G were captured aboard the *Fanny*, twenty-four-year-old Gross would be counted as the only private taken prisoner at Hatteras from Herron's company.[501] Private Leonard H. Riley of Company E, LaPorte County, Indiana, also on detached service as a hospital cook, became an early prisoner of war that day.[502]

When Colonel Brown called his officers together and informed them of the retreat orders, "we fell in at once," recalled Lieutenant Gilbreath with Company I. As the Twentieth was about to begin its march, Gilbreath remembered that First Sergeant John C. Brown of Captain Reed's Company K, a forty-two-year-old shoemaker from White County,[503] "took position on a sand dune and sung 'Our Flag is there'. After the song, which was the only defiant thing we did except shake our fists, we started on the march."[504]

Colonel Brown giving the order to fall back, kept Company F, under Lieutenant Logan, forward of the regiment.[505] Logan's men had already been thrown out to the south the day before and were about five miles ahead of the regiment when the retreat began.[506] Company K would be the rear guard to hold off any advance of the enemy on the fleeing Hoosiers.[507] Reed's company was "detailed for rear guard with directions to zealously look after all straying from the command and over no account suffer himself to be cut off from the main body of the Battalion."[508]

The sun was shining bright and the heat was staggering on the retreat. The Twentieth had not yet eaten, when the Rebel attack commenced. Its food was on the fire as the volunteers swiftly abandoned camp. Blankets were left spread out in the sand with playing cards dealt out for a morning game. One thing working in favor of the Indiana boys that day was the tide. The tide was out when the retreat began. The wet and compact sand below

"Loyal Inhabitants of Hatteras Island, Expelled from Their Homes by the Rebel Troops, Overtaken by the 20th Indiana Regiment, while Retreating to Fort Hatteras for Protection, October 4th, 1861." Original in *Frank Leslie's Illustrated News*, November 2, 1861. Colonel William Brown can be seen allowing a local Hatteras woman to ride his horse. The regiment is seen in orderly ranks moving down the beach. *Outer Banks History Center.*

the high water mark along the ocean beach allowed a relatively swift escape, while the sand everywhere else was of a loose consistency.[509]

Twentieth Indiana sergeant Thomas Stephens wrote, "This day I shall never forget." As part of Company K Stephens was ordered to remain behind as rear guard. Stephens recalled the Rebel yell not far behind them as the Hoosiers fled Live Oak and Chicamacomico. Soon after the camp was shelled, Stephens "heard them yelling like demons. They had possession of our camp."[510]

The regiment marched south, catching up with Logan's Company F near the landing south of Chicamacomico, and halted.[511] Colonel Brown, often accused of being a "rigid disciplinarian,"[512] would, this day, be remembered for his compassion and self-sacrifice. He ordered the men to rest, and then the "line of march was resumed" with Logan's company leading about five hundred yards ahead. Brown would later point out that this was the Tall Twentieth's "first march and under the circumstances was a sad and painful one…many of the citizens had previous to our retreat abandoned their homes." However, within a few hours, the Banker families were overtaken by the regiment moving south along the beach.[513]

The silk ensign of the USS *Monticello*, embroidered with the name of the vessel and her commander, "Lieut. Da' L. Braine USN." With an eight-foot hoist and twelve feet on the fly, it is the only silk naval flag from this period known to exist. *Graveyard of the Atlantic Museum.*

The USS *Monticello*. Painting by Clary Ray. *U.S. Naval Historical Center.*

"It was a march I shall never forget," exclaimed one Twentieth Indiana officer. Of all the "sorrowful sights," the officer recalled—including men staggering and fainting from the heat, nothing to drink and Colonel Brown giving up his own horse to be ridden by a sick soldier—

> *the most sorrowful sight of all was the Islanders leaving their homes from fear of the enemy. They could be seen in groups, sometimes with a little cart carrying their possessions, but mostly with nothing, fleeing for dear life. Mothers carrying babes, fathers leading along the boys, grandfathers and grandmothers straggling along from homes they had left behind. Relying on our protection they had been our friends, but in an evil hour we had been compelled to leave them. When will we learn that guns and men are necessary to enforce the law? When shall we learn that our protection cannot be given, unless by gunboats and batteries?*[514]

By 11:00 a.m., the retreating Hoosiers observed the Rebel fleet following along inside the sound. The Bankers informed Brown the Rebels would attempt to cut off the regiment another ten miles down the island. Knowing this, Brown pushed to get the regiment south "as fast as the heat and sand would permit."[515]

Initially, news of the Third Georgia landing came to Colonel Hawkins through Lieutenant Bankhead who turned back to the *Stars and Stripes* anchored inside the inlet and signaled the news.[516] The message from the *Stars and Stripes* was that 2,500 Rebels—regiments wrongly identified as from Georgia, Virginia and South Carolina—had come from the mainland on six steamers and schooners with flatboats and attacked Camp Live Oak.[517] Lieutenant Reed Werden of the USS *Stars and Stripes* received a corrected report from Hawkins in the late afternoon that stated, "The enemy have landed above from six steamers, a sailing vessel, and some scows, and that the Indiana regiment are in full retreat, the natives flying before them."[518]

Werden immediately informed Captain Lardner, in command of the USS *Susquehanna*, that Colonel Hawkins was requesting support from both the *Susquehanna* and the USS *Monticello* to cover the retreat of the Twentieth Indiana along with the loyal families from Chicamacomico. The *Stars and Stripes* from "the shipping" could see Confederate vessels across the island inside the Pamlico. Werden wanted Lardner and the commander of the *Monticello*, Lieutenant Daniel L. Braine, to "haul in a little above the fort." As a cautionary note, Werden added that the three tugs typically available were either grounded or disabled and would not be able to assist.[519]

Ninth New York lieutenant colonel George Betts's command of four companies at Camp Wool joined the Zouaves who had started marching north at 5:00 p.m. and had already marched the two miles up to Camp Wool from Fort Clark. The *Monticello*, at that time, could be seen steaming north along with the Zouaves on the beach between Fort Clark and Camp Wool,[520] as both the navy and the Ninth New York raced to meet the retreating Twentieth Indiana and support them against the Rebel attack. The *Susquehanna* also immediately responded to Hawkins's request and weighed anchor. Lardner reported that his ship and the *Monticello* were both under way at once, as soon as he received word late in the afternoon that the enemy had landed "in large force" at Chicamacomico and Kinnakeet.[521] Actually, the Rebels had not yet landed at Kinnakeet, but by this hour, it was apparent that was their intention. By 7 p.m., three hours after Jardine arrived at Fort Clark with news of the assault, the vessels were under way,[522] steaming north up close to shore at Hatteras Cove. They dropped anchor near the Hatteras Lighthouse until morning.[523]

Not everyone was aware that the Union tugs *Ceres* and *General Putnam* were out of commission and unengaged in this attempt to support the fleeing Twentieth and citizens of Chicamacomico. Zouave private Charles Johnson's diary indicates that the two gunboats may not have been disabled or grounded as Lardner reported. Johnson knew that these two light-draft vessels should have been steaming up the sound opposite the *Monticello* and *Susquehanna*. Why they were not moving north to aid the retreating Hoosiers, Johnson "could not comprehend. These vessels were made ready for action, and considerable indignation was felt by the men on board, as well as by us on shore, at their inactivity."[524]

The retreat order given, Brown was left no time to return to camp to "secure or destroy the same."[525] Sergeant Major Charles Hammond Comly and the chaplain of the Twentieth, Dr. William Clay Porter, though, volunteered soon into the retreat to return to Live Oak to bring in the pickets[526] and "look after the sick, start the cooks in retreat, break up a lot of cartridges and destroy certain papers."[527] At this point, the Rebel first wave had not made it down to Live Oak from their landing at Loggerhead Inlet, and the second wave was still wading in from the sound directly west of camp and its shattered windmill.

Charley Comly, a civil engineer in private life, was handpicked by Colonel Brown to be sergeant major. Chosen from one of the strong, influential and religiously devout new families of Cass County, Indiana, Comly was ready for service. The twenty-four-year-old, five-foot-nine sergeant major was more Buckeye than Hoosier and more "Fighting Quaker" than either. Born and raised in Ohio, Comly's family had only recently moved from Dayton to Logansport, Indiana, after his publisher father sold his stake in the *Dayton Journal*. Both sides of his family were Quakers, politically outspoken Republicans and well represented in the military. His mother's family, the Sanders, from North Carolina and Virginia, were part of the Southern Quakers who migrated west and founded Richmond, Indiana, in 1806. Comly's paternal roots were in Pennsylvania.

Sergeant Major Comly's family was immersed in the newspaper business. His father, Richard, came to Dayton from Cincinnati in October 1830 and bought a stake in the *Dayton Journal*. In 1834, Richard Comly's brother William bought out the remaining interest in the *Journal*. Together, the Comly brothers built the paper to become "the dominant organ of the Republican party in the southern district of Ohio."[528] In March 1861, President Lincoln appointed the sergeant major's uncle postmaster of Dayton.[529] Charley Comly's father, only days after the Twentieth left Indiana, was nominated by Secretary of War Simon Cameron "to be commissary of subsistence with rank of captain."[530] Sergeant Major Comly went to war just as his younger brother, Clifton, was beginning his final year as a cadet at West Point.

The sergeant major quickly collected two sick men as he moved south from the abandoned Live Oak camp. One private, William Stickley of Company C, had been recuperating from a badly injured right arm. The nineteen-year-old from Tippecanoetown, Marshall County, Indiana, had carelessly stuck his right arm out of the rolling passenger car traveling from Cockeysville to Baltimore, Maryland, and caught it on a water pipe leading to a railroad water tank overhead.[531]

Comly "had a slight rush of blood to the head" while on the move, felt faint and needed to take only a short nap. He lay down and overslept thirty minutes longer than intended. Waking, he found himself surprisingly six to eight miles to the rear of the regiment and immediately started again toward the lighthouse. After another half mile south, Comly saw a group of men approaching whom he mistook for Hoosiers. They were, in fact, Georgians calling for him to surrender. Comly could not bring himself to give up so easily without an attempt to escape.[532] Chaplain Porter, though, saved one of the pickets "only by snatching him in his arms, and carrying him out of the range of the pursuers."[533]

Chaplain William Porter was an immigrant from the tiny Isle of Jersey in the English Channel. The twenty-seven-year-old chaplain was the son of a Presbyterian pastor who brought his family from England to the United States

Chaplain Dr. William C. Porter, Twentieth Indiana. *Richard F. Carlile Collection.*

Lieutenant Erasmus C. Gilbreath, Twentieth Indiana, Company I. *Richard F. Carlile Collection.*

in 1856.[534] Porter earned a Doctor of Divinity from Wabash College in Crawfordsville, Indiana, the following year in 1857.[535] Chaplain Porter soon became known as the "fighting chaplain."[536]

One of the Georgians calling Comly to surrender was none other than their Colonel Rans Wright, who was riding a Banker pony,[537] having already covered considerable ground since leading the first landing at Loggerhead Inlet. The Third Georgia officers did not bring horses with them for the assault. Instead, they went to nearby houses, and "procured marsh ponies and old saddles." Adjutant Turner very clearly remembered years later his error of choosing to walk and not use a pony. After running himself literally into the sand from exhaustion, Adjutant Turner was picked up by Lieutenant Colonel Reid: "A nice figure too, the Lieutenant Colonel and Adjutant cut, two tall men, on a small pony, their legs nearly dragging the sand." Turner procured his own pony later that evening.[538]

Colonel Wright overtook a group of some thirteen Indianans in all, including Sergeant Major Comly, about six miles from his Loggerhead landing, on his Banker pony in advance of his command.[539] Ordered to surrender, Comly managed to take his musket from his shoulder and get off two shots. One ball missed completely while the other hit the pony Colonel Wright rode.[540] The pony fell beneath the colonel, and Comly began ramming down a third round.[541] Georgian reports state Wright then grabbed "the smallest of the Yankees, who was very near him—a mere boy," and used him as a shield against Comly's threat to fire again.[542] Wright was able to thus advance on Comly with a revolver and captured the sergeant major with four other Hoosiers.[543] Corporal Nathan B. Easton was captured there and later wrote in an 1888 letter to Third Georgia private Dexter about the shooting of Wright's Banker pony. Easton wrote, "If the ball had elevated—as they were trained to believe—and not have gone true to the point aimed at, [Comly] would have shot Col. Wright through the hips, as he sat upon the horse."[544]

Private William Stickley, injured as he was, was captured,[545] as was civilian cook Nathan Brady, of Baltimore, who was serving the men of Company D, predominantly from Fountain County, Indiana.[546] Private John H. Hoffman of Company D, seventeen, born in Attica, Indiana, had been on assignment as a cook for his company. Hoffman in 1853, at the age of nine, had crossed the Rockies in a wagon train from Covington, Indiana, along the Oregon Trail to the Rogue River Valley, where his family settled. It appears he returned to Indiana just to serve alongside Hoosier comrades.[547]

The "mere boy" Wright used to save his own life and capture the retreating Indianians, was one of two boys who left their Lancaster, Pennsylvania homes "without the consent of their parents" and joined with the regiment at Cockeysville, Maryland. Henry Hines was but thirteen years old and served as Captain Lytle's "boy." Hines was captured with another youth from his Lancaster neighborhood, George W. Gerber. Gerber was fifteen years old and was the "colonel's boy." Each had been left behind at camp, evidently, in the initial movement of the regiment south of Live Oak. With no time to return to camp to get the boys, Colonel Brown and Captain Lytle left them to make their own way south. The "very respectable parents" of Hines and Gerber would discover the whereabouts of their sons when their names appeared in the newspapers. Another young private of Lytle's company was also captured in this "skirmish." Private John C. Drury, who called Wabash, Indiana, home, turned fourteen two weeks before his enlistment in Indiana. Drury, nearly six feet tall,[548] was now a prisoner of war.[549]

Comly, in retelling the story of his capture to his mother, did not mention the boy used as a shield. The sergeant major did say that, surrounded after shooting Wright's pony, he realized escape was impossible. He lamented, "Bitter as was the idea, I surrendered, as I would have been taken dead or wounded."[550] Southern papers actually praised Comly as "the only evidence of bravery evinced by the whole party" and reported that Colonel Wright treated him very courteously for his bravery.[551] Comly took his capture in stride, later writing his mother, "I have the satisfaction of knowing that I have done all in my power for my God and my country, and submit to my fate with good spirit."[552]

The pursuing Georgians would pick up a few Yankees hiding in bushes and tidal pools here and there as the day wore on. Upon capture, prisoners were escorted back to Live Oak and loaded onto boats. Third Georgia quartermaster Alexander Phillips was also loading the Twentieth Indiana's camp furnishings onto the boats. The "Yankee plunder" included all of the blankets, shoes, hats, clothes and muskets the Hoosiers tossed aside along their route south. Some of the despised altered muskets had met their fates by being bent around trees.[553] Southern reports were that several hundred muskets and many pistols were gathered from the fleeing Hoosiers.[554] Colonel Wright had detailed Private George N. Dexter, an assistant to the quartermaster, to gather every fishing boat he could find from the area. Dexter pulled in "one hundred and four boats, including a 2 masted schooner" belonging mostly to the Bankers at Chicamacomico. Those were all taken back to Roanoke Island.[555]

First Lieutenant Gilbreath later wrote,

> *We kept it up during the day without much rest and felt that it was a race with the boat we had seen go south to get past the landing place before they could come on shore. We could see with our glasses too that they were landing men at our Camp at Chickamicamico, which was an additional spur to lively action on our part…as we had no transportation of any kind, not even a horse at Chicamiomico, we left everything we had there.*[556]

He also wrote, "There was no water except as we dug for it. We had no tin cups (all captured) but had found some large shells which answered the place of cups, and we used them in digging for water. We thus supplied ourselves with enough."[557]

The Indiana men could see early on that the Rebel fleet intended to cut off their retreat by landing farther south. There were several potential landing sites along the route, and it wasn't clear which site would be used. After the second Rebel landing directly at Live Oak, the CSS *Empire* and the other steamers had moved south. The *Cotton Plant*, however, remained off Chicamacomico throughout the day. The first objective of the Confederate assault, including the first two landings, was to render it impossible to hold a position at Camp Live Oak. The second objective was to capture the retreating Hoosiers in a "net" farther south at Big Kinnakeet. Eighteen miles south of Camp Live Oak, toward Hatteras Light, was Barnes Mill, a windmill, where the Rebels intended to land. With this plan, the Confederates would "by bringing their artillery to bear, take us in flank, as well as in front, thus cutting off our retreat should we attempt it, and bagging us, as it were, in a net."[558]

The 650 men of the Eighth North Carolina had been towed on barges behind the steamer *Empire* from Roanoke Island to a few miles off Live Oak camp and then finally to a landing at Big Kinnakeet. Colonel Wright had directed Shaw to land his men "at the wind mill to intercept the Federals." That was Barnes Mill. The lighthouse was about eight miles farther south of the intended landing site. While the Third Georgia and the Seventh North Carolina had attacked Live Oak from the north and directly from the west, the Eighth North Carolina was to disembark from the barges and intercept the retreating Indiana Regiment at a landing farther south.[559]

The CSS *Empire* (later renamed CSS *Appomattox*) was a 120-ton wooden-hulled screw steamer, built in Philadelphia in 1850. The *Empire* was eighty-six feet long, twenty feet wide and had a draft of seven and a half feet.[560] *Empire* was originally chartered by the Virginia State navy as a tug, which towed ballast ships, to obstruct rivers between the forts at Norfolk. Later it acted as a flag-of-truce vessel under then captain T.T. Hunter before coming in under the Confederate States navy.[561]

The Eighth North Carolina arrived at the Kinnakeet landing ahead of the Twentieth but without enough time to make shore successfully and catch the Indiana regiment in its net. Brown, seeing he had some time, brought the column to rest again, then pushed on a few more miles toward the lighthouse. Above Kinnakeet, from a clearing where the sound was visible, the enemy was strangely nowhere to be found, and the Hoosiers thought the Rebels had abandoned their attempt to cut them off. The Twentieth stopped yet again for water and rest when an islander informed Brown that the Confederates had gone further down the sound and were anchoring five miles south in preparation for a landing. The Banker told Brown "that the place selected was the best between camp [Live Oak] and Hatteras Light, and urged us to take the Atlantic beach and push forward." Brown rested there briefly and then pushed the regiment forward again as quickly as possible, though the men moved quite slowly.[562]

CSS *Empire*, later renamed CSS *Appomattox. Frank Leslie's Illustrated Newspaper*, July 20, 1861.
Bruce Long Collection.

The Twentieth's column stopped yet again at 4:00 p.m., one mile above the expected Rebel landing at Big Kinnakeet. The CSS *Empire* was visible at anchor two miles out in the sound. Colonel Brown sent ahead Twentieth Indiana major Benjamin H. Smith who "reconnoitered and found [the enemy] barges and launches ready for disembarking." Once again, Brown rested the regiment but this time for two hours, fully refreshing the men and preparing for the possibility of a fight. All the stragglers were called in, and "all arms were examined and put in condition for use." Here, a mile above the windmill at Big Kinnakeet, Brown formed the Twentieth into a line of battle, skirmishers on the flanks in front of the column, and the Hoosiers marched for the lighthouse.[563] Lieutenant Gilbreath recalled years later that the skirmish line across the island was "to guard against running into the enemy should he succeed in landing. I was in charge of a part of the line, and never did harder work."[564] It was dusk and light was fading.[565]

The Rebels at Big Kinnakeet, two miles out in the sound, could be seen by the Twentieth when the regiment arrived. The Rebels were "well lighted up" and were trying to land their forces, Brown observed. The Twentieth moved forward, frequently resting, and after another five hours, reached the lighthouse. Once there, Brown immediately sent another messenger to inform Hawkins of the Confederate assault at Live Oak, the same dispatch Jardine was to have carried south. Brown had not seen any evidence yet of Hawkins Zouaves marching north to reinforce his retreating Hoosiers. Brown was not certain of either "the success or failure of Captain Jardine's mission" since Brown had last seen him about 9:00 a.m. at Live Oak.

At about 1:00 a.m., Jardine came into the camp at the lighthouse and informed Brown of Hawkins's presence along with his Zouaves.[566] Jardine was the first sign of relief Brown had seen all day from either the army or navy. Ordered to assist the Twentieth in its retreat, Captain Jardine had returned north again after his 4:00 p.m. October 4 report to Hawkins at Fort Clark. Rush Hawkins, thirty years later at a reunion of the Ninth New York and Third Georgia, referred to this day as the beginning of a friendship—"the beginning of the interweaving"—not between the Ninth New York and the Twentieth Indiana but between Hawkins Zouaves and the Third Georgia Regiment.[567] There would be no such "interweaving" between Zouaves and the Hoosiers.[568]

The Eighth, under command of Colonel Shaw, found itself two miles from land, unable to make a landing because of the shoals.[569] From its vantage point, though, the Eighth could see the Hatteras Lighthouse as well as the Federal vessels at Hatteras Inlet.[570] Shaw transferred the regiment's guns to a flat boat. Finding the water shallow enough at one location, the soldiers were so anxious to get into a fight that they attempted to wade toward shore. A smaller boat went ahead to take soundings, but the regiment "found it impossible to land owing to the peculiar formation of the flats."[571] Regimental drummer, Private H.T.J. Ludwig, Company H, recalled, "After wading about a mile, a deep channel, too deep to cross, was met. The order was given to return to the barges. In the meantime, the tide began to rise, and by the time the last of the men arrived at the barges, the water was up to their armpits and chins."[572] If the Eighth North Carolina had had an opportunity to land at Big Kinnakeet, it had passed them by.

The Eighth North Carolina abandoned the attempted landing and was back on the barges at dark. Eighth North Carolina captain Edward Clement Yellowley, Company G, was disappointed at how close the men had come to a real victory, and wrote, "the enemy was completely in our power and had we landed they would have surrendered without a shot."[573] The captain explained the circumstances surrounding the failed assault at Kinnakeet, stating:

Night overtook us by the time we re-embarked and we could not try to land any more that day. We were about twenty-five miles distant from the Yankees' camp at Chicamacomico…We heard next day that they saw our regiment trying to land, and being broken down running from the Georgians, who were pursuing them, they prepared to surrender to us, by stopping and shooting off their guns. The people on the island told this. They got rested before the Georgians came up with them and went on…Had we landed, we would have taken them all prisoners and blown up Hatteras light house. Bad generalship on the part of Colonel Wright prevented it. He had made boats, but would not let us have them to land in. He kept them to make good his retreat…owing to his bad management and want of military skill, we failed to catch them.[574]

Eighth North Carolina captain Jonas Cook, of Company H, in a later narrative of his Civil War service, categorizing the various actions in which the regiment participated, merely identified the Chicamacomico Affair as a "Demonstration & Engagement."[575] There was no further elaboration. Other Eighth North Carolina troops would refer to the engagement at Hatteras as "the Folly Affair."[576]

The North Carolinians were not aware of the visual advantage of the retreating Hoosiers after sunset: "Happily every movement of the force attempting to reach the shore was thrown out with singular and perfect distinctness by the illuminated western sky, while their own motions, and even their figures, were obscured by the blue and now darkening eastern heavens, which formed their background." And so, most of the Twentieth Indiana was able to slip by the Eighth North Carolina's intended Kinnakeet landing and make the final eight miles to the safety of Hatteras Lighthouse.[577] On the evening of October 4, the sky was clear, and providentially for the Hoosiers, the moon was new.[578]

Colonel Brown commended Captain Reed's Company K, of Monticello, Indiana, saying that "my rear guard nobly gallantly performed his perilous task and at 12 at night brought his entire command into camp."[579] The Monticello and Susquehanna sent provisions to shore for the Indiana troops camped at the lighthouse for the night.[580] Lieutenant Gilbreath remembered, "Beautiful as our glorious flag is at all times, it seemed never so beautiful as when displayed on the water, especially if on one of the old fashioned men of war. The [Monticello] accompanied us to Hatteras Light House and the first thing solid we got to eat there was Hard Bread and dried apples, sent to us from her stores."[581]

Officers of the Eighth North Carolina Regiment. Colonel Henry Marchmore Shaw, *top center.*
Histories of the Several Regiments and Battalions from North Carolina in the Great War 1861–5.

Men of the Eighth North Carolina Regiment. Private H.T.J. Ludwig, drummer, *top center*. *Histories of the Several Regiments and Battalions from North Carolina in the Great War 1861–5.*

Nearly fifty families fled Chicamacomico with the Indiana regiment. Retreating ahead of the Twentieth nearly to the lighthouse, these loyal citizens left behind all worldly possessions. They were "glad to escape with life alone, and knowing nothing of what the future had in store them."[582] One mother "trudged twelve miles through the sand" with her three-day-old baby.[583]

The Third Georgia field and staff became aware before nightfall of the probably failed landing of Shaw's troops. The Hoosier retreat had not been cut off as planned. The reason for the failure the Third Georgia would not understand until later.[584]

Private George E. Ritchie, Eighth North Carolina Volunteers, Company H, The Cabarrus Phalanx. *Eastern Cabarrus Historical Society Museum.*

On the heels of the Twentieth Indiana throughout the day, the Georgians had become hungry and took raw vegetables from the patches of the native islanders who had fled their homes in a panic. When night fell, the Georgian field and staff were settling in at a few houses at Kinnakeet that had been deserted earlier in the day. For dinner, a lamb was slaughtered and stewed together with flour dumplings seasoned with salt pork, cooked in two large wash pots. Freshly baked corn bread and roasted sweet potatoes were also on the menu that lent itself nicely to a deep and deserved sleep. Most slept on the sand while others staked their claim for the floors, but all most assuredly "sank into a profound slumber."[585]

Despite Captain Reed's best efforts, stragglers were left behind the Twentieth Indiana's rear guard, Company K. Two young privates were among those picked up by the Georgians. Both just fifteen years old, Private Henry Unruh,[586] Company C, from Valparaiso, Indiana, and a freckle-faced Private Eli Snyder, Company E, of Warsaw, Indiana, were escorted back to Live Oak and the flatboat waiting offshore.[587]

Speakman, the Twentieth Indiana sutler, and three other men made it as far south as the vicinity of the proposed Eighth North Carolina landing, eight miles north of the lighthouse. Their feet tortured by the loose sand and miles of running, Speakman and the others could barely limp along and stopped for a few hours of rest about midnight. Waking near three in the morning, the Hoosiers were on their way again toward the lighthouse when they were spotted by the Rebels and captured. Speakman however was able to get free, escaping into the early morning darkness unharmed[588] after having run "the gauntlet of seven bullets."[589]

The Ninth New York Volunteers, coming to the rescue from Fort Clark and Camp Wool, were played out by midnight after the intense march through the deep sand with little drinking water. Many stopped to sleep about three or four miles short of the Hatteras Lighthouse.[590]

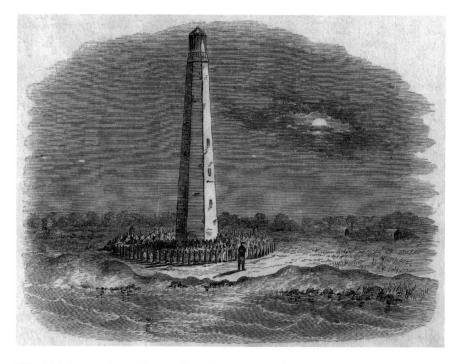

"The Lighthouse at Cape Hatteras, Round Which the 20th Indiana Regt., Bivouacked after Their March of 25 Miles from Chicamacomico, on the Night of Friday, Oct. 4, 1861." A rather inaccurate depiction of the 150-foot lighthouse tower. Source unknown. *Outer Banks History Center*.

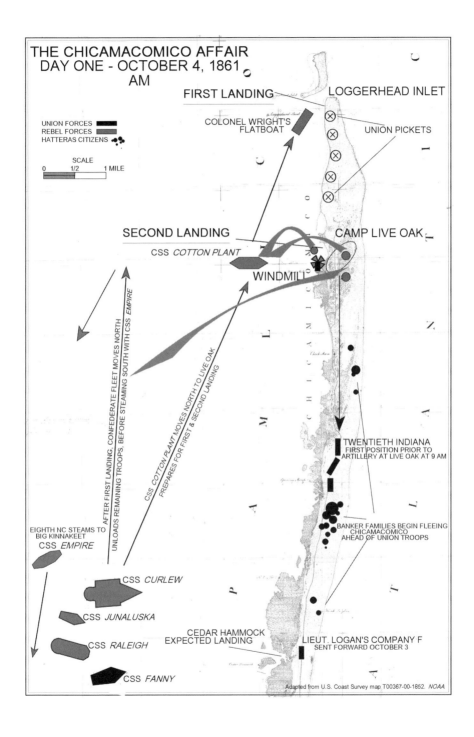

THE CHICAMACOMICO AFFAIR
DAY ONE - OCTOBER 4, 1861
AM

FIRST LANDING

LOGGERHEAD INLET

COLONEL WRIGHT'S
FLATBOAT

UNION PICKETS

UNION FORCES
REBEL FORCES
HATTERAS CITIZENS

SCALE
0   1/2   1 MILE

SECOND LANDING

CAMP LIVE OAK

CSS *COTTON PLANT*

WINDMILL

AFTER FIRST LANDING, CONFEDERATE FLEET MOVES NORTH
UNLOADS REMAINING TROOPS, BEFORE STEAMING SOUTH WITH CSS *EMPIRE*

CSS *COTTON PLANT* MOVES NORTH TO LIVE OAK
PREPARES FOR FIRST & SECOND LANDING

TWENTIETH INDIANA
FIRST POSITION PRIOR TO
ARTILLERY AT LIVE OAK AT 9 AM

EIGHTH NC STEAMS TO
BIG KINNAKEET
CSS *EMPIRE*

BANKER FAMILIES BEGIN FLEEING
CHICAMACOMICO
AHEAD OF UNION TROOPS

CSS *CURLEW*

CSS *JUNALUSKA*

CEDAR HAMMOCK
EXPECTED LANDING

LIEUT. LOGAN'S COMPANY F
SENT FORWARD OCTOBER 3

CSS *RALEIGH*

CSS *FANNY*

Adapted from U.S. Coast Survey map T00367-00-1852. *NOAA*

149

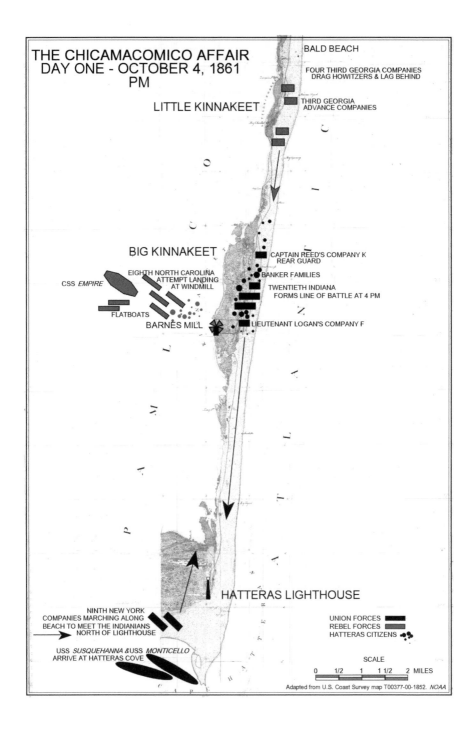

THE CHICAMACOMICO AFFAIR
DAY ONE - OCTOBER 4, 1861
PM

BALD BEACH

FOUR THIRD GEORGIA COMPANIES
DRAG HOWITZERS & LAG BEHIND

LITTLE KINNAKEET

THIRD GEORGIA
ADVANCE COMPANIES

BIG KINNAKEET

CAPTAIN REED'S COMPANY K
REAR GUARD

EIGHTH NORTH CAROLINA
ATTEMPT LANDING
AT WINDMILL

CSS EMPIRE

BANKER FAMILIES

TWENTIETH INDIANA
FORMS LINE OF BATTLE AT 4 PM

FLATBOATS

BARNES MILL

LIEUTENANT LOGAN'S COMPANY F

HATTERAS LIGHTHOUSE

NINTH NEW YORK
COMPANIES MARCHING ALONG
BEACH TO MEET THE INDIANIANS
NORTH OF LIGHTHOUSE

UNION FORCES
REBEL FORCES
HATTERAS CITIZENS

USS SUSQUEHANNA &USS MONTICELLO
ARRIVE AT HATTERAS COVE

SCALE

0   1/2   1   1 1/2   2 MILES

Adapted from U.S. Coast Survey map T00377-00-1852. NOAA

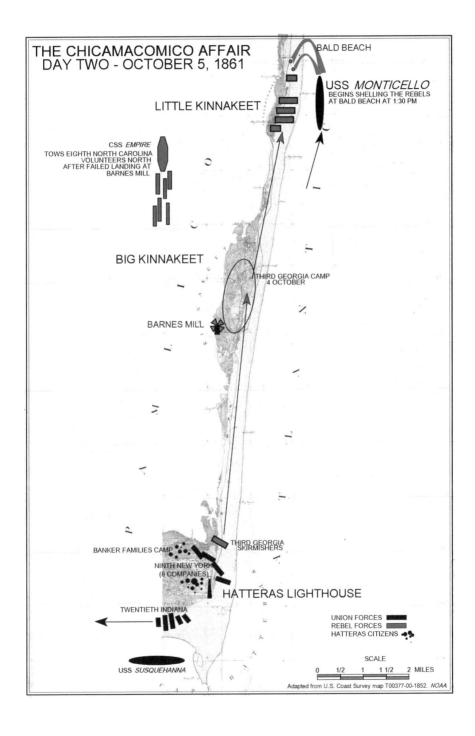

THE CHICAMACOMICO AFFAIR
DAY TWO - OCTOBER 5, 1861

BALD BEACH

USS *MONTICELLO*
BEGINS SHELLING THE REBELS
AT BALD BEACH AT 1:30 PM

LITTLE KINNAKEET

CSS *EMPIRE*
TOWS EIGHTH NORTH CAROLINA
VOLUNTEERS NORTH
AFTER FAILED LANDING AT
BARNES MILL

BIG KINNAKEET

THIRD GEORGIA CAMP
4 OCTOBER

BARNES MILL

THIRD GEORGIA
SKIRMISHERS

BANKER FAMILIES CAMP

NINTH NEW YORK
(8 COMPANIES)

HATTERAS LIGHTHOUSE

TWENTIETH INDIANA

UNION FORCES
REBEL FORCES
HATTERAS CITIZENS

SCALE

0   1/2   1   1 1/2   2 MILES

USS *SUSQUEHANNA*

Adapted from U.S. Coast Survey map T00377-00-1852. *NOAA*

Twentieth Indiana lieutenant Gilbreath remembered, "We camped about Hatteras Light House the night of October 4th, and in the morning of the 5th found that we had not only been followed by a Georgia regiment, but that they had succeeded in landing during the night, four or five miles from us soon after we had passed the point of landing place."[591]

Chapter Eleven

"I Expected Every Minute to Be Blown to Atoms"

Sergeant Thomas White Stephens, of Captain Reed's Company, the regiment's rear guard the previous day, ate hardtack for breakfast, courtesy of Hawkins Zouaves. He climbed the lighthouse and looked out on the waters of the Atlantic to the East before starting at 8:00 a.m. on the twenty-mile march through the sand toward the inlet.[592]

After a scanty breakfast, Colonel Brown had acted on Hawkins's orders for the Twentieth to continue its march farther south to Fort Clark.[593] The Twentieth would eventually make it to Fort Clark around 8:00 p.m., enjoying a supper of hot coffee and crackers on arrival.[594] About the facilities at Fort Clark, Brown said, "We were without tents and so camped our men under old sail cloths which had been taken from the Rebels at the time the Forts were captured."[595]

The Third Georgia was already awake when day broke on October 5. Within a few hours, some of the Georgians, including Adjutant Turner, had forced themselves on toward the lighthouse. A few miles from the tower, it was discovered that the Twentieth Indiana had camped there. A few Georgians went very near to the temporary encampment, near enough to find, in addition, the Ninth New York Zouaves had provided reinforcement overnight.[596]

The Hawkins Zouaves had made a hasty march overnight to the lighthouse. Just like the Georgians coming south, the Zouaves also dragged two field pieces north from Fort Clark sixteen miles through the "deep sands of the Hatteras Sand hills," ready for "the stand, and, if necessary, battle in the vicinity of Hatteras Light." Hawkins arranged his "line of battle along the edge of the wood, the right resting near the lighthouse, with guns on flank to meet the coming attack of the Third Georgia which never came." Hawkins remembered later "probably the happiest moment in the history of the Ninth was when the gallant sons of Georgia were seen to face to the rear and move in the new direction. If their advance had continued to our line there certainly would have been an interesting meeting." The Zouaves felt that the Georgians deserved repayment for their attack on the Twentieth and the capture of Union stores and equipment aboard the *Fanny*. "There was a rather clear determination on the part of the Ninth," that morning of October 5, "to do if not to die." Still, the Hawkins Zouaves were "considerably relieved when they discovered that the 3rd Georgia had changed its mind."[597]

Colonel Wright's intention was to bring up the remainder of the Third Georgia and the single company of the Seventh North Carolina to make an assault on the lighthouse. Its destruction was one of the primary objectives of Wright's plan. Having already called for the rear to move forward, Wright changed his mind and "started the advance back to meet the rear."[598] Colonel Wright passed the point at Big Kinnakeet where he expected Eight North Carolina colonel Henry Shaw with his 650 men to cut off the Hoosiers the night before and saw that Shaw had been unable to land any of his men. The Twentieth Indiana having been reinforced by the Ninth New York Zouaves overnight, Rans Wright withdrew to the position he had held the previous evening.[599] The regiment was back together around noon at Big Kinnakeet, recouping their strength in the shade of the woods, and the colonel found a house nearby for use as a "headquarters."[600]

Permission had been granted one of the Georgia captains to move his men back toward the boats waiting in the sound, and he was swiftly "far on his way." Other captains saw that Wright had agreed and began requesting to move north as well. Hesitating, as Adjutant Turner later recalled, Wright said something to the effect of, "You may take the whole command back, but there must be no stragglers in front or rear. Company 'G' may go forward, as skirmishers (it was thought there were Yankees still lurking in the marshes) but they must not go more than a half a mile ahead." The Georgians started north across what is known as the "bald beach," a piece of sand without "a shrub obstructing the view of the Sound to Ocean, although there were thickets behind and before us." Turner became aware of a "huge vessel" which suddenly appeared very close to the beach on the Atlantic side. Lieutenant Colonel Reid, riding on his Banker pony, had taken the regimental flag from the color-bearer and was carrying it himself.[601]

The "handsome silk flag" had been painted by a Norfolk artist. Rans Wright's wife, Carrie C. Hazlehurst Wright, had commissioned the artist and had presented these colors in her name to the regiment. The Third Georgia carried them throughout the first year of the war.[602]

Alexander Langston, color bearer of the Third Georgia Regiment, in front of the first regimental flag. *Georgia Capitol Museum Collection.*

The drum of the Third Georgia Regiment, which entered service with the first and only regimental drummer, Seaborn Barnwell of Company C (Dawson Grays). *Georgia Capitol Museum Collection.*

Sergeant Martin L. Bridwell of Company G questioned Turner as they moved north along the beach, "Adjutant, what is that?" Bridwell was at the same time pointing at a huge vessel remarkably close to the beach. Not more than a minute after Bridwell's question, the cannon of the ominous steamer "belched forth its thunder, and a shell whizzed over our heads. Take it altogether, we felt in an awkward position. It was the first time most of us were under fire."[603]

At 12:30 p.m. on October 5, Lieutenant Daniel Braine, commanding the USS *Monticello*, was steaming north through the inner channel of the

Hatteras shoals, staying close to shore.[604] The lighter-draft vessel was able to cross the shoals extending from the cape and establish enemy positions.[605] An hour later, aloft in the *Monticello*, Braine's lookout spotted sails across the woodlands at Kinnakeet inside the sound. At the same time, a Rebel flag was spotted in the midst of a regiment marching north out of the woods at Kinnakeet.[606] The crew of the *Monticello* assumed the Confederates had just given up the chase, "satisfied at [the Twentieth Indiana's] superiority in running" and started back north.[607] Two tugs flying Confederate colors also showed in the sound beyond.[608]

As soon as the Rebels came out of the Kinnakeet woods, the *Monticello* opened up a fiery hell on the Rebels from three-quarters of a mile. One Georgian on the receiving end of the bombardment wrote that the *Monticello* "commenced pouring into our temporary encampment her fiery shot and shell. I expected every minute to be blown to atoms."[609] Another volunteer described in a letter to his father being "shot at 300 Times with all Kinds of shot that seeamed to threten us with speady destruction at the Time [*sic*]."[610] When the first shell fell in the middle of the retreating Rebels, they immediately rolled up Mrs. Wright's "handsome silk flag" and scattered, moving at a brisk pace northward into the next grove of trees that would receive them.[611]

Some of the Rebel stragglers, though, came out on the beach and began firing at the lookout on the *Monticello*'s mast, who scrambled quickly down, convincing the Georgians that their Enfields were somewhat accurate at a half mile or more. Some of the Rebels taunted the Federal steamer with their flags planted on the beach.[612] One of the two Confederate howitzers had already been loaded onto a schooner waiting in the sound. The other howitzer had been abandoned somewhere north, as the men dragging the gun had been thoroughly exhausted hauling it through the loose sand. The Georgians, therefore, had nothing with which to return fire at the *Monticello* except their Enfields. Those men with muskets were particularly impotent.[613] Adjutant Turner described vividly the experience under fire:

> *And so, the shelling continued all that blessed summer afternoon. In our covert, grape, from shrapnel, fell thick and fast. First would come the report from the cannon, then that shrill scream of the missile through the air… then the explosion, during the passage, and, lastly, the 'bip-bip-bip' of the separate shot, and fragments, as they fell in the sand, all around us.*[614]

The *Monticello* continued its three-gun reign of terror on the confused and panicked Rebel retreat. Small boats emerged in the sound loaded with troops trying in earnest to make it out to their steamers. Three additional steamers moved south, opposite the woods, and returned fire on the *Monticello*, coming up short except for three shots. Two sloops were also receiving fire from the Federal steamer. The shelling continued, almost continuously from 1:30 p.m.[615]

Mid-afternoon, at 3:30 p.m., two men appeared on the beach signaling to the *Monticello*,[616] one waving a white handkerchief.[617] They were assumed to be Twentieth Indiana, so an armed boat was sent off to pick them up while the *Monticello* provided cover fire. Seeing the launch coming for them, the two jumped into the surf and swam out to meet their rescuers. The two grateful men were Private Charles White and Private Warren O'Haver, both from Company H.[618] Unfortunately while the rescuers were pulling O'Haver into the boat, White went under and drowned in the breakers. Private White was known to have been a good swimmer, but in need of food and exhausted from the ordeal, the young immigrant patriot sank "to rise no more."[619]

Private Warren O'Haver, known as "Boone," originated from Kentucky and was remembered for his ability to spin a good yarn.[620] This would become one of his best. O'Haver had been suffering on the previous morning from an attack of erysipelas, a kind of cellulitis that caused his legs to swell whenever he had "to perform heavy labor, or even ordinary exercise of drilling." His condition had gone unnoticed by Captain George Geisendorf during enlistment in Indiana. In bad shape, unable to walk and left behind in the camp hospital at Live Oak, Boone had been taken prisoner[621] early in the assault on the morning of October 4. O'Haver, White and another private from Company H, Lucius Bennett, stayed behind at Live Oak and were busily destroying anything of value that could be useful to the Confederates if it were captured. O'Haver in error would report Bennett had been "shot dead in an attempt to escape."[622] Bennett was neither shot nor killed[623] but was left behind in the camp hospital at Live Oak, having contracted the measles. Bennett, like Private White, had made it off the *Fanny* onto Captain Bailey's launch on October 1 but was unable to outrun the Georgians the morning of October 4.[624]

O'Haver also inaccurately reported to Lieutenant Braine once aboard the *Monticello* that several Rebel officers had also been killed. In fact, none had been killed. O'Haver saw rider-less ponies running about and apparently assumed, or hoped, the worst. O'Haver also claimed to have just escaped that morning before appearing on the beach, having shot one of the Confederate captains. There were certainly no deaths on either side from enemy fire. Neither were there later any reported bullet wounds among the Confederates. There were plenty of inaccurate reports made of the events of that week.[625]

O'Haver's account states that he and White were tied and put under the watch of a certain "Captain Wilson of the Georgia Seventh [*sic*]."[626] O'Haver reported that Captain Wilson and some other soldiers had "liberated" some ducks from the poor islanders and were cooking them near dusk on October 4. Hungry and brave enough to speak up, he asked for some of the duck to eat. The Confederates, calling him a "black republican son of a b———," told him that they "don't eat with n———rs."[627] Thus, O'Haver remained hungry.

Just before daybreak on October 5, O'Haver claimed, he broke his hands free and released Private White. O'Haver claimed to have hidden a small revolver between his shirts, which he used to then shoot "Captain Wilson," before making it to a nearby marsh and being pursued by Georgian troops. The escapees buried themselves up to their faces in the marsh, avoiding recapture, while the Rebels were only steps away. O'Haver was certain the Rebels would have executed him on the spot if recaptured. Fortunately, the bombardment took the attention off the two Indianians, scattering the Rebels and giving O'Haver and White an opportunity to make it to the beach where the *Monticello* was standing in command.[628]

O'Haver recalled the Rebels were in a state of confusion, running into the sound and making for the vessels in an attempt to escape the unrelenting bombardment of the *Monticello*. He pointed out where the Rebels were massing to escape the island, and Braine opened fire again, scattering the Confederates. The Rebel retreat was stretched out over four miles. The *Monticello*'s Parrott thirty-pounder rifled cannon was let loose on the six enemy steamers just off the western edge of the narrow island. Braine reported that one of those six steamers was the *Fanny*, now a part of the secessionist fleet, and that he hit the *Fanny* probably once. The Parrott gun, however, was not as accurate or effective as anticipated.[629]

Colonel Wright would later report with great specificity that 441 shells were thrown by the *Monticello* before his men got out of range. Assuming Braine's report—that he bombarded the Rebel retreat for three hours straight—was correct, between two and three shells per minute fell on that narrow strip above Kinnakeet, terrorizing the Georgians. Despite initial Federal reports to the contrary, there were no deaths caused by the shelling.[630] Not a single one. The USS *Monticello* ceased fire at 5:25 p.m.,[631] at which time it rejoined the *Susquehanna*, both vessels returning to Hatteras Inlet and arriving at 8:30 p.m.[632]

Flag Officer William Lynch's squadron in the Pamlico Sound on the afternoon of October 5, 1861, off Kinnakeet. From the *Pictorial Dictionary of the War of 1861. Outer Banks History Center.*

Private Charles Henry White's body was never recovered. Word eventually made its way back to Oxford, Indiana, where White had been last working in the fields before enlisting, that he had been "swallowed up by a shark."[633] White's German-immigrant mother, Louisa, living in Genesee County, New York, was not informed of White's death by her son's captain, George W. Geisendorff of Company H. In fact, Mrs. Weidt wrote a letter to her son as late as December 13, not yet aware he was dead or even missing. Louisa Weidt's letter came into Camp Hamilton, outside Fort Monroe, on December 21, a couple weeks after Geisendorff resigned the regiment. Company H's new captain, George W. Meikel, had taken command on December 4 and wrote an incredibly moving letter to White's mother explaining the death of her only son, Charles:

> *Camp Hamilton Dec 21ˢᵗ 1861*
> *Mrs. Louisa White*
> *Dear Madam,*
>
> > *Your letter of the 13ᵗʰ inst. addressed to your son Charles came to hand today and was opened by me. I am deeply sorry that I am unable to give you such an answer as I would wish, for I can imagine how much pain and sorrow my words will bring to your heart. Your son is no more.*
> > *I will try and give you briefly the facts in the case: We left Cockeysville for Fort Hatteras in September and on our arrival then were ordered to Chickamacomico [sic]. We had been at Chickamacomico but a few days, when we were attacked by the Rebels and were ordered to retreat. Charles and another of my men named [O'Haver] fell behind and unfortunately*

were taken prisoners. They managed however to make their escape and seeing the gun boat—Monticello, on the Atlantic, near them, they plunged in and attempted to swim to her. The breakers however were very strong and ere the boat from the Monticello could reach them. Charles was taken under, and was never seen again. This is the statement of the man that was with him and although I have tried often to persuade myself that it was not true, yet from all that I can learn I am forced believe [sic] it [is] too true. We had some forty prisoners taken on that occasion and I have seen all their names published in the Rebels prints and I looked in vain for your son's name among them. This convinces me that there is no hope.

There was no man in my company for whom I entertained a higher regard as a man and as a soldier, and I assure you the intelligence of his loss was received by all of us, with the sincerest sorrow; and I can imagine ~~how~~ with what terrible weight this sad affliction must fall upon his mother.

Charles is entitled to pay from the first of September to the 4th of October and also his bounty of $100.00 and perhaps a Land Warrant, should Congress make the allowance. I have written to the man O'Haver, for a sworn statement so that you can draw this pay. When I get that I will take such steps as will secure you the pay. If you have any instruction in regard to the matter be kind enough to drop me a line.

Again expressing my sympathy with you in this deep affliction which has come upon you

I am

> *Sincerely your friend*
>
> > *Captain George W. Meikel*
> > *Co. H 20th Reg't Ind. Vol's*
> > *Fortress Monroe Va*

P.S.
G.W. Geisendorff our former Captain has resigned.
GWM[634]

The Eighth North Carolina just sat and watched the show on October 5. From its isolated vantage point aboard barges towed by the CSS *Empire* on the Pamlico Sound, the regiment could observe the *Monticello* on the Atlantic side firing its guns. Colonel Shaw, though, eventually went ashore while ordering Captain Yellowley to take part of Company G—some forty men, as well as Company G's first lieutenant Amos J. Hines—and return by land to Chicamacomico and complete the loading of the captured Twentieth

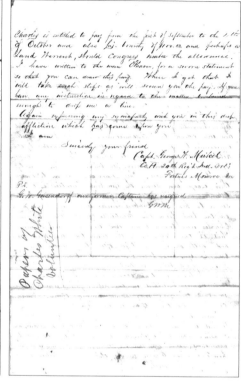

Above: "Dear Madam." The December 21, 1861 letter of Captain George W. Meikel to Mrs. Louisa White, the mother of Private Charles H. White, who drowned swimming out to the USS *Monticello* the afternoon of October 5, 1861. This original manuscript was submitted as a supporting document in Mrs. White's Dependents Pension Application. *National Archives.*

Left: Captain George W. Meikel, Twentieth Indiana. *Richard F. Carlile Collection.*

Indiana property. Yellowley remarked, "The appearance of the camp gave evidence of the fright and haste of the enemy."[635]

Edward Clements Yellowley, nearing forty, was the son of a British immigrant to the United States, who came to Martin County, North Carolina, soon after the Revolutionary War. Yellowley was a lawyer, having graduated from University of North Carolina at Chapel Hill in 1844. In October 1847, he was drawn into a duel, which took place in Virginia, between Portsmouth and Elizabeth City, North Carolina along the Dismal Swamp Canal. After firing his pistol in the air on the first shot, Yellowley took aim on the second, shooting his opponent, a Mr. H.F. Harris, directly through the heart, killing him instantly. Originally opposed to secession, after the election of Lincoln, Yellowley raised his own military company and joined Shaw at the Warrenton, North Carolina rendezvous.[636]

Georgian reports stated during the five-hour shelling by the USS *Monticello*, one man received a bruise trying to dodge a ball that rolled over his leg. Another soldier reportedly received a slight scratch on his face from the explosion of a shell.[637] Private J.G. Turner of Greenville, South Carolina, fighting as a member of the Third Georgia's Company G wrote a few days later, "Not one was hurt or tuched By [*sic*] shot whistling close to our Ears and throwing Sand in our faces."[638]

The company rosters are a record of the true casualties, however. The company roster entry of Morgan County, Georgia private Henry C. Moore of Company D, the Madison Home Guards, noted Moore was "Wounded, Chickamicomico Island, N.C. October 5, 1861." Moore had been "bruised by a spent shot." One member of the Third Georgia died of exhaustion during the chase, late in the day on the fifth. Private

Captain Edward C. Yellowley, Eighth North Carolina Regiment. *Sarah Ann Matilda Yellowley Collection.*

163

Captain Rufus A. Barrier, Eighth North Carolina Regiment. *Eastern Cabarrus Historical Society.*

Private Guilford Hatley, Eighth North Carolina Volunteers, Company H, the Cabarrus Phalanx. *Ben F. Callahan Collection.*

Benjamin K. Smith of Houston County, Georgia, was a member of Company E, the Governor's Guard. His body was loaded onto the *Junaluska* and taken to Norfolk. Smith was the "first member of the regiment to perish on the field of battle."[639]

There were various reports of the death of one native islander who was shot "by mistake" when he was ordered to halt.[640] It was also reported that Chicamacomico storeowners, "Mr. and Mrs. Goodwin," were shot by the Georgians.[641] Another report in the *New York Tribune* said that "the Confederates burned all the property of the inhabitants and killed several who remained behind. One old gentleman, Mr. Goodin, was shot dead while attempting to reach his family, who had taken refuge with Colonel Brown's men."[642] The *New York Herald* reported an old man seventy years old "was shot in cold blood by a devil incarnate from Georgia."[643] The most convincing report of a Banker death is by Third Georgia historians who recorded that just after sunrise on October 5, skirmishers of Companies A, C, D and F, who had stayed behind with the two artillery pieces, came upon what they thought was a squad of the Twentieth Indiana hiding in the grass at Little Kinnakeet. They would not come out or answer, so the Georgians shot, and one person was killed. The Federal "squad" turned out to be a group of Bankers.[644] With Union and

"The 'Monticello' Shelling the Rebels near Hatteras, October 5, 1861." *Harper's Weekly*, October 26, 1861. An inaccurate depiction of events based on the official report of Lieutenant Daniel L. Braine, commander of the *Monticello*, and the narrative of Twentieth Indiana private Warren O'Haver. *Oxford Collection.*

Confederate reports alike noting this civilian death, it appears to have based in fact, though the details are elusive.[645]

Many of the Georgians trudged the full distance back to Chicamacomico on foot, along with the two brass howitzers and their limbers. Dragging these pieces through the foot-deep sand became too much for the Georgian gun crews, and they gave up the attempt to keep up with the regiment. Others who could not maintain the chase simply stayed behind with the guns. One piece was left behind until the return north on October 5.[646] First reports in Norfolk newspapers exaggerated the stamina and determination of the Georgians and reported the howitzers were dragged the entire pursuit of twenty-five miles and back, stopping eighteen miles south at Kinnakeet overnight. The brass nemeses were finally loaded on October 5 on the *Curlew*, which had steamed back north from Kinnakeet and was waiting off Chicamacomico. The flag officer had earlier ordered the *Cotton Plant* to remain at Chicamacomico to take on the entire camp equipment of the Twentieth Indiana, as well as all the troops that made it back on the ground.[647]

The spoils of Camp Live Oak included three hundred tents, carriage boxes, haversacks, canteens, cooking utensils and provisions, in addition to the Hoosiers' private clothing and papers they were unable to take due to the great rush to retreat.[648] The personal property at Camp Live Oak, captured and carried away by the Rebels, included the most precious possessions of any soldier in the field, far away from home[649]—Bibles[650] and personal mail. The Southern soldiers soon found "these Yankee troops had not been long from Cockeysville, Md., as letters found in their possession are directed to that point, and are of a very late date."[651] Captain Yellowley seemed somewhat surprised that the letters "all breathed hostility to the South."[652] Third Georgia musician Alva Spencer wrote home "we seldom get any mail, and have no chance to send off any of our letters." Capturing the vacated Federal camp revealed an unanticipated but welcomed treasure: "I wish you could have seen some of the Yankee letters we found at Hatteras. They represented themselves as fighting for their flag. Some say they were forced into it, others that they were fooled into it." Some of the Georgia men sent this captured mail home for their families and friends to see. After seeing what happened to the Twentieth Indiana's personal effects, Private Spencer determined that he would burn his letters from home rather than allow them to fall into "Lincolnite" hands and be read and enjoyed by "Lincolnite" eyes. Writing home to a Dooly County, Georgia friend of the family about his decision, Private Spencer hoped they would understand why he would treat these "letters with such disrespect."[653] Some of the letters were partly written the day of the attack,[654] left unfinished and un-mailed, which the Rebels "kept and read. Some were funny, some vulgar."[655]

Daguerreotypes of mothers, fathers, sisters and sweethearts were left behind. The Eighth North Carolina's captain Yellowley concluded, "The panic must have been as great as Manassas, and yet they escaped."[656] The Rebels mailed home other personal items captured at Live Oak. Spencer noted that he had sent captured items home and still had others in his possession. He intended to send a captured snuffbox for his Aunt Nancy to use for storing tooth powder.[657] Captain Yellowley wrote home to a relative on October 8, using writing paper captured from the Hoosiers. "This paper I am writing on was taken from them. You must keep it as a relic."[658]

It was midnight on October 5 before the majority of the Third Georgia was back to Chicamacomico.[659] The entire Rebel expedition had returned to Roanoke Island by midnight on Sunday, October 6.[660] When the Third Georgia returned to Roanoke Island, a young corporal, R.A. Whitman, from Company K,[661] the Athens Guards, was found missing, left behind somewhere near Chicamacomico. When he was last seen, the soldier had been "delirious and idiotic from excessive fatigue"[662] and had wandered off from the regiment. Private Joel A. Rice of Company H, the Young Guards of Newton County, Georgia, answered Colonel Wright's call for a volunteer to return in search of the young soldier.[663] Rice took a small skiff and returned alone across the Pamlico Sound to Chicamacomico. On October 9,[664] after several days and "many adventures," Rice returned on the skiff on a rainy and windy day to Roanoke Island along with his lost comrade, alive and safe.[665]

On Sunday, October 6, the Hoosiers trudged from Fort Clark another two miles back up to Camp Wool, sleeping that night on the cold, damp sand. On Tuesday, October 8, they received mail, and Sergeant Stephens of Company K wrote, "God bless our friends at home for remembering us."[666]

Among the missing when the regiment reached Fort Clark and presumed to be among those captured was Private Robert Stoddard. As a musician in the band, Stoddard's name appears among the list of "Missing Men" drawn up by Hawkins as late as October 8.[667] Stoddard had been sick for a while prior to the attack, and the retreat from Live Oak was too much for him.[668] News of Stoddard's return was recorded in Ninth New York private Charles Johnson's diary on October 9: "Information just received that an Indianan is at the house of one of the inhabitants, sick from exposure, having passed some days in the swamps without food while getting away from the Rebs."[669] Knowing Stoddard's name had been in the newspapers, Twentieth Regiment lieutenant Erasmus Gilbreath wrote home to Valparaiso revealing Stoddard had not been captured after all. The son of William Stoddard of Tassinong had been hiding in bushes for two days. With nothing to eat and the enemy passing within feet of him, the young soldier finally found his way to safety, though he "lost his coat and shoes and everything almost, but saved himself."[670]

The *New York Weekly Tribune* also listed among the "Missing Men" a Twentieth Indiana private Henry A. Munk of Company C, listed as "lost during the retreat."[671] This appears to have been a mistaken listing, however, as there was no "Munk," "Monk" or any name similar on the Twentieth's muster rolls. The name did not appear on Hawkins's list of October 7 either.[672]

Thirty-one men and boys—soldiers and civilians—from the Twentieth Indiana's Camp Live Oak were captured on October 4 and 5. They were taken out to the CSS *Cotton Plant* sitting off Chicamacomico, awaiting transport to meet up with the forty-two men of the Twentieth Indiana and the Hawkins Zouaves captured aboard the U.S. gunboat *Fanny*. This combined lot of seventy-three Union prisoners of war was the greater part of all the casualties on Hatteras, Union or Confederate, despite the slaughter communicated in the remarkable official report of the USS *Monticello*'s commander Lieutenant Daniel L. Braine.

Chapter Twelve

"The Most Remarkable Naval Report of the War"

B oth Northern and Southern newspapers published highly distorted reports of the events that took place that week on Hatteras. The account published in Washington's *Daily National Intelligencer* told it as most in the North wanted to hear it:

> *For upward of three hours the Monticello's guns raked the bare beach, bare of everything save the terrified, fleeing imploring, and dying rebels. Some idea may be gathered of what the slaughter must have been, from the fact that in about three hours the Monticello fired three hundred and seventy-five shells, at a range so short that in order to give the three-second fuses full time she had to draw off and take up position at a greater distance. Any body who has seen a shell burst—those terrible ten-inch shells that come as near to something infernal as anything imaginable—can form some idea of what must have been the effect of planting in the midst of a thousand or fifteen hundred men two of them every three seconds.*[673]

The distorted stories in Northern newspapers were primarily the product of two erroneous reports. These were the official navy report of Lieutenant Daniel Braine, in command of the USS *Monticello*, and the narrative of Twentieth Indiana private Warren "Boone" O'Haver who escaped capture and swam to safety aboard the *Monticello*. These two errant narratives had an ongoing impact on the retelling of the capture of the U.S. gunboat *Fanny* and

"Lieutenant Braine, U.S.N., Commanding the 'Monticello'". Cover of *Harper's Weekly*, October 26, 1861. *Oxford Collection*.

the Chicamacomico Affair, even to the present day. Histories continue to be written perpetuating the errors contained in these documents.

Brigadier General Joseph K.F. Mansfield (who would later conduct the government's initial investigation of the two October 1861 engagements on Hatteras after taking command from Colonel Hawkins) in an October 14 letter to Major General Winfield Scott made it clear that he was aware of the gross misrepresentation of the facts in Lieutenant Braine's official navy report. Mansfield stated flatly, "I do not understand the report of the Navy in this matter."[674] The report was brought to life in dramatic engravings such as the one appearing in *Harper's Weekly* on October 26, 1861. Lieutenant Braine was lionized, with a bold engraved portrait, on the cover of the same issue of *Harper's Weekly* as well. [675]

U. S. Navy Admiral David Dixon Porter continued repeating the falsehoods of the Braine report as late as Porter's 1886 book, *The Naval History of the Civil War*. Porter repeated as fact the false report that two Confederate boats filled with fleeing Rebel soldiers were struck by shells and destroyed, that

U. S. S. MONTICELLO,
Off Cape Hatteras, North Carolina, October 5, 1861.

SIR: I have the honor to inform you that in obedience to your order of this morning I stood through the inner channel of Hatteras Shoals at 12:30 p. m., and stood close along shore to the northward, keeping a bright lookout from aloft. At 1:30 p. m. we discovered several sailing vessels over the woodland Kinnakeet, and at the same time a regiment marching to the northward, carrying a rebel flag in their midst, with many stragglers in the rear; also two tugs inside flying the same flag. As they came out of the woods Kinnakeet we ran close inshore and opened a deliberate fire upon them at the distance of three-quarters of a mile. At our first shell, which fell apparently in their midst, they rolled up their flag and scattered, moving rapidly up the beach to the northward. We followed them, firing rapidly from three guns, driving them up to a clump of woods, in which they took refuge, and abreast of which their steamers lay.

We now shelled the woods and could see them embarking in small boats for their vessels, evidently in great confusion and suffering greatly from our fire.

Their steamers now opened upon us, firing, however, but three shots, which fell short. Two boats filled with men were struck by our shells and destroyed. Three more steamers came down the sound and took position opposite the woods we were shelling; also two sloops. We continued firing deliberately upon them from 1:30 p. m. until 3:30 p. m. when two men were discovered on the seabeach making signals to us. Supposing them to be two of the Indiana regiment, we sent an armed boat and crew to bring them off, covering them at the same time with our fire. Upon the boat nearing the beach they took to the water. One of them was successful in reaching the boat, Private Warren O'Haver, Company H, Twentieth Regiment Indiana troops; the other man, Private Charles White, Company H, Twentieth Regiment Indiana troops, was unfortunately drowned in the surf. Private O'Haver informed me that he was taken prisoner on the morning of the 4th; that he witnessed our fire, which was very destructive. He states that two of our shells fell into two sloops loaded with men, blowing the vessels to pieces and sinking them. Also that several of the officers were killed. Their horses were seen running about the track. He had just escaped from his captors after shooting the captain of one of the rebel companies. He states that the enemy were in the greatest confusion, rushing wildly into the water, striving to get off to their vessels. Private O'Haver now directed me to the point where the rebels were congregated, waiting an opportunity to get off. I opened fire again with success, scattering them. We were now very close, in 3 fathoms water, and 5-second shell told with effect. Six steamers were now off the point, one of which I recognized as the *Fanny*.

At 5:25 p. m. we ceased firing, leaving the enemy scattered along the beach for upwards of 4 miles.

I fired repeatedly at the enemy's steamers with our rifled cannon, a Parrot 30-pounder, and struck the *Fanny*, I think, once. I found the range of this piece much short of what I had anticipated, many of the shot turning end over end, and not exceeding much the range of the smoothbore 32-pounders.

I enclose you herewith memorandum of the ammunition expended to-day.

I am, respectfully, your obedient servant,
D. L. BRAINE,
Lieutenant, Commanding U. S. S. Monticello.

Captain J. L. LARDNER,
Comdg. U. S. S. Susquehanna, off Cape Hatteras, North Carolina.

Official report of Lieutenant D.L. Braine on the USS *Monticello* bombardment of the Third Georgia, October 5, 1861. *Official Records of the Union and Confederate Navies in the War of the Rebellion,* 1, 6:291–92.

several officers were killed and that "the shore for a distance of four miles was strewn with killed or wounded."[676] John Thomas Scharf rightly assessed Braine's report in his *History of the Confederate States*, when he stated, "This U.S. naval report of this affair is one of the most remarkable made during the war."[677]

Early Southern reports based on Confederates accounts claimed the Rebels not only captured forty fleeing Indiana troops in the Affair at Chicamacomico but also killed seven or eight other "flying Hessians."[678] These Confederate reports of Union deaths continued long after the war as well. At the Reunion of the Third Georgia at Union Point, Georgia, on July 30–31, 1874, Colonel Claiborne Snead repeated the errant casualty statistics of the Chicamacomico Affair. Snead reported, "A loss to them of eight killed and forty two captured."[679] These reports, official and unofficial, lived on despite the facts in an early Southern letter that appeared in the papers. Dated October 5 from Elizabeth City, North Carolina, and addressed to a man in Richmond, Virginia, the letter confirmed not a "single man killed on either side, as the cowardly rascals did not stand long enough to fire their pieces."[680]

In Washington on Thursday, October 10, news of "the late affair near Hatteras Inlet," considered a Union victory, was the talk of the town. The news was again filled with Braine's report of the supposed slaughter of Rebels during the October 5 *Monticello* bombardment: "The terrific repulse of the Rebels by the gunboat *Monticello*, and the successful retreat of the Twentieth Indiana, is the theme of the day in the Department corridors and the lobbies of the hotels. It was heard of in the camps this afternoon, and gave great enthusiasm to the troops."[681]

With victory in the nostrils of anyone reading the newspaper accounts from Hatteras and Chicamacomico, there was little interest in casting blame on anyone for the Union failures. However, in the earliest attempts to lay blame for the mistakes at Chicamacomico on someone other that Colonel Rush Hawkins, the *New York Tribune*, in its October 8 issue, placed suspicion on a cook. He was said to be a civilian in the service of an anonymous Twentieth Indiana officer accused of treasonous behavior, taken aboard the *Fanny*, suspected of informing the Rebels and thus aiding them in the subsequent assault at Chicamacomico:

> *Among the prisoners taken was a cook, from Baltimore, in the employ of one of our officers, who, it is thought, is a Secessionist, and from whom it is supposed the enemy obtained all the information desired in relation to our force here, and much other information, which will doubtless be of great*

value to them. In fact, it is thought the second attack by the enemy…was made upon the strength of the news received by this Baltimore cook.[682]

The newspapers were obviously referring to cook William Vogel of Cockeysville, Maryland, who was attached to Company G.[683] No further coverage, however, is found about Vogel after this initial report.

Colonel Brown and the men of the Twentieth Indiana, though, knew exactly who to blame. Even among the ranks of Hawkins's Zouaves, there were those in agreement with the Hoosiers. A quite perceptive Private Charles Johnson, on October 5, confided to his diary the first words Colonel Brown spoke to his superior, Colonel Rush Hawkins, on meeting him after the retreat from Live Oak: "You sent me up there with my hands tied!" To Johnson it was obvious that Brown was angry with Hawkins for having set up the Twentieth for potential disaster without adequate cover. The Zouave private did not blame Brown for complaining either, "for the policy of having an outpost some forty miles from its base of supplies, without a cannon or the protection of a gunboat, and within hailing distance of the enemy, is certainly questionable."[684] Regardless of who was at fault for the fiasco at Live Oak, the *New York Times* still concluded Brown's "narrow escape" was a "masterly movement."[685]

"We had been placed in a false position," Brown flatly stated in a personal letter home to a close friend. A false position, in military parlance, is simply a piece of ground that cannot be held or defended under attack. It was clear to Brown and his officers why Live Oak could not be held. Brown had about "500 effective men" among the seven companies of the Twentieth Indiana on Hatteras at the time of the October 4 assault on Live Oak. In the end, Brown estimated the Confederate force to have been about three thousand (not two thousand as he first estimated on October 4). In fact, the combined Confederate forces on October 4, were indeed closer to two thousand. The Hoosiers carried altered smoothbore muskets and were "nigh 50 miles from help," and "that [help], from experience, doubtful." As Brown matter-of-factly put it, "our rebel friends in possession of the sound, the race commenced."[686]

Other reports shouted treachery and incompetence and began to trickle out to Indiana hometown newspapers. Company I captain James M. Lytle of Valparaiso told the editor of the *Valparaiso Republic* in no uncertain terms: "The fact is, that the 20th Regiment has been most shamefully 'sold.'"[687] One Hoosier wrote to the Logansport *Journal*, revealing, "We were wholly unprepared to resist an attack with artillery, or to make a successful retreat.

We had no guns, no baggage wagons...and we had nothing but the old fashioned muskets to fight artillery and resist a landing, and not food enough to last one day."[688] The Twentieth would not see the promised Enfield rifles until December 5.[689]

Twentieth Indiana adjutant Israel Stiles recorded at the time, "It has been pronounced an outrage that we should have been placed in such a position, without steamers, and out of reach of reinforcements."[690] Colonel Brown was reported to have said that the prisoners from the Twentieth consisted of the "sick and wounded, and twenty pickets, who could not be called in."[691] Brown's casualty statistics in a letter home included twenty-five prisoners taken, of which six had been sick "since the day previous." Brown revealed that it was fortunate that he had sent off the sick and most of "the baggage" the day before. These had been loaded on the *Ceres* and *General Putnam* with the Bankhead expedition on the third.[692] Brown was not counting civilian cooks and boys in this number, however, as a total of thirty-one men and boys were taken during the Chicamacomico Affair alone. There were thirty-two Union casualties total, including the drowning of Private Charles White who drowned attempting to swim out to the safety of the USS *Monticello*.

The troops of the Twentieth Indiana and the Ninth New York were not the only men complaining about the "Chicamacomico Affair." Eighth North Carolina captain Yellowley was one who was especially unhappy with the execution of the expedition despite the capture of the valuable camp equipment from Live Oak, and Yellowley bitterly blamed Colonel Wright. Recalling the misery associated with the Eighth's failed landing, he wrote, "I passed three nights...on a boat without cover or blanket, lived upon fired meat and crackers...without whiskey or coffee...have 25 sick men, most cases of measles...a day before our departure to attack the enemy."[693] It was not quite the "jolly crowd...jolly time" the Eighth was promised.

The North Carolina captain admitted that Colonel Wright was evidently a brave leader. But Yellowley charged that Wright

> is without military tact...had he landed between the enemy's position and Hatteras or had [he] supplied us with flat boats to make our landing... we could have captured every one of the enemy and succeeded in blowing up Hatteras lighthouse...we would have stormed and taken Fort Hatteras and blew it up...the Georgians are self-satisfied with what was done...Colonel Wright did not communicate at any time his designs...[including with] Colonel Shaw.[694]

The government was also interested in finding those responsible, and General Wool did not hesitate to investigate the command problems at Hatteras. When Wool gained a clearer picture of what occurred in regard to the *Fanny* capture, he took immediate action, even before the Chicamacomico Affair came to light. Rush Hawkins did not report to Wool, as required, until October 8, a full week after the *Fanny* capture and several days after the retreat from Live Oak.[695] It was Commander Rowan, instead, who submitted his own report to Newport News, Virginia, on October 4, en route to the Washington Navy Yard. He also landed the civilian captain and crew of the *Fanny*. Rowan was due at Washington Navy Yard with the *Pawnee* the following day.[696]

General Wool was in Washington when the *Pawnee* steamed into Newport News, but Wool returned to Fort Monroe the morning of October 5 to resume his command there.[697] In Wool's absence, Brigadier General Mansfield went from Fort Monroe to Newport News straight away and took statements from the civilian crew members of the *Fanny*—including Captain Morrison, First Mate Ridgely, the engineer and a deck hand. Mansfield personally examined each separately. It was dark when he finished gathering the statements, and he returned to Fort Monroe too late to send his report up the Potomac to the Adjutant General's Office in Washington. The next day, October 5, that report was sent to the Headquarters of the Army.[698] This delay in getting the bad news did not sit right with Wool, especially as it was not coming from his own army commander, Colonel Hawkins at Hatteras.[699] There was not a word from Rush Hawkins.

Captain Morrison was prevented from going to Baltimore on October 5. After all, he was held at Fort Monroe until further particulars could be gleaned regarding the capture and his role in it. Morrison's testimony on the fifth at Fort Monroe turned out to be materially different than that of the previous day at Newport News when under examination by Brigadier General Mansfield. Many regarded Morrison as a coward. It was publicized that, sometime previous, while U.S. Navy lieutenant Peirce Crosby commanded the *Fanny*, Morrison had attempted to run the vessel ashore under Rebel guns, and Lieutenant Crosby had had to hold a gun to his head to prevent him from compromising the tug.[700] The truth of that accusation was never substantiated. To Morrison's credit, in his statement before a House Investigating Committee, the civilian captain was so confident of his reputation with the navy lieutenant that he appealed to Crosby as a character reference.[701]

Brigadier General Mansfield had years of experience with military investigations and audits. He had been appointed inspector general of the army in May 1853.[702] Eight years as army inspector general took Mansfield from coast to coast auditing government programs and installations. On April 27, 1861, two weeks after the first fire at Fort Sumter, he was appointed to the command of the Department of Washington through August 17.[703] Soon after taking that command, Mansfield received an appointment as Brigadier General.[704]

Major General Wool, having received Mansfield's Newport News report of October 5, ordered the former inspector to proceed immediately to Hatteras aboard the *Spaulding* and take command from Hawkins on arrival. He was authorized to make whatever troop deployments necessary for the defense of the station. The new commanding general was also ordered to report back immediately by "return of steamer."[705] Mansfield was finally able to leave Fort Monroe on October 6, arriving at the inlet on the morning of October 7.[706]

Brigadier General Mansfield arrived at Hatteras Inlet along with five hundred additional troops including the remaining two Ninth New York companies, B and K, under Major Edgar Kimball that had been waiting back at Camp Butler in Newport News[707] and the three companies of Twentieth Indiana Volunteers under Lieutenant Colonel Charles Murray that had been held at Fort Monroe.[708] The addition of these troops brought the forces at Hatteras to about two thousand men.

Mansfield was Wool's temporary solution to the Hatteras command problem until the arrival of Brigadier General Thomas Williams. A widely unknown fact is that General Williams had already received orders to take command at Hatteras days before the twin disasters involving the gunboat *Fanny* and Live Oak. General Mansfield would only be there long enough to get a fix on what had gone wrong in the capture of the *Fanny*, however. As Mansfield had just retired from his command of the Department of Washington and Washington City, it was the perfect opportunity for him to put on his inspector-general hat and investigate the *Fanny* capture, which had become front-page news in Washington, New York and throughout the country. Mansfield knew how to get answers. If there was mismanagement, poor command decisions or a traitor in the ranks, Mansfield was the man to uncover it.

As soon as Mansfield was on the ground at Hatteras, he realized things had gone from bad to worse, receiving the news of the more recent Chicamacomico Affair. Reporting back to Wool with the return steamer became impossible when the *Monticello* and *Susquehanna* left the inlet the night of October 7, to Mansfield's surprise.[709]

The first news Mansfield received was that the Twentieth Indiana regiment had fallen back to the inlet.[710] Then, initially accepting the official statement in the Braine report, Mansfield immediately "dispatched four hundred men up the beach to the scene of annihilation, probably to look after the dead and wounded left by the rebels, and secure the arms which it is represented they threw away as they took to the water, at least such of them as were not killed."[711]

Wool recognized that the failures associated with the *Fanny* capture were probably not isolated and could very well mean the beginning of

Brigadier General Joseph K.F. Mansfield, United States Army, Department of Virginia. *U.S. Naval Historical Center.*

the eventual loss of Hatteras Inlet and perhaps Newport News for that matter. Even as Mansfield was shoving off for Hatteras, Wool informed Lieutenant General Winfield Scott that this was Rush Hawkins's "great error." The surrender of the *Fanny* was "disgraceful," wrote Wool, apart from any other tactical errors made by Hawkins. Wool chalked up the loss of the gunboat *Fanny* to Hawkins's placing the Twentieth Indiana encampment too far away from his artillery batteries. This was an error that would not have been made had a general officer been in command as earlier intended. Wool confessed to Scott, "I regretted extremely the withdrawal of Brigadier-General Reynolds."[712]

Wool also sensed that with the withdrawal of Commander Rowan and the *Pawnee* to the Navy Yard, the naval force on which the army batteries of Forts Clark and Hatteras depended for protection had become so vulnerable as to open the possibility of other disasters. The additional troops who arrived at Hatteras with General Mansfield would give short-term protection to the stores and batteries until Wool could make a more permanent deployments to hold the inlet. The loss of the inlet, Wool thought, would be unfortunate to say the least.[713]

Mansfield, at Hatteras, quickly cleared Colonel Brown, concluding he responded correctly in the face of the enemy at Live Oak. Adjutant Stiles said, "Indianians will be most proud to know that the 'old veteran' [Mansfield] sustains most fully Colonel Brown in all his views and acts in the late expedition." Colonel Hawkins, on the other hand, seemed to be blaming Brown and the Hoosiers for the failures at Live Oak. Exposing Hawkins, Stiles wrote that "the author of this calamity, in all meanness, has circulated falsehoods and wronged the regiment." As a result of the strain that was brewing between Brown and Hawkins, Mansfield ordered Hawkins to move out of Fort Clark and move up to the more primitive Camp Wool. Colonel Brown and the Twentieth then moved in and occupied Fort Clark.[714]

Assistant Adjutant General William D. Whipple, on October 8, before receiving news of the newest disaster at Chicamacomico, ordered Brigadier General Thomas Williams immediately to relieve General Mansfield at Hatteras. Mansfield had arrived at the inlet only a day earlier, on the morning of the seventh, but Wool and others were getting restless about the lack of information coming from the inlet. A report from Rush Hawkins had not been received, and no clear picture existed of the condition of the troops. Still unaware of the events of October 4 and 5, Whipple ordered Williams to "send a special report of the condition of the troops and conduct of those who preceded General Mansfield, and to report how it happened that the *Fanny* was so disgracefully surrendered to the enemy, and the losses sustained by the Government." The department's anger over the failures at Hatteras was reaching its peak, and there was no hiding it from Williams. Whipple made certain that there was no ambiguity in the orders. He stated, "We have not yet received any returns from the regiments nor any reports of their condition. These will receive your attention as soon as practicable, and you will transmit such reports and returns to these headquarters." Williams was warned to be certain not to separate regimental camps farther apart than was necessary to provide support for one another and was charged to treat the loyal islanders with "care and kindness."[715]

General Williams arrived at Hatteras Inlet on the morning of October 13 after multiple delays in departure. Not able to leave immediately the night of October 8 after finally getting news of the retreat of the Twentieth Indiana from Chicamacomico, Williams again attempted to leave on October 9 but a storm prevented the U.S. Revenue Cutter *Dale* from getting off.[716] The *Spaulding*, with Williams aboard, left Fort Monroe the night of October 12 and arrived at the inlet the next morning amid the cheers of hundreds of Federal soldiers waiting for mail from family and sweethearts and a large shipment of quartermaster and commissary stores.[717]

Colonel Rush Hawkins's first official report arrived in General Wool's hands on October 11, ten days after the capture of the *Fanny* and a full week after Third Georgia colonel Rans Wright set foot on the beach below Loggerhead Inlet. Wool was not pleased. Hawkins's report is difficult to read, even a century and a half later, without cringing. General Wool, on forwarding a copy of the document to Winfield Scott, in his prefacing remarks, is more than gracious to Hawkins by stating, "His language is highly insubordinate, and which I shall not fail to treat in a proper manner." For effect, Wool repeats this introductory statement as a remark on the enclosure. Wool chalked up the two embarrassments at Hatteras to Hawkins's "bad management in sending the Indiana regiment, commanded by Colonel Brown, out of supporting distance."[718]

Hawkins, when finally drafting his own highly inflammatory report, was certainly aware that General Mansfield was reporting on the facts uncovered concerning the *Fanny* and the "affair" at Chicamacomico. Knowing this, Hawkins was more intent upon providing excuses for the delay of his report and transferring blame from himself to the military hierarchy and even the Lincoln administration.[719]

Hawkins explained that no report on the *Fanny* had been sent because he had not been able to "get at the truth relating to her capture." In addition, Hawkins waited in order to write a report "the truth of which could be relied upon." Hawkins also claimed Commander Rowan, before finally leaving the inlet on October 3, said he didn't plan on stopping the *Pawnee* at Fort Monroe en route to his new assignment at Washington. Hawkins clearly shifted blame to the navy commander. Rowan, Hawkins implied, just was not willing to take the report of the *Fanny* capture to Wool. Then Hawkins took a swipe at Brigadier General Joseph Mansfield, who had relieved him of command the previous day:[720]

Sending a new commanding officer here to step into my shoes, after all the dirty work has been done, to supersede me, indicates that all confidence in my ability has been lost. This touches my pride. Next to doubting my integrity this is the most tender point in my nature, and now I have only to say that if by return mail you should inform me that you will accept my resignation, I will send it at once. One word more and I have done. I do not seek promotion. Brigadier-generals are made of such queer stuff nowadays, that I should not esteem it any very great honor to be made one. I had supposed, when I entered the service, that, if I should live to the end of my term, I might come out a very respectable colonel, but nothing more.[721]

Contrary to Hawkins's accusations in his official report, Commander Rowan actually did stop at Newport News (as previously noted) where he had landed the civilian captain and crew of the *Fanny* on Friday afternoon, October 4. Arriving in the *Pawnee*, Morrison and his crew were about to embark on the steamer *Adelaide* for Baltimore about 6:00 p.m. However, regular army quartermaster Grier Tallmadge recommended that the crew of the captured vessel report themselves to the guardhouse and wait to be examined on the circumstances of the disaster. Navy officers present at Newport News were "exceedingly mortified at the affair." Certainly, these officers' declarations that the surrender "was the result of gross negligence and inattention to duty" had influence on the decision to hold the crew for further questioning.[722] It was the opinion of many at Fort Monroe that the loss of the *Fanny* was under such circumstances that would convict Morrison and the crew of "deliberately throwing the vessel into the hands of the rebels" or, at the very least, "of abandoning her in a manner that makes the case but little better for them." Tallmadge was determined that the Philadelphia Transportation Company would not be paid for the lost boat until the circumstances of the surrender were thoroughly investigated.[723]

Commander Rowan also had with him in the *Pawnee* the official statements given Hawkins from both the acting master of the *Fanny*, John H. Morrison, and its first mate, George Ridgely. Rowan, unlike Hawkins, had evidently gathered enough facts before his October 3 departure from the inlet. These were sufficient facts for Rowan to put together his October 5 reports from Washington.[724] Furthermore, it was Hawkins who had most assuredly ordered the reports of the master and mate, drafted on October 2 at the inlet. The civilian crew of the *Fanny*, having left Chicamacomico about 6:00 p.m. on October 1, finally arrived at the inlet by small boat near 7:00 a.m. on October 2.[725] The crew remained at the inlet thirty-four hours until departing with Rowan on the *Pawnee* at 5:00 p.m. on October 3,[726] more than forty-eight hours after the capture of the *Fanny*. Hawkins did have sufficient access to the facts of the capture from the crew before their departure. In addition, because the crew of the *Fanny* was under the direct command of the army, not the navy, it most certainly would not have been permitted to leave the inlet without orders from Hawkins. With the suspicious nature of the surrender of the tug, a close watch should have been kept on these men. Navy commander Rowan would have respected Hawkins's command over that civilian crew.

Hawkins later became indignant about "the tone" of Wool's October 6 letter, which was drafted in response to Rowan's report in the absence of one from Hawkins. Hawkins complained, "A change in your feelings towards me has taken place." Indignation quickly turned to threats of exposing what the colonel characterized as "the criminal neglect of the Government." Hawkins felt that if he was going to be blamed for the disasters, he was "ready, eager and willing" to take his case to the public. Besides, after all the personal sacrifice he had made for his country, it seemed to him that the government had let him down: "But how different is the feeling now. I feel that I have an ungrateful and unappreciating [*sic*] Government at my back, which cannot or cares not to discern the difference between those of its servants who have its interests truly at heart and those who work for pay only."[727]

Twenty-five years later, Hawkins would write blandly about how the government "felt" about him: "The news of the loss of the *Fanny* created some excitement both at Fort Monroe and at Washington, and I was severely censured for having divided so small a force, and was superseded by Brigadier-General J.K.F. Mansfield."[728] Hawkins, even later, did not understand that Mansfield was a temporary substitute for General Williams, who had been ordered to replace Hawkins even prior to his "bad management" in the case of the Twentieth Indiana at Chicamacomico. Williams's orders to take command of Hatteras were given before news of the *Fanny* capture or the Chicamacomico Affair. The government wanted a general officer, not a colonel, commanding at Hatteras from the earliest days of the Union capture of the forts. Hawkins never seemed to understand this. Though it was public knowledge as early as September 13 that Wool intended to replace Hawkins with a general officer, Hawkins, even years later, attributed being relieved of command to his error of separating the Twentieth too far north of the inlet. The *New York Times* reported on September 8 from Fort Monroe, "The Government is preparing to follow up the late victory of Hatteras with vigorous measures. Brig.-Gen. JOHN F REYNOLDS having been designated will soon repair to that post and assume command under Major-Gen. WOOL."[729]

Washington and Fort Monroe were not the only voices censuring Hawkins for the failures of Live Oak. Newspaper publisher Horace Greeley joined the chorus of critics who came out against what seemed an elementary tactical error. Greeley considered posting the Twentieth Indiana at Camp Live Oak a "perilous division" of Hawkins's forces. He criticized Hawkins's desire to protect the loyal islanders at Chicamacomico who had taken the oath of allegiance, calling it an "excuse" for placing the Hoosiers in peril. Ninth New York regimental historian J.H.E. Whitney took issue with Greeley's criticism of his Zouave colonel, stating that Greeley "has no knowledge of the *excuse* offered." Whitney praised Hawkins's establishment of Camp Live

Oak in the end: "It became now the part of prudence to fix a camp at Chicomocomico [*sic*], and the seven companies of the Twentieth Indiana at Fort Clark were dispatched to the upper end of the Island for that purpose which…was a wise one."[730]

Rush Hawkins's problems were not limited to Live Oak and the *Fanny*, though. On Monday, October 7, the day Hawkins was relieved of command at Hatteras by General Mansfield, he faced another assault on his command related to neither of the previous events. Traveling along with the recently arrived two Ninth New York companies under Major Kimball and the three Twentieth Indiana companies under Lieutenant Colonel Murray was a Captain Leon Barnard, appointed to a captaincy in the Ninth by New York governor Edwin D. Morgan. Barnard was being transferred from the First New York Regiment to the Ninth over Hawkins's head. None of this sat well with Hawkins, who was accustomed to imposing his will on others—not the other way around. Colonel Hawkins readied his sharpened pen for the second time that day, firing off yet another indignant letter to General Wool and threatening his resignation.[731]

Hawkins was struggling under scrutiny, and with what came to be known as the "Barnard Affair,"[732] his stress hit a crescendo. In 1900 when the aged Rush Hawkins as a remembrance of his Zouaves wrote the foreword to Matthew Graham's regimental history of the Ninth Regiment, five of his twenty pages were dedicated to documents and description of events related to the "Barnard Affair." His remembrance of Antietam, Suffolk and all other engagements did not amount to five pages combined.[733] The reasons why Hawkins so vividly recalled the details related to Barnard may or may not be all too important to those studying the career of Rush Hawkins. However, it does reveal some of the impact the events the first couple of weeks of October had on on his mind and emotions.

Looking to escape public humiliation and military scrutiny, Hawkins reached out in a quick personal note to Major General Butler in Boston at the headquarters of the Department of New England. Butler, who had brought him to Hatteras, could possibly get him out:

From Colonel Rush C. Hawkins
HATTERAS INLET, N.C. Oct. 10th, 1861
Major General B. F. BUTLER, Com'd'g Dept. of N. E.

DEAR SIR: I am sick of Hatteras Inlet. Will you help me to get my regiment out of this infernal place? I would prefer to go with you, and I

think that this may be the wish of my regiment, in fact I know it is. I would like to return to Newport News, or be placed under the command of General Dix, until you get ready to use me. Do be kind enough to give this matter your attention and let me hear the result.
Ever most faithfully yours,
RUSH C. HAWKINS[734]

The young colonel most definitely was sick of Hatteras Inlet. By October 10, the date his letter to Butler was drafted, Hawkins had probably caught wind of Wool's decision to send General Thomas Williams that week to succeed General Mansfield in command of the troops not only at the inlet but throughout North Carolina.[735] Hawkins omitted a few items when asking for Butler's help: loss of command, loss of the *Fanny*, the Chicamacomico Affair, his issues with the governor of New York over Captain Barnard and the constant hum of negativity that was circulating about his leadership lapses.

General Mansfield, after remaining at Hatteras one full week, boarded the *Spaulding* again for his return north at 4:00 p.m., Sunday, October 13. Before his departure, Mansfield transferred command to Brigadier General Thomas Williams, who had finally arrived that morning on the *Spaulding* from Fort Monroe.[736] The Ninth New York's regimental historian Matthew Graham recalls that Mansfield left Hawkins in command for a short time before Williams arrived.[737] However, Graham was in error, as that command was transferred directly to Williams. Mansfield arrived back at Camp Hamilton on October 14 and took command of the post that day.[738]

Brigadier General Thomas Williams was ordered to the command at Hatteras Inlet by Winfield Scott's Special Order W 160. General Wool had received the order assigning Williams to the command on October 2. The order was issued entirely separate from and prior to the events concerning the *Fanny* and Chicamacomico. Wool was anxious to get Williams to the inlet at the earliest possible date, originally intending to send Williams south aboard the *Spaulding* on October 3. Wool, on receipt of Order W 160 from Scott, replied to the Lieutenant General, stating he would even "detain the vessel a day in the hope that he will arrive the next day. I do this because we are greatly in want of a General at Hatteras Inlet. I hope, General, if it is possible you will send General Williams at once. So anxious am I on the subject I send this by special messenger, Major W.P. Jones."[739]

General Thomas Williams, at forty-six, had "the appearance of a gentleman."[740] As a major with the Fifth Artillery, he had been appointed brigadier general on September 28, only two weeks before his arrival at

Hatteras. Williams, an 1837 graduate of West Point, was the son of the first elected mayor of Detroit, John R. Williams. An artillery officer before the war, Williams served as commandant of Fort Mackinac from 1852 to 1856.

Conditions quickly became testy between Hawkins and Williams, then between the Ninth New York and Williams and finally between the Ninth New York and the Twentieth Indiana. Williams praised the Hoosiers when writing to Mansfield, saying that "the Indiana men can undergo more fatigue, wade deeper water, go bare footed, ragged and hungry longer and finally eat more, build more breastworks, sing louder while at it and complain less than any class of men that I ever met."[741] Ninth New York regimental historian Matthew Graham remembered General Williams as the "inconsiderate martinet." Williams, wrote Graham, "managed affairs on Hatteras in a vigorous manner by issuing a series of orders which completely changed previous conditions."[742]

Navy secretary Gideon Welles was not as quick to criticize the capture of the *Fanny* as he was to disavow any knowledge of or relationship with the army quartermaster vessel and its civilian captain John H. Morrison. In an October 8 letter, John F. Potter, chairman of the House Investigating Committee, questioned Welles about his knowledge of Morrison and the veracity of newspaper reports concerning whether or not Morrison had refused to take an oath of allegiance.

Potter, a Wisconsin Republican congressman, chaired what was known as the Potter Investigating Committee, which investigated the loyalties of government employees, ferreting out those with secessionist leanings. By early September 1861, the Potter Committee was already being celebrated and was in the public eye for identifying some 220 Federal employees as "traitors in government service."[743] The committee would later report that, among the departments having secessionists on the payroll, the Navy Yard was found to have its fair share.[744] At the conclusion of the Potter Committee's business in January 1862, over five hundred Federal workers had been identified as being disloyal.[745]

Secretary Welles was obviously conflicted, holding to the Lincoln administration's and Navy Department's official policy that the navy's role on the North Carolina Coast was one of blockade, not joint amphibious operations. At the same time, if Captain Morrison had not taken the oath of allegiance, Welles possibly concluded, there would be no reason to imply that the navy had not been watching for employees or contractors with treasonous sentiments. Perhaps just a brief denial of any knowledge would put to rest any question as to whether or not Welles was off script on naval blockading policy.

Welles responded to Potter's inquiry about Captain Morrison in a brief October 9 Navy Department dispatch: "This Department has no knowledge of him whatsoever." The Navy Department, however, did in fact know that Commander Rowan, Colonel Hawkins and Captain Chauncey had been intent on combined operations between the army and navy forces on the coast. Welles knew Rowan had employed the *Fanny* for naval use in the bombardment of Fort Ocracoke and that a navy lieutenant was in command of the *Fanny* during that engagement. Welles's disavowal was entirely untrue but hit the Washington papers the next day. No time was being lost by the Navy Department in making certain the public thought the *Fanny* was not under the command of regular navy officers at the time of its shameful surrender or anytime prior.[746] The Navy Department may not have had official knowledge of civilian Captain John H. Morrison, but certainly the navy secretary knew that the naval officers at Hatteras cooperated with him.

After the war, criticism of Morrison's loyalties continued to float about. Hawkins

THE STEAMER FANNY, CAPTURED BY THE REBELS.

The *Day Book* states that the barge containing the Union prisoners arrived at Norfolk on Wednesday night. The steamer Empire, which had the barge in tow, ran aground in North Landing river. The steamer G. B. White, which arrived here early in the morning, was sent out and took the barge in tow. The prisoners number seventy-three; forty-two of them were taken in Pamlico Sound, on board the Fanny; the remainder were captured at Chicamacomico, on the 4th inst., by the Third Georgia regiment, under Colonel Wright. The march of the prisoners through the city, under a guard from a detachment of the Third, on their way to the jail attracted much attention, but nothing was said or done that was out of place. The following is a list of the names of the prisoners:—

LIST OF PRISONERS CAPTURED ON BOARD THE STEAMER FANNY, OCTOBER 1, 1861.

Lieut. F. M. Peacock, U. S. N., commanding Fanny.
Lieut. Isaac W. Hart, Quartermaster 20th Ind. regiment.
Corporal J. E. Tuttle, Co. C, 9th reg. N. Y. vols., Hudson county, N. J.
Corporal E. Everard, Co. G, 9th reg. N. Y. V., Hudson county, N. J.

Privates, Ninth Regiment New York Volunteers.

J. S. Rowan, Company C, Hudson county, N. J.
J. R. Havens, Company C, Hudson county, N. J.
W. H. Edsall, Company G, Hudson county, N. J.
W. H. Cunningham, Company C, Richmond, N. Y.
J. V. H. Page, Company C, Essex county, N. J.
D. Dougherty, Company C, Essex county, N. J.
John Carson, Company G, New York city.
Jas. Beith, Company G, New York city.
Frank Trottes, Company H, New York city.

Twentieth Indiana Regiment.

Sergeant F. M. Bartlett, Company G, Porter county.
Corporal C. W. Keder, Company K, Monticello, Ind.

Privates.

John Helson, Company C, Marshalleo.
J. W. Sparks, Company I, Indianapolis.
J. H. Andrews, Company H, Rosaville, Ill.
Robert Inglis, Company C, Marshall county, Ind.
F. F. B. Parsons, Company H, Hamilton county, Ind.
Elias Oxford, Company H, Vermillion county, Ind.
G. W. Clark, Company C, Marshall county, Ind.
Hiram Hyde, Company I, Valparaiso county, Ind.
Van Hinds, Company K, White county, Ind.
Abel Oblenia, Company C, Marshall county, Ind.
John Jones, Company I, Dauphin county, Pa.
John A. Meek, Comaany K, Wabash county, Ind.
M. Casper, Company K, Jasper county, Ind.
John Mustro, Company G, Switzerland.
N. Kelley, Company K, White county, Ind.
J. A. Comingore, Company F, Logansport, Ind.
N. Braum, Company G, Valparaiso, Ind.
W. P. Wendell, Company H, Manchester, Ind.
H. C. Wilkerson, Company F, Logansport, Ind.
Jacob Rice, Company G, Michigan City, Ind.
G. H. Smith, Company K, White county, Ind.
F. B. Sackett, Company H, Van Buren county, Ind.
G. C. Kerns, Company H, Logansport, Ind.
H. Watson, sutler's clerk, Wabash county, Ind.
Wm. Vagel, cook, Company F, Cockeysville, Md.
J. Chaffar, cook, Company G, Chester county, Pa.
G. H. Edwards, colored boy, Laney's Valley, Md.

The New Orleans *Delta* states that no communication is to be allowed with the federal prisoners, and none will be admitted to see them except the officers of the prison.

The New Orleans *Crescent* of Tuesday states that Captain Andrew O'Murphy, of the rebel schooner Antonio, arrived at New Orleans on Monday from a cruise in the Gulf off the southwest coast, and that the Antonio made an important capture within a mile and a half of the steam frigate Powhatan, and that documents have been seized seriously implicating persons in New Orleans.

"List of Prisoners Captured on Board the Steamer Fanny, October 1, 1861." The *New York Herald*, October 14, 1861, front page. *Oxford Collection.*

Zouaves historian J.H.E. Whitney maligned Morrison in 1866, reviving the rumor that the Brooklyn resident had refused to take the oath: "The captain of the *Fanny*, had, some time previous [to the capture], been arrested and lodged in Fortress Monroe for refusing to take the oath of allegiance, and the manner in which the vessel was surrendered left no doubt that it was a conspired navy freak on his part."[747]

Despite Welles's disavowal of Morrison, the official record shows without a doubt that Morrison had, as he stated, been under the direct naval command of Rowan, Lieutenant Pierce Crosby and lieutenants James Maxwell and Thomas Eastman. It was also true that Morrison and the rest of his civilian crew received pay not from the Navy Department or even the army itself but from the steamer company from whom the army quartermaster leased the *Fanny*, the Philadelphia Transportation Company.[748] Maxwell and Eastman had taken short-term command of the *Fanny* after Crosby left Hatteras to eventually assume command of the USS *Pembina*. The *Pembina* command was a promotion following Crosby's commendable service on the *Fanny* during the Butler Expedition. Flag Officer Silas Stringham had no question as to the navy's involvement with the *Fanny* in his official report to Gideon Welles on September 2 and put the *Fanny* together with the other vessels and their captains that had taken part in the Hatteras Expedition. Stringham stated these were "all of the United States Navy."[749]

Chapter Thirteen

"Volunteer Navy Lieutenant Francis M. Peacock, Commanding the *Fanny*"

T he wind and the rain picked up after the Rebels returned to Roanoke Island. Men were sick with chills and fever from measles and were generally worn down from the "run." There was no reason to just sit on the captured quartermaster stores when his men were sick, so Wright divided the one thousand captured blankets among his men on October 8. On October 19, names were taken from among the Third Georgia of who needed a winter overcoat, and they were distributed among the men the following day, a day conspicuously noted in Private Marion Moss's diary.[750]

The blue overcoats perhaps saved a life or two later in April 1862 at the Battle of South Mills, North Carolina. Captain J. Merrill Linn, Company H, Fifty-first Pennsylvania Volunteers, wrote about an encounter with the Third Georgia in an article for the *National Defender* of Norristown, Pennsylvania: "We had met the 3d Georgia, but as they wore blue overcoats [captured on the *Fanny*] some one cried out we were firing on our own men." Firing was halted long enough to determine that the men were indeed Rebels, then "the colors were lowered, and we went to work. It was hot work, and bloody."[751] The blue overcoats would continue to identify the Third Georgia for some time, as in Richmond the following summer. Since the "Yankee overcoats were considerably sprinkled about," the people of Richmond surmised the Georgians had encountered a "large body of Hessians, and possessed themselves of some of their toggery."[752]

The Rebel steamer *Junaluska* arrived at Norfolk on Tuesday, October 8, bringing confirmation of the attack at Camp Live Oak and carrying the body of Third Georgia Volunteer Benjamin Smith who died of exhaustion.[753]

Marquis de Lafayette Kinneard, First Sergeant, Twentieth Indiana, Company D. Captured during the retreat from Live Oak. *Craig Dunn Collection.*

The Federal prisoners were then sent up to Norfolk on October 8 by Colonel Wright,[754] under a guard commanded by Lieutenant Thomas M. Daniel of Company K.[755] The prisoners reached Norfolk Wednesday night, October 9, on a "large barge drawn by the steamer *Empire*, and were in pretty good condition." Large crowds, curious and excited, gathered as the Yankee prisoners marched along the street from the wharf to the city jail. The prisoners were treated pretty well by these crowds, except for "a gang of boys who followed in the rear cheering for Jeff. Davis." After just two days in Norfolk, the prisoners reported they had been treated very kindly, "much better than they anticipated."[756]

Huger reported to Adjutant and Inspector General Samuel Cooper on October 10 about the arrival of seventy-three prisoners from the *Fanny* capture and the Chicamacomico Affair. Not hearing back from Cooper by October 15, the general wrote again, reminding the War Department chief of his recommendation to parole the privates among the prisoners. Brigadier General Huger was ready to send the prisoners to Richmond

Left: Private Robert A. Inglis, Twentieth Indiana, Company C. Captured aboard the *Fanny*. *Inglis Family Collection.*

on Thursday, October 17, if he didn't hear back from Cooper beforehand.[757] Indeed, there was no need to send dozens of prisoners to Richmond when they would come right back down to Norfolk to board a boat under a flag of truce. Cooper's response to Huger the following day was quick and to the point: "Send the prisoners here; parole not authorized."[758]

Company K's corporal Calvin Keefer clearly remembered the conditions in the Norfolk jail, stating that even the sick prisoners were "confined in <u>dark</u> <u>damp</u> <u>Iron</u> <u>grated</u> cells." Private Mike Casper, captured aboard the *Fanny* and suffering from measles, Keefer said was "still sick and grew worse while there. I don't remember of his receiving any medical attention while there from the rebels and I will say that those damp cells were no place for a sick man to be confined."[759] Rations at the Norfolk city jail "consisted of meat and bean soup for dinner, and for breakfast…some salt mackerel and corn bread."[760]

The Rebel ironclad CSS *Virginia* (*Merrimack*) was clearly visible in the Rebel Navy Yard to the *Fanny* and Chicamacomico prisoners[761] as they left Norfolk jail late in the day on October 19 to board a train for Richmond.[762] In addition to seeing the ironclad itself, the men spied out freight cars, filled with iron

Private Van Buren Hinds, Twentieth Indiana, Company K. Captured aboard the *Fanny*. *Van Buren Hinds Family Collection*.

Private Frederick Plummer Sackett, Twentieth Indiana, Company H. Sackett, shown here with his sister Alsafine Pluma Sackett, was a musician playing fife for the company. He was captured along with the company drummer, John H. Andrews, aboard the *Fanny*. *Mary Ellen Sackett Wills Collection*.

Private Abel O'Blenis, Twentieth Indiana, Company C. Captured aboard the *Fanny*. *Craig Dunn Collection*.

plates, which were marked *MERRIMACK* and which were in clear view.[763]

The captives arrived in Richmond on Saturday night, October 19, via the "Southern train" from Norfolk. The *Richmond Dispatch* announced their arrival in the Rebel capital under the Confederate guard commanded by Colonel John Mullin. The seventy-three *Fanny* and Chicamacomico men were among eighty-two prisoners moved from Norfolk to Richmond that day,[764] and they were all marched nearly twenty blocks through the streets from the rail station to the corner of Main and Twenty-fifth Streets.[765]

On October 21, the *Richmond Dispatch* announced the arrival of the Hatteras prisoners from Chicamacomico and the *Fanny* capture. The first line of the report was quite revealing, stating, "The party is a large one, consisting of F.M. Peacock, lieutenant of the *Fanny*." Sergeant Major Peacock was from the moment of his capture addressed as "Volunteer Navy Lieutenant Francis M. Peacock, commanding the *Fanny*." It appears that this was not a title he created in order to receive favor with his captors. Instead, it seems that at the time of the *Fanny*'s departure from Hatteras Inlet to Live Oak, since there was a shortage of regular navy lieutenants and midshipmen, Rowan made some kind of temporary arrangements with Hawkins. Peacock signs each of his letters from prison as "lieutenant, commanding the steamer *Fanny*."

The *Fanny* prisoners' arrival in Richmond on October 19 was the tipping point for Confederate secretary of war Judah Benjamin's prison overcrowding dilemma. It took only two days before Benjamin was sending out requests for prison space throughout the South. On October 23, Benjamin's similar requests were sent via telegraph to the governors of Alabama, Georgia and South Carolina. The secretary was looking for a "safe" location in the interior of each governor's state to hold "a few hundred prisoners." He expected to pay a "fair rent" for whatever property was obtained. Available facilities in Richmond were overtaxed with Confederate and Union sick and wounded. The prison population in the capitol was "inconveniently large." Benjamin confided in Alabama governor A.B. Moore, "We are greatly embarrassed by our prisoners, as all accommodations here are required for our sick and wounded. It would be a great public service if you can find a place for some if not all of our prisoners. We have now over 2,000 here."[766]

Within a month, all but a handful of the Hatteras prisoners were sent south, the majority to the Columbia Military Prison, also known as the Richland County Jail in Columbia, South Carolina. Quartermaster Hart would be exchanged within a matter of months. Peacock and a couple of the Twentieth Indiana were sent to Tuscaloosa, Alabama, to a new prison in a former hotel downtown. A couple, John H. Hoffman and young Henry Hines, were shipped to New Orleans's Parish Prison. Most of these men and boys, returning to Richmond at the end of winter, in late February 1862, were the first to walk through the doors of the newly opened and later notorious Libby Prison. They were paroled on May 12, 1862. The story of their imprisonment, particularly that of Francis Milford Peacock, is an incredible one that will have to be told another time.

Indeed, it was Lieutenant Francis Milford Peacock, Volunteer Navy, who surrendered his sword to Flag Officer William F. Lynch aboard the CSS *Curlew* the afternoon of October 1, 1861, off Camp Live Oak at Chicamacomico, North Carolina. It was Peacock's sword that John Taylor Wood delivered to Confederate president Jefferson Davis at his home in Richmond late in the evening of March 9, 1862, together with the trophies of the captured USS *Congress*.

State of Illinois } ss
Vermilion County } John H. Andrews
being duly sworn deposes and says
that he was well acquainted with
Elias Oxford, that he was a member of the
same company and Regt, in the United
States Army, both being members of Co.
"H" 20th Indiana Volunteers Infantry and
that further the said John H. Andrews
deposes and says that Elias Oxford
was taken prisoner of war at Republics
Sound North Carolina, on the 14th March 1861 thence taken to Norfolk
thence to Richmond Virginia; thence to
Columbia South Carolina, thence back
to Richmond Virginia; remaining there
until paroled, when he was transfered
to Washington D.C. the said John H Andrews
being with him all this time. and that they
arrived at Washington on the 12" day of May
1862. And that the said Elias Oxford
Died on or about the 18th day of May 1862
and that John H. Andrews was present at
the time of his death and that he did see
him after death, and that Elias Oxford
was a Private of said Co "H" 20" Ind. Vol. Infty.
And further that the John H Andrews was
discharged as a Drummer, He John H.
Andrews further deposes and says that he has
no interest in this matter whatever
                    John. H. Andrews.

This affidavit of John Henry Andrews, filed December 8, 1869, was found in Dependents Pension File of Elias Oxford, Twentieth Indiana. Andrews states he was with Oxford throughout his captivity and at the time of his death at the Patent Office. *National Archives.*

Epilogue

Twice unlucky with marriage and a father of four, at thirty-four years of age, Elias Oxford had been one of the older private soldiers in the Twentieth Indiana. Of the original seventy-three men and boys captured October 1 at Hatteras aboard the U.S. gunboat *Fanny*, and October 4 and 5 during the subsequent retreat from Chicamacomico, North Carolina, Oxford was one of only three who would die during or immediately following Rebel captivity. The other two Twentieth Indiana men, Theodore M. Bartlett and Abraham Van Horn, died while in the Richland County Jail at Columbia, South Carolina, where most of the Hatteras prisoners waited out the winter months, from November 1861 to the end of February 1862.

On Sunday, May 18, 1862, Private Oxford died in bed number forty-two, ward three, of the "Indiana Hospital." Assistant surgeon in charge J.C.C. Downing hastily scratched "fibris typhoides" in his report as the cause of death. Private Andrews was there at that moment and remained for some time thereafter.[767] The *Indianapolis Daily Journal*, on May 29, printed four brief lines buried on page three reporting the Hoosier's death: "Elias Oxford, Co. H, 20th Indiana, died at the General Hospital, Washington, May [18]th. He was taken prisoner in October last at Hatteras, N. C., and had just been released."[768]

Private Elias Oxford's body was not brought home to Indiana or Iroquois County, Illinois, but was instead carried north from the Patent Office the following day to a cemetery across from the Soldiers' Home in northeast Washington, some four miles distant. The Indiana private was buried with military honors at a spot along Harewood Road, just a stone's throw from President Lincoln's summer cottage, along one of the walks Mary Lincoln found so "delightful."[769] Oxford's grave was marked with a walnut headboard, painted white and numbered, and bearing "the name, company, and regiment of the dead soldier sleeping below."[770] President and Mrs. Lincoln had already retired for the summer to their cottage sanctuary near the Soldiers' Home, a week before Oxford's death and burial. The president on horseback and young Tad on his pony would ride the area of Soldiers' Home together each morning at 9:00 a.m.[771] Lincoln, in the coming weeks, would begin writing and later that fall would put the final touches to the Emancipation Proclamation there at the hilltop cottage, overlooking the new graves of the Union dead.[772] George Templeton Strong described that scene from the president's cottage, writing, "In the graveyard near at hand there are numberless graves—some without a spear of grass to hide their newness—that hold the bodies of volunteers. While we stood in the soft evening air, watching the faint trembling of the long tendrils of waving willow, and feeling the dewy coolness that was flung out by the old oaks above us, Mr. Lincoln joined us, and stood silent, too, taking in the scene."[773]

Locating Camp Live Oak at Chicamacomico (Rodanthe), North Carolina

The 1852 U.S. Coast Survey map of the eastern coast of North Carolina (sheet number fourteen, surveyed by Hull Adams in March and April 1852) is a key to the true historic location of Live Oak Camp at Chicamacomico. A portion of this 1852 map is used for an illustration on the marker at the Salvo (North Carolina) Day Use Area that commemorates the capture of the U.S. gunboat *Fanny*.

In April 2011, I contacted the Outer Banks History Center (OBHC) in Manteo, North Carolina, and curator KaeLi Schurr located the Hull Adams map in the OBHC archive, which was used for the Salvo display located at mile point 53.6 along Route 12. It was soon obvious that the Salvo marker was in error, with a "You Are Here" label pointing to the center of three "clumps," which was in Waves not Salvo. The marker actually stands at roughly 35° 32' 3.6" North latitude. The "You Are Here" label is pointing to approximately 36° 34' 41.1'" North latitude. That error is about two and a quarter miles difference, roughly. The Salvo marker does not say that Live Oak was located there, though, just that the *Fanny* was captured three miles out into the sound west of that point.

The Midyett windmill at Chicamacomico has always been important in locating the Twentieth Indiana's encampment. The windmill, the only one in the Chicamacomico area at that time in the nineteenth century, is clearly marked on the Hull Adams map, and its coordinates are listed in the legend as a "station" for navigation purposes. The windmill was to the left of camp as one faced north in 1861.

Composite map of correct location of Midyett's windmill and Camp Live Oak at the north end of Chicamacomico, now Rodanthe, North Carolina. The windmill site has modern coordinates of 35° 35' 54.5"N - 75° 28' 19.3"W. This composite was prepared by NOAA's Office of Coast Survey for the author's illustrative purposes only and includes the 1852 Hull Adams Coast Survey map overlaid with a 2012 satellite image. This product contains nautical information reproduced from NOAA's National Ocean Service Chart "Eastern Coast of North Carolina," chart #T00367-00-1852, 1852. *Courtesy of NOAA.*

I concluded that Live Oak was immediately north and east of the windmill, which stood at 35° 35' 54.5" North to 75° 28' 19.3" West (these are corrected coordinates provided by cartographers from the Office of Coast Survey and are reflected in the placement of the windmill marker in the map shown above). One can see the windmill was directly behind where the Island Convenience store is located at the time of this publication. This placed the Twentieth Indiana Regiment fully north of all the populated areas of Chicamacomico in October 1861 and is consistent with the stated distances from the historic location of Loggerhead Inlet.*

*U.S. Office of Coast Survey. "U.S. Coast Survey Map of the Eastern Coast of North Carolina." Sheet No. 14. A.D. Bache, superintendent. Topography surveyed by Hull Adams, esq. March and April 1852. Historical Map & Chart Collection. Office of Coast Survey. National Oceanographic and Atmospheric Administration.
http://historicalcharts.noaa.gov/historicals/preview/image/T00367-00-1852 (accessed April 1, 2013).

Union Prisoners Captured Aboard the U.S. Gunboat *Fanny* on October 1, 1861, in the Pamlico Sound off Chicamacomico, North Carolina

TWENTIETH INDIANA VOLUNTEER REGIMENT

NAME	RANK	AGE	DATE OF BIRTH	PLACE OF BIRTH	DATE DEAT
Field and Staff					
Hart, Isaac W.	Quartermaster	47	October 1, 1814	Troy, Ohio	March 1873
Company C: Marshall County					
Clark, George W.	Private	38			
Helsel, John	Private	30	April 15, 1831	Johnstown, Pennsylvania	July 22, 1909
Inglis, Robert A.	Private	16	July 1, 1845	Ireland	April 4, 1926
O'Blenis, Abel	Private	32	March 18, 1829	Ohio	Februar 1870
Company F: Cass County					
Comingore, John A.	Private	20	about 1841	Indiana	after 18
Wilkinson, Henry C.	Private	16	1845	Miami, New York	Februar 15, 190
Company H: Marion County					
Meek, James A.	Corporal	20	August 15, 1841	Indiana	May 3, 1909
Andrews, John H.	Private: Musician, Drummer	24	May 14, 1837	St. George Parish, Southwark, County of Surrey	March 1879
Kerns, James C.	Private	25	December 13, 1835		
Oxford, Elias	Private	34	August 1827	Vermillion County, Indiana	May 18 1862
Peirsons, Frank B.	Private	19	about 1842		
Sackett, Frederick P.	Private: Musician, Fifer	24	June 25, 1837	Indiana	Octobe 1905
Wendle, William P.	Private	21	July 16, 1840	Muncy, Pennsylvania	Octobe 20, 192

E OF DEATH	CEMETERY	*RESIDENCE	NOTES
lle, Illinois	Village Cemetery, Attica, Indiana	Attica, Indiana	
		Marshall Co., Indiana	
n, Indiana	Marion National Cemetery, Marion, Indiana	Marshall Co., Indiana	
ld, nsin	Greenwood Cemetery, Bayfield, Wisconsin	Marshall Co., Indiana	
County, na	IOOF Cemetery, Richland Center, Indiana	Marshall Co., Indiana	
		Logansport, Indiana	
lle, Illinois	Danville National Cemetery, Danville, Illinois	Logansport, Indiana	
Lake, na	South Pleasant Methodist Church Cemetery, North Manchester, Indiana	Wabash Co. Indiana	
lle, Illinois	Springhill Cemetery Danville, Vermilion County, Illinois	Rossville, Illinois	
		Logansport, Indiana	
ington, D.C.	U.S. Soldiers' and Airmen's Home National Cemetery, Washington, D.C.	Vermillion County, Indiana	
		Hamilton County, Indiana	
s, Michigan	Earl Cemetery, Kendall, Michigan	Van Buren County, Indiana	
n, sylvania	Muncy Cemetery, Muncy, Pennsylvania	Manchester, Indiana	

NAME	RANK	AGE	DATE OF BIRTH	PLACE OF BIRTH	DATE OF DEATH
Company I: Porter County					
Bartlett, Theodore M	Sergeant	24	August 24, 1837	Illinois	Februar 1861
Baum, Napoleon	Private	21	June 23, 1840	Morgan, Indiana	March 1910
Hyde, Hiram	Private	27	October 1834	New York	Septem 2, 1904
Jones, John N.	Private				
Muster, John	Private	32	about 1829	Switzerland	Octobe 1887
Rice, Jacob	Private	26	about 1835	Baden, Germany	March 1915
Sparks, John W.	Private	19	1843	Hendricks County, Indiana	May 2, 1864
Company K: White County					
Keefer, Calvin W.	Corporal	20	March 1841	Ashland County, Ohio	Februar 10, 191
Casper, Michael	Private	26	August 3, 1835	Coblenz, Germany	January 1915
Hinds, Van Buren	Private	22	July 13, 1839	Jennings County, Indiana	Februar 10, 192
Kelley, Noah E.	Private	39	January 1823	Virginia	Februar 1903
Smith, James B.	Private	25	1836	Indiana	Februar 27, 187
Citizens Attached to the Twentieth Indiana Regiment					
Watson, Hugh	Sutler's Clerk				
Chaffer, Joseph	Cook, Company G				
Vogel (Vagel, Volger, Vogler), William	Cook, Company G				
Edwards, J.H.	Free "Colored Boy"				

CE OF DEATH	CEMETERY	*RESIDENCE	NOTES
ral Hospital	Hospital Cemetery, Columbia, South Carolina	Porter Co., Indiana	
mbia, South lina	Location Unknown		
r County, na	Luther Cemetery Valparaiso, Indiana	--	
on, Indiana	Marion National Cemetery, Marion, Indiana	Valparaiso, Indiana	
		Dauphin County, Pennsylvania	Enlisted at Cockeysville
san, Indiana	Valparaiso, Indiana—Unknown Cemetery	Switzerland	
y, Nebraska	Valley Cemetery, Valley, Nebraska	Michigan City, Indiana	
phis, essee	Memphis National Cemetery Memphis, Tennessee	Indianapolis, Indiana	Cleft palate—noted heavy drinker
on, Indiana	Marion National Cemetery, Marion, Indiana	Monticello, Indiana	
Cicott, son Township, na	Mount Hope Cemetery Logansport, Indiana	Jasper Co., Indiana	
na, Arizona	Oak Grove Cemetery, Searcy, Arizona	White County, Indiana	
on, Kansas	IOOF Cemetery, Clifton, Kansas	White County, Indiana	
ski County, na	Indian Creek Cemetery, Winamac, Indiana	White County, Indiana	
		Wabash County, Indiana	
		Chester County, Pennsylvania	
		Cockeysville, Maryland	
		Dulaney Valley, Maryland Baltimore County	

NINTH NEW YORK VOLUNTEER REGIMENT: "HAWKINS ZOUAVES"

NAME	RANK	AGE	DATE OF BIRTH	PLACE OF BIRTH	DATE OF DEATH
Field and Staff					
Peacock, Francis Milford	Sergeant Major	30	1831	Macao, China	after April 1864
Company C					
Tuttle, Joel E.	Corporal	22	about 1839		
Cunningham, William H.	Private	21	December 1839	New York	December 5, 1924
Doherty, Daniel	Private	22	about 1839		
Havens, John R.	Private	21	April 1841	New York	January 1907
Page, Joseph Van Kirk	Private	22	April 1839	New Jersey	August 1906
Rowan, John S.	Private	23	February 11, 1838	New Jersey	December 5, 1913
Company G					
Everard, Gardiner	Corporal	26	April 4, 1834	St. Edmonds, Suffolk, England	March 5 1875
Beith, James	Private	19	August 1843	Scotland	July 13, 1910
Carson, John	Private	20	about 1840		after September 13, 1882
Edsall, William H.	Private	29	about 1832	New York City	April 28 1902
Company H					
Trotter, Francis "Frank" E.	Private	20	about 1841		after 189

*Residence—This is the hometown or residence that was given to the Rebels on capture and publi listed. However, Attica, Indiana, was consistently recorded elsewhere as his hometown. Sergeant M

**The author is not attempting to apply the Genealogical Proof Standard.

E OF DEATH	CEMETERY	*RESIDENCE	NOTES
		Hudson Co., New Jersey	
klyn, New	Greenwood Cemetery, Brooklyn, New York	Richmond, New York	
		Essex County, New Jersey	
oken, New y	Hoboken Cemetery, North Bergen, New Jersey	Hudson County, New Jersey	
, New York	Bath National Cemetery, Bath, New York	Essex County, New Jersey	
ter Heights, sylvania	Woodlands Cemetery Philadelphia, Pennsylvania	Hudson County, New Jersey	
Brighton, sylvania	Grove Cemetery, New Brighton, Pennsylvania	New York City	
y, sylvania		New York City	
ed away from , New York ers Home never heard again		New York City	
water, New y	Edgewater Cemetery, Edgewater, New Jersey	Hudson Co., New Jersey	
		New York City	

newspapers. Napoleon Baum was not listed, and Quartermaster Hart's hometown was not
ock's hometown was not listed in the newspapers.

Union Prisoners Captured During the Chicamacomico Affair on October 4–5, 1861, During the Retreat from Camp Live Oak at Chicamacomico, Hatteras Island, North Carolina

TWENTIETH INDIANA VOLUNTEER REGIMENT

NAME	RANK	AGE	DATE OF BIRTH	PLACE OF BIRTH	DATE OF DEATH
Field and Staff					
Comly, Charles Hammond	Sergeant Major	21	February 11, 1837	Dayton, Ohio	July 31, 1878
Company A: Miami County					
Dangerfield, William	4th Corporal, Color Guard	26	about 1835		December 28, 1864
Company C: Marshall County					
Stickley, William M.	Private	19	October 22, 1841	Ohio	April 8, 1929
Unruh, Hiram "Henry" Augustus	Private	15	November 1, 1845	Valparaiso, Indiana	December 16, 1916
Company D: Fountain County					
Kinneard, Marquis De Lafayette	1st Sergeant	31	May 22, 1830	Georgetown, Maryland	April 9, 1876
Engel, Ferdinand	3rd Sergeant	31	about 1830	Erfurt, Germany	1882–88
Brady, Nathan	Civilian Cook				
Gerber, George W.	Colonel's Boy	15	about 1846	Lancaster, Pennsylvania	
Glover, Francis M.	Private	24	1837		December 24, 1897
Hoffman, John Horace	Private: "Cook"	17	December 27, 1843	Attica, Indiana	January 1905
Probus, Washington	Private	20	1841	Butler County, Ohio	January 1863
Company E: Laporte County					
Easton, Nathan B.	8th Corporal	18	May 8, 1843	Pulaski, New York	May 2, 1928
Jones, Charles E.	Private				
Parker, George M.	Private	16	December 25, 1844	Smithville Flats, New York	December 15, 1927

CE OF DEATH	CEMETERY	*RESIDENCE	NOTES
Antonio, s	San Antonio National Cemetery, San Antonio, Texas	Logansport, Indiana	
t Station, ssippi	Corinth National Cemetery, Corinth, Mississippi	Peru, Indiana	
erton, na	Woodlawn Cemetery, Walkerton, Indiana	Marshall County, Indiana	
dia, ornia	Evergreen Cemetery, Los Angeles, California	Wanatah, Indiana	
a, Indiana	Old Hillside Cemetery, Williamsport, Indiana	Fountain County ,Indiana	
ably Santa Fe, Mexico		Fountain County, Indiana	
		Baltimore, Maryland	
		Lancaster, Pennsylvania	
ngton, na		Fountain County, Indiana	
onville, on	Historic Jacksonville Cemetery Jacksonville, Oregon	Fountain County, Indiana	
outh, Virginia	Unknown	Fountain County, Inidiana	
vater, homa	Forest Lawn Memorial Park, Glendale, California	New Buffalo, Michigan	
		LaPorte County, Indiana	
ably Battle k, Michigan	Unknown	Michigan City, Indiana	

Name	Rank	Age	Date of Birth	Place of Birth	Date of Death
Riley, Leonard H.	Private: Detached as Cook for camp hospital	26	February 1835	New York	November 9, 1901
Ruff, Lawrence	Private	45	1816	Germany	
Snyder, Eli	Private	15	April 22, 1846	Sandy, Stark County, Ohio	January 1909
Company F					
Maddox, James (or Joseph)	Private	42	about 1819	Mifflin County, Pennsylvania	
Company G: Tippecanoe County					
Gross, Charles M.	Private Detached for Hospital Service	24	1838	Butler County, Ohio	July 10, 1883
Company H: Marion County					
Bennett, Lucius L.	Private	22	1838	Ohio	October 1880
Clayton, James	Private	23			
Serach, Christian (Sherrick?)	Private	27	about 1834		
Shoaf, Jacob	Private	28	March 1833	Bavaria	November 22, 1908
Van Horn, Abraham	Private: Standing picket	26	October 2, 1835	Hickory Creek, Kankakee, Illinois	November 25, 1861
Company I: Porter County					
DeMotte, Charles W.	Fourth Sergeant	19	April 1843	DuBois County, Indiana	March 6, 1908
Johnston, Hiram B.	Second Sergeant	20	about 1841	Eaton, Michigan	March 25, 1865
Bernhart, Paul		18	about 1843		
Berringer, John F.		20	October 1841	Prussia/ Germany	February 1904

CE OF DEATH	CEMETERY	*RESIDENCE	NOTES
enworth as	Leavenworth National Cemetery, Leavenworth, Kansas	LaPorte County, Indiana	
		Lafayette County, Indiana	
on, Indiana	Oakwood Cemetery, Warsaw, Indiana	Warsaw, Indiana	
		Pulaski County, Indiana	
ecanoe ty, Indiana	Battle Ground Cemetery, Tippecanoe, Indiana	Lafayette County, Indiana	
eld, Indiana	Albright Cemetery, Kokomo, Indiana	Howard County, Indiana	
		Marshall County, Indiana	
		Indianapolis, Indiana	
ille, Indiana	Union Cemetery, Huntington, Indiana	Wabash County, Indiana	
ral Hospital mbia, South ina	Hospital Cemetery, Columbia, South Carolina Location Unknown	Cook County, Illinois	
lena, rnia	Pomona Cemetery and Mausoleum, Pomona, California	Valparaiso, Indiana	
sburg, nia battlefield al	Unknown	Wanatah, Indiana	
		Chicago, Illinois	
rvliet, en, Michigan	Watervliet City Cemetery, Watervliet, Michigan	Cedar Lake, Indiana	

Name	Rank	Age	Date of Birth	Place of Birth	Date of Death
Drury, John	Captured in skirmish on retreat	14	July 12, 1847	New Brighton, Beaver, Pennsyvlania	Arpil 3, 1910
Hines, Henry	Captain Lytle's boy	13	1849	Lancaster, Pennsylvania	
Pearsall, Henry Parent		21	December 10, 1839	LaPorte County, Indiana	October 20, 1904

*Residence—This is the hometown or residence that was given to the Rebels upon capture and pul
**The author is not attempting to apply the Genealogical Proof Standard.

E OF DEATH	CEMETERY	*RESIDENCE	NOTES
nd, Jay y, Indiana	Green Park Cemetery Portland, Indiana	Wabash, Indiana	
		Lancaster, Pennsylvania	
rte City, Hawk, Iowa	Westview Cemetery La Porte City Black Hawk County, Iowa	Wanatah, Indiana	

ie newspapers.

Notes

Introduction

1. Secretary of the Navy, *Official Records*, Mallory report to Davis, March 11, 1862, 42.
2. Symonds, "Battle of Hampton Roads."
3. Davis, *Jefferson Davis*, 221.
4. *New York Times*, "Obituary Notes," July 20, 1904.
5. George Weber to his brother, March 10, 1862, George Weber Papers.
6. Secretary of the Navy, *Official Records*, Phillips to Jones, March 8, 1862, 42.
7. Wood, "First Fight of Iron-Clads," 746.
8. Davis, *Jefferson Davis*, 221.
9. Tayloe, *Tayloes of Virginia*.
10. Dennis Tuttle to his wife, March 16, 1862. Dennis Tuttle Papers. Twentieth Indiana quartermaster Dennis Tuttle reported the *Congress* had already struck its colors and run up the white flag following a few broadsides from the CSS *Virginia* (*Merrimack*) from within fifty feet. Both the Tuttle Manuscript and the Lewis Manuscript agree that the Confederates sent row boats to take off prisoners and that first attempt was repulsed under fire from the Twentieth Indiana from the shore. The manuscripts further agree that after this, a Rebel officer removing the federal colors was shot. These accounts differ from Confederate navy commander Parker of the Beaufort who says two of his midshipmen retrieved both the colors and a "ship's cutlass" representing the sword of the Congress's commander.
11. Tayloe, *Tayloes of Virginia*, 60–1.

Chapter One

12. Whitman, *Notebooks*, 583–5.
13. Gaff, *On Many a Bloody Field*, 65.
14. Whitman, *Wound Dresser*, 3.

15. U.S. National Archives, Case Files of Approved Pension Applications, Elias Oxford, private, Company H, Twentieth Indiana Infantry, Certificate No. 140,676.

16. *New York Times*, "Important Reports of Released Prisoners," May 15, 1862.

17. Merrill, *Soldier of Indiana*, 499.

18. Secretary of the Navy, *Official Records*, "Abstract Log of the U.S.S. Port Royal," May 12, 1861, 722.

19. *New York Times*, "The Rebellion," May 17, 1862.

20. Merrill, *Soldier of Indiana*, 499. Charles DeMotte indicates the prisoners arrived in Washington on the fifteenth. It seems, however, this must have been late the evening of the fourteenth as indicated in *New York Times*, "The Rebellion," May 17, 1862. The 885 POWs were divided at Fort Monroe, some of the men going up the Chesapeake to Baltimore the morning of the thirteenth on the Federal steamers *Kent* and *Hero*. Those released prisoners boarded trains at Baltimore and arrived in Washington that evening at the Soldiers' Rest. It appears that all of the Indiana men arrived together on the fourteenth.

21. "Our Washington Correspondence," May 20, 1862.

22. *New York Tribune*, "Reports from Rebeldom by Released Prisoners," May 17, 1862.

23. U.S. National Archives, Case Files of Approved Pension Applications, Elias Oxford, private, Company H, Twentieth Indiana Infantry, Certificate No. 140,676; ibid., Burial Registers of Military Posts.

24. Muenchausen, John Henry Andrews Family Group Sheet and Notes; Ross, *History of the Coldstream Guards*, 107–17; Muenchausen, John Henry Andrews Family Group Sheet and Notes.

25. Whitman, *Wound Dresser*, 3–4.

26. Teresa Riordan, "Patents: Models That Were Once Required in the Application Process Find a Good Home," *New York Times*, February 18, 2002.

CHAPTER TWO

27. *Marshall County Republican*, "At Fortress Monroe," October 3, 1861; ibid., "Letter from Hatteras Inlet," October 10, 1861.

28. Gilbreath, manuscript, 6.

29. Ibid., 7.

30. Ibid., 8.

31. Coggins, *Arms and Equipment*, 32.

32. *Valparaiso Republic*, "From the 20th Regiment," August 15, 1861.

33. *Marshall County Republican*, "Letter from Hatteras Inlet," October 10, 1861.

34. Gilbreath, manuscript, 6.

35. Ibid.

36. *Valparaiso Republic*, "Camp Belger," September 26, 1861.

37. Main, "Civil War Record," 2.

38. *Valparaiso Republic*, "Camp Belger," September 26, 1861.

39. Ibid., "From the 20th Regiment," October 24, 1861.

40. Lincoln, "Proclamation 85."

41. Secretary of the Navy, *Official Records*, Goldsborough order for day of fasting and prayer, September 25, 1861, 253.

42. *The Independent*, "Notes from the Capital," October 3, 1861. See article for Fast Day in Washington and the clergy's lack of commitment to the Union cause and destruction of slavery.

43. Powell, *History of Cass County Indiana*, 674.
44. *Nashville Union and American*, "A Yankee Account of a Visit to Gen. Floyd's Outposts," September 11, 1861.
45. Gilbreath, manuscript, 8.
46. *Lafayette Journal*, August 13, 1861.
47. U.S. Congress, Senate, *Journal of Executive Proceedings*, 491.
48. These companies were not present on Hatteras until after the first week of October 1861.
49. *Marshall County Republican*, "Letter from Hatteras Inlet," October 10, 1861.
50. Main, "Civil War Record," 2.
51. U.S. National Archives, Case Files of Approved Pension Applications, Robert A. Inglis, acting assistant engineer, U.S. Navy, Certificate No. 00020236.
52. Wisconsin, Bayfield, "Robert Inglis."
53. U.S. National Archives, Case Files of Approved Pension Applications, Robert A. Inglis, acting assistant engineer, U.S. Navy, Certificate No. 00020236.
54. Ibid., Charles H. White, Certificate No. 209.509.
55. *Valparaiso Republic*, "From T.M. Bartlett, Who Was Taken on Board the Fanny," October 24, 1861.
56. *Marshall County Republican*, "Letter from Hatteras Inlet," October 10, 1861.
57. *Valparaiso Republic*, "From T.M. Bartlett," October 24, 1861.
58. Ibid., "From the 20th Regiment."
59. Ibid., "From T.M. Bartlett."
60. Ibid., "From the 20th Regiment"; "From T.M. Bartlett"; *New York Times*, "Important from Hatteras Inlet," October 6, 1861; Spears, "Sand-Waves," 507; Duffus, *The Lost Light*.
61. *Valparaiso Republic*, "From T.M. Bartlett," October 24, 1861; *New York Times*, "Important from Hatteras Inlet," October 6, 1861.
62. Ibid.
63. Secretary of the Navy, *Official Records*, Chauncey report to Welles, September 28, 1861, 262.
64. *Valparaiso Republic*, "From T.M. Bartlett," October 24, 1861.
65. *Marshall County Republican*, "Letter from Hatteras Inlet," October 10, 1861.
66. Merrill, *Soldier of Indiana*, 486.
67. *Valparaiso Republic*, "From T.M. Bartlett," October 24, 1861.
68. Ibid.
69. *Marshall County Republican*, "Letter from Hatteras Inlet," October 10, 1861.
70. *Valparaiso Republic*, "From the 20th Regiment," October 24, 1861.

CHAPTER THREE

71. Johnson, *Long Roll*, 9.
72. Sons of the Revolution, "Membership Roll," 80.
73. Aldrich and Holmes, *History of Windsor County, Vermont*, 968.
74. Dana, *History of Woodstock, Vermont*, 470.
75. Aldrich and Holmes, *History of Windsor County*, 732; Sons of the Revolution, "Membership Roll," 80. Notes that Dexter Hawkins served in the "3d Regiment, Rhode Island Infantry, Colonel Archibald Cary [*sic*]"; Hawkins, Headstone;

Stillwell, "General Hawkins," 79; Aldrich and Holmes, *History of Windsor County*, 738–9; Vermont, Pomfret, "Lorenzo Don [*sic*] Hawkins."

76. Stillwell, "General Hawkins," 77–9; Johnson, *Twentieth Century Biographical Dictionary*, "Hawkins, Rush Christopher;" Stillwell, "General Hawkins," 78. Several short biographies of Colonel Rush Hawkins were published following the Battle of Roanoke Island that contained considerably misinformation concerning his early education and Mexican War service. Hawkins was not educated at Alden Partridge's Norwich, Vermont academy. Hawkins never served on a sloop-of-war under William F. Lynch on the Dead Sea Expedition or on any other vessel.

77. "Vermont, Vital Records," Lorenzo Don [*sic*] Hawkins; Stillwell, "General Hawkins," 77–9.

78. Ibid., 78; Hawkins, files, "Biographical Sketch of General Rush C. Hawkins;" Gilman, *Bibliography of Vermont*, 135.

79. Johnson, "The Liberty Party in Vermont," 261, 269; *Boca Raton News*, "Historians Trace Slaves' Underground Railroad," January 30, 1977. I have found no reference by Hawkins indicating his knowledge of the Hutchinson home being used as a station along the Underground Railroad.

80. Hawkins to Lieutenant Colonel H.R. Roberts, Acting President of Norwich University, October 8, 1919. Rush Christopher Hawkins Papers.

81. Ibid.

82. Ibid.

83. Stillwell, "General Hawkins," 79–80; Ancestry.com. U.S. Army.

84. Stillwell, "General Hawkins," 79–80.

85. Hawkins to Lieutenant Colonel H.R. Roberts, acting president of Norwich University, October 8, 1919. Rush Christopher Hawkins Papers; Stillwell, "General Hawkins," 79–80; Graham, *Ninth Regiment*, 633.

86. *New York Herald*, "Hawkins' Zouaves," February 16, 1862; Frank Leslie's *Illustrated Newspaper*, "Colonel Rush C. Hawkins," March 22, 1862.

87. Stillwell, "General Hawkins," 79–80.

88. Ibid.

89. Ibid., 81–3.

90. Pollard, "General Rush C. Hawkins," 171–8.

91. Stillwell, "General Hawkins," 84; Lincoln, "Proclamation 80;" Hawkins, files, "Biographical Sketch of General Rush C. Hawkins;" Stillwell, "General Hawkins," 84–5.

92. Butler, *Butler's Book*, 282.

93. U.S. War Department, *War of the Rebellion*, Butler report to Wool, August 30, 1861, 581–6

94. Graham, *Ninth Regiment*, 79–83; Butler, *Butler's Book*, 284; Graham, *Ninth Regiment*, 79–83.

95. Ibid, 84; U.S. War Department, *War of the Rebellion*, Hawkins report to Wool, September 7, 1861, 607–9.

96. Ibid.

97. Ibid.; Hawkins, "Early Coast Operations." 636; U.S. War Department, *War of the Rebellion*, Hawkins report to Wool, September 7, 1861, 607–9.

98. Hawkins, "Early Coast Operations," 635.

99. U.S. War Department, *War of the Rebellion*, Hawkins report to Wool, September 7, 1861, 607–9.

100. Ibid., September 21, 1861, 619–20; ibid., September 7, 1861, 607–9. Hawkins recalled this as a September 6 report, though in fact it was September 7.

101. U.S. War Department, *War of the Rebellion*, Wool to Cameron, September 3, 1861, 604.

102. Butler, *Butler's Book*, 287-288.

103. U.S. War Department, *War of the Rebellion*, Wool to Cameron, September 4, 1861, 606; ibid., Cameron to Wool, September 5, 1861.

104. Ibid., Hawkins report to Wool, September 7, 1861, 607–9; ibid., Wool report to Scott with enclosures, September 13, 1861, 607–12.

105. *New York Times*, "Affairs at Fortress Monroe," September 13, 1861. *New York Times* correspondent wrote from Fort Monroe on Sunday, September 8, 1861.

106. U.S. War Department, *War of the Rebellion*, Wool report to Scott with enclosures, September 13, 1861, 607–12; ibid., Wool to Thomas, September 14, 1861, 613.

107. Johnson, *Long Roll*, 50.

108. Hawkins, "Early Coast Operations," 635.

109. U.S. War Department, *War of the Rebellion*, Hawkins report to Wool, September 19, 1861, 617–9.

110. *New York Times*, "Obituary: Col. Lewis O. Morris," June 9, 1864.

111. Clark, *Heroes of Albany*, 216–7.

112. U.S. War Department, *War of the Rebellion*, Hawkins Report to Wool, September 17, 1861, 617–9; Parker, *Recollections of a Naval Officer*, 232. Confederate navy captain William Harwar Parker, long after the war in his 1883 autobiography, expressed agreement with Rush Hawkins's assessment that the Union should have taken the offensive immediately following the capture of Hatteras. Parker, who commanded the CSS *Beaufort* on the Neuse River in 1861, wrote, "The enemy made a great mistake in not taking possession of the sounds immediately after capturing Hatteras. There was nothing to prevent it but two small gunboats, carrying one gun each. Two of the small steamers, under Flag-Officer Stringham, should have swept the sounds, and a force should have occupied Roanoke Island."

113. Not to Secretary of War Simon Cameron as Hawkins later recalled in Hawkins, "Early Coast Operations," 634.

114. U.S. War Department, *War of the Rebellion*, Wool report to Scott with enclosures, September 22, 1861, 616–20; ibid., Wool to Lincoln, September 18, 1861, 614–5; ibid., Thomas to Scott, September 24, 1861, 617.

115. *Marshall County Republican*, "Cockeysville…Marching Orders," October 3, 1861.

116. Kimball to Hawkins, September 27, 1861. Rush Christopher Hawkins Papers.

117. U.S. War Department, *War of the Rebellion*, Hawkins report to Wool, September 21, 1861, 619; Hawkins, "Early Coast Operations," 636.

118. U.S. War Department, *War of the Rebellion*, Hawkins report to Wool, September 21, 1861, 619.

119. Ibid.

120. Hawkins, "Early Coast Operations," 637.

121. Secretary of the Navy, *Official Records*, Maxwell report to Rowan, September 18, 1861, 223; ibid., Rowan report to Welles, September 20, 1861, 240–1; ibid., Chauncey Report to Stringham, September 19, 1861, 224–5; ibid., Rowan Report to Welles, September 20, 1861, 240–1.

122. *Baltimore Sun*, "The Capture of the Fanny—Statement of a Passenger," October 7, 1861.

123. Moore, *Rebellion Record*, 155; *Baltimore Sun*, "The Capture of the Fanny—Statement of a Passenger," October 7, 1861; Duyckinck, *National History*, 548; Moore, *Rebellion Record*, 155. In the official statement for the Potter Commission, a separate statement from the October 1 statement for Rowan, Captain Morrison noted that after the capture of Fort Hatteras, control of the *Fanny* was given jointly to both Captain Rowan of the navy and Colonel Hawkins of the Ninth New York. But there is every indication that Morrison was relating the practical agreement between Rowan and Hawkins that followed the Ocracoke Expedition.

124. Secretary of the Navy, *Official Records*, Rowan report to Welles, September 20, 1861, 240–1.

125. U.S. War Department, *War of the Rebellion*, Hawkins Report to Wool, September 19, 1861, 617–9.

126. Secretary of the Navy, *Official Records*, Chauncey to Stringham, September 20, 1861 238–40.

127. Ibid., Rowan report to Welles, September 20, 1861, 240–1.

128. Ibid., Welles Letter of Commendation to Rowan, September 25, 1861, 225.

129. Welles to John F. Potter, October 9, 1861.

130. Secretary of the Navy, *Official Records*, Welles orders to Rowan, September 18, 1861, 234.

131. Ibid., Goldsborough Orders to Acting Elliott, September 23, 1861, 249.

132. "Ceres," *Dictionary of American Fighting Ships*; "William G. Putnam," ibid.

133. Secretary of the Navy, *Official Records*, Rowan Report to Goldsborough, September 30, 1861, 270–1.

134. *Vermont Chronicle*, "A Colonel Defeated," July 1, 1871.

135. *New York Times*, "Our Hatteras Inlet Correspondent," October 6, 1861.

136. Ibid.

137. *Valparaiso Republic*, "From T.M. Bartlett," October 24, 1861.

138. Ibid.

CHAPTER FOUR

139. Merrill, *Soldier of Indiana*, 486; *Valparaiso Republic*, "From the 20th Regiment," October 24, 1861; Hawkins, papers, W.L. Brown report to Hawkins, October 6, 1861, 68; Merrill, *Soldier of Indiana*, 486.

140. *Valparaiso Republic*, "From T.M. Bartlett," October 24, 1861.

141. Ibid., "From the 20th Regiment," October 24, 1861; Merrill, *Soldier of Indiana*, 486; *Valparaiso Republic*, "From the 20th Regiment," October 24, 1861; Merrill, *Soldier of Indiana*, 486–7; *Valparaiso Republic*, "From the 20th Regiment," October 24, 1861; *Marshall County Republican*, "Letter from the 20th Indiana," October 3, 1861.

142. Ibid.; Merrill, *Soldier of Indiana*, 487; Dawson, "Coastal Algonquian Vocabulary;" Gerhardt, "Permaculture Design on the Edge."

143. Hawkins, papers, W.L. Brown report to Hawkins, October 6, 1861, 68; *Valparaiso Republic*, "From the 20th Regiment," October 24, 1861; Hawkins, papers, W.L. Brown report to Hawkins, October 6, 1861, 68; *Valparaiso Republic*, "From the 20th Regiment," October 24, 1861.

144. *Howard Tribune*, "The 20th In A Close Place," October 22, 1861; This windmill was most likely owned at that time by Jethro Anderson Midyett of Chicamacomico (1820–66); "Midyett's Mill" is listed in the Hyde County section

of *Branson's North Carolina Business Directory for 1872*; Merrill, *Soldier of Indiana*, 487; *Valparaiso Republic*, "From the 20th Regiment," October 24, 1861; *New York Times*, "Our Hatteras Inlet Correspondent," October 6, 1861.

145. *Daily National Intelligencer*, "Fort Clark, At Hatteras Inlet," October 5, 1861.

146. Hawkins, papers, W.L. Brown report to Hawkins, October 6, 1861, 68

147. Spears, "Sand-Waves," 507, 511.

148. Lindsey and Andrews, "Third Georgia Regiment."

149. *New York Times*, "Our Hatteras Correspondent," October 6, 1861.

150. *Valparaiso Republic*, "From the 20th Regiment," October 24, 1861.

151. U.S. War Department, *War of the Rebellion*, Hawkins Report to Wool, September 21, 1861, 619–20.

152. *New York Times*, "Our Hatteras Inlet Correspondent," October 6, 1861.

153. *Valparaiso Republic*, "From the 20th Regiment," October 24, 1861.

154. Ibid.

155. *New York Times*, "Our Hatteras Inlet Correspondent," October 6, 1861.

156. *New York Tribune*, "From North Carolina," October 19, 1861.

157. Hawkins, papers, W.L. Brown report to Hawkins, October 6, 1861, 68

158. Secretary of the Navy, *Official Records*, Rowan report to Stringham, September 13, 1861, 207.

159. *Daily National Intelligencer*, "From Fortress Monroe," October 4, 1861.

160. *Valparaiso Republic*, "From the 20th Regiment," October 24, 1861.

161. Secretary of the Navy, *Official Records*, Goldsborough to Rowan, September 25, 1861, 253.

162. U.S. War Department, *War of the Rebellion*, Hawkins Report to Wool, September 21, 1861, 619.

CHAPTER FIVE

163. *Valparaiso Republic*, "From T.M. Bartlett," October 24, 1861.

164. Hawkins, "Early Coast Operations," 637.

165. Secretary of the Navy, *Official Records*, Rowan report to Goldsborough, September 30, 1861, 270–1.

166. Moore, *Rebellion Record*, 156.

167. *Valparaiso Republic*, "From T.M. Bartlett," October 24, 1861.

168. U.S. National Archives, Case Files of Approved Pension Applications, Charles H. White, Certificate No. 209.509.

169. Ibid., Lucius L. Bennett, private, Company H., Twentieth Indiana Infantry, Certificate No. 393,405.

170. Ibid., Michael Caspar [*sic*], private, Company K, Twentieth Indiana Infantry, Certificate No. 812,452; ibid., 1880 U.S. census, ibid.; ibid., 1900 U.S. census, ibid.; U.S. National Archives, Case Files of Approved Pension Applications, Michael Caspar [*sic*], Certificate No. 812,452.

171. Ibid., Charles H. White, Certificate No. 209.509.

172. Ibid.

173. *New York Times*, "Prisoners of the Twentieth Indiana Regiment," October 13, 1861.

174. *New York Tribune*, "From North Carolina," October 19, 1861.

175. *Baltimore Sun*, "The War News," October 8, 1861.

176. Secretary of the Navy, *Official Records*, Welles orders to Goldsborough, September 25, 1861, 253.

177. Ibid., Goldsborough orders to Rowan, September 26, 1861, 255.

178. Ibid., Goldsborough orders to Elliott, 249.

179. *Marshall County Republican*, "Letter from Hatteras Inlet," October 10, 1861.

180. Secretary of the Navy, *Official Records*, Morrison statement to Rowan, October 1, 1861, 276.

CHAPTER SIX

181. Maryland, Vansville, 43A.

182. Parker, *Recollections of a Naval Officer*, 228.

183. Secretary of the Navy, *Official Records*, Forrest orders to Hunter, August 28, 1861, 719.

184. Turner, "3rd Georgia First Twelve Months."

185. "Address by Colonel Claiborne Snead," Third Georgia Volunteer Infantry Website.

186. Turner, "3rd Georgia First Twelve Months," June 14, 1864.

187. Warner, *Generals in Gray*, 345.

188. "William Ambrose Wright," *Memoirs of Georgia*, 965–6.

189. Atkinson, "We Are Now Complete Masters of the Field," 211.

190. "William Ambrose Wright," *Memoirs of Georgia*, 965–6.

191. "William Ambrose Wright," *Georgia's Public Men*.

192. Turner, "3rd Georgia First Twelve Months," June 14, 1864.

193. *Covington News*, "Mr. Moss's Diary," June 8, 1916.

194. Turner, "3rd Georgia First Twelve Months," June 14, 1864.

195. Spencer, Wiggins, and Cone, *My Dear Friend*, 29.

196. Turner, "3rd Georgia First Twelve Months," June 14, 1864.

197. Wyllie, *Confederate States Navy*, 95.

198. Turner, "3rd Georgia First Twelve Months," June 14, 1864.

199. Parker, *Recollections of a Naval Officer*, 228.

200. Turner, "3rd Georgia First Twelve Months," June 14, 1864.

201. Spencer, Wiggins and Cone, *My Dear Friend*, 29.

202. *Covington News*, "Mr. Moss's Diary," June 8, 1916.

203. Spencer, Wiggins and Cone, *My Dear Friend*, 29.

204. Ibid.

205. Parker, *Recollections of a Naval Officer*, 229.

206. Turner, "3rd Georgia First Twelve Months," June 14, 1864.

207. Ibid.

208. Spencer, Wiggins and Cone, *My Dear Friend*, 29.

209. Turner, "3rd Georgia First Twelve Months," June 14, 1864.

210. *Covington News*, "Mr. Moss's Diary," June 8, 1916.

211. Turner, "3rd Georgia First Twelve Months," June 14, 1864.

212. Spencer, Wiggins and Cone, *My Dear Friend*, 29.

213. "Junaluska," Dictionary of American Fighting Ships.

214. Turner, "3rd Georgia First Twelve Months," June 14, 1864.

215. Scharf, *History of the Confederate States Navy*, 277.

216. Turner, "3rd Georgia First Twelve Months," June 14, 1864.

217. Parker, *Recollections of a Naval Officer*, 231.
218. Lindsey, *Report on Coastal Defenses*.
219. Barrett, *Civil War in North Carolina*, 47.
220. Lindsey, *Report on Coastal Defenses*.
221. Ibid.
222. Ibid.
223. Ibid.
224. Barrett, *Civil War in North Carolina*, 47.
225. Parker, *Recollections of a Naval Officer*, 231.
226. Barrett, *The Civil War in North Carolina*, 47.
227. Parker, *Recollections of a Naval Officer*, 231.
228. Turner, "3rd Georgia First Twelve Months," June 21, 1864.
229. North Carolina, State Legislature, *Report of the Adjutant General*, 11.
230. Lindsey, *Report on Coastal Defenses*.
231. Turner, "3rd Georgia First Twelve Months," June 21, 1864.
232. Parker, *Recollections of a Naval Officer*, 231.
233. Turner, "3rd Georgia First Twelve Months," June 21, 1864.
234. Spencer, Wiggins and Cone, *My Dear Friend*, 27.
235. Secretary of the Navy, *Official Records*, Forrest orders to T.T. Hunter, August 28, 1861, 719.
236. Scharf, *History of the Confederate States Navy*, 277; Turner, "3rd Georgia First Twelve Months," June 21, 1864; Scharf, *History of the Confederate States Navy*, 277; Turner, "3rd Georgia First Twelve Months," June 21, 1864.
237. Fearing, "Federal Attack on Hatteras," 110–1; Lindsey, *Report on Coastal Defenses*.
238. ORN, 1, 6:721-722, Forrest to Hunter, September 4, 1861.
239. Turner, "3rd Georgia First Twelve Months," June 21, 1864.
240. Spencer, Wiggins and Cone, *My Dear Friend*, 29.
241. Turner, "3rd Georgia First Twelve Months," June 21, 1864.
242. Ibid.
243. U.S. War Department, *War of the Rebellion*, Wright Letter to Huger, September 6, 1861, 642–3.
244. *Covington News*, "Mr. Moss's Diary," June 8, 1916.
245. Scharf, *History of the Confederate States Navy*, 277.
246. Spencer, Wiggins and Cone, *My Dear Friend*, 26.
247. U.S. War Department, *War of the Rebellion*, Wright Letter to Huger, September 6, 1861, 642–3.
248. Spencer, Wiggins and Cone, *My Dear Friend*, 26, 30.
249. Scharf, *History of the Confederate States Navy*, 277.
250. Spencer, Wiggins and Cone, *My Dear Friend*, 28.
251. *Covington News*, "Mr. Moss's Diary," June 8, 1916.
252. Turner, "3rd Georgia First Twelve Months," June 21, 1864.
253. Secretary of the Navy, *Official Records*, T.T. Hunter Letter to Huger, September 10, 1861, 725.
254. North Carolina, State Legislature, *Report of the Adjutant General*, 11.
255. U.S. War Department, William F. Lynch to S.R. Mallory, January 22, 1862.
256. Ibid., Wright to Huger, September 11, 1861, 647.
257. Ibid.
258. Ibid., Wright to Huger, September 22, 1861, 655.
259. Spencer, Wiggins and Cone, *My Dear Friend*, 28.

260. Ibid., 32.
261. Ibid., 33.
262. *Covington News*, "Mr. Moss's Diary," June 8, 1916.
263. U.S. War Department, *War of the Rebellion*, Wright to Huger, September 22, 1861, 655.
264. Lindsey and Andrews, "Third Georgia Regiment."
265. Secretary of the Navy, *Official Records*, Minor to Jones, September 4, 1861, 722–3. Minor informs Jones that "Captain Lynch has just been sent to fill Barron's place."
266. Eicher and Eicher, *Civil War High Commands*, 86.
267. Scharf, *History of the Confederate States Navy*, 277.
268. Lynch, *Naval Life*, 9.
269. "Biographies in Naval History."
270. William Francis Lynch, *Narrative of the United States' Expedition*, 16.
271. Ibid., 424.
272. *Daily National Intelligencer*, "An Interesting Volume," June 22, 1849.
273. Secretary of the Navy, *Official Records*, Magruder to Lynch, September 19, 1861, 653–4. Even at this late date, after Lynch's detachment from the Bureau, he is being addressed as "Chief of Bureau."
274. Secretary of the Navy, *Official Records*, Lynch orders to Simms, September 2, 1861, 721.
275. Eicher and Eicher, *Civil War High Commands*, 86.
276. Parker, *Recollections of a Naval Officer*, 233.
277. Secretary of the Navy, *Official Records*, Lynch report to Mallory, September 12, 1861, 726–7.
278. Ibid., Forrest orders to Sinclair, September 5, 1861, 723–4.
279. Ibid., Lynch report to Mallory, September 12, 1861, 726–7.
280. Ibid., Forrest to Lynch, September 23, 1861, 732–3.
281. *New York Times*, "Burnside at Work," February 11, 1862.
282. *New York Times*, "The Burnside Expedition…Commodore Lynch's Mosquito Fleet Demolished…," February 12, 1862.
283. Secretary of the Navy, *Official Records*, Wise report to Huger, February 17, 1862, 762–5
284. Hawkins, papers, Commodore W.F. Lynch official report to S.R. Mallory, October 3, 1861.
285. Suther, "George E. Ritchie," 1.
286. Powell, *Dictionary of North Carolina Biography*, 323. The Indiantown area of Currituck County was later named Shawboro in his honor.
287. Owens, "Story of the Confederate Flag."
288. Powell, *Dictionary of North Carolina Biography*, 323.
289. U.S. Congress, *Biographical Dictionary*, "Shaw, Henry Marchmore, (1819-1864)."
290. Powell, Dictionary of North Carolina Biography, 323.
291. Owens, "Story of the Confederate Flag."
292. Suther, "George E. Ritchie," 1.
293. Yellowley, "8th NC Infantry Letter."
294. State of North Carolina, Adjutant General's Department, *Register of North Carolina Troops*.
295. Spencer, Wiggins and Cone, *My Dear Friend*, 34.
296. U.S. War Department, *War of the Rebellion*, Wright to Huger, September 22, 1861, 655.

297. *Covington News*, "Mr. Moss's Diary," June 15, 1916.
298. Spencer, Wiggins and Cone, *My Dear Friend*, 34.
299. *Covington News*, "Mr. Moss's Diary," June 15, 1916.
300. Yellowley, "8ᵗʰ NC Infantry Letter." Yellowley's date of the receipt of information conflicts with both Wright's and Lynch's official reports.
301. U.S. War Department, *War of the Rebellion*, Wright report to Huger, *October 2, 1861*, 596–7.

CHAPTER SEVEN

302. U.S. War Department, *War of the Rebellion*, Wright report to Huger, *October 2, 1861*, 596–7.
303. Scharf, *History of the Confederate States Navy*, 378.
304. "Raleigh," *Dictionary of American Fighting Ships*.
305. Scharf, *History of the Confederate States Navy*, 378.
306. Spencer, Wiggins and Cone, *My Dear Friend*, 35.
307. Hawkins, papers, Commodore W.F. Lynch official report to S.R. Mallory, October 3, 1861.
308. Ibid.
309. Ibid.
310. Private Taylor, who died at Malvern Hill, is pictured at the far left in the portrait on the back cover of this book; Lindsey and Andrews, "Third Georgia Regiment."
311. Scharf, *History of the Confederate States Navy*, 277.
312. Hawkins, papers, Commodore W.F. Lynch official report to S.R. Mallory, October 3, 1861.
313. U.S. War Department, Mansfield report to Townsend, October 5, 1861, 595.
314. Hawkins, papers, F.M. Peacock Report to Hawkins, October 8, 1861, 68.
315. U.S. War Department, Mansfield report to Townsend, October 5, 1861, 595.
316. Hawkins, papers, F.M. Peacock Report to Hawkins, October 8, 1861, 68.
317. U.S. War Department, Mansfield report to Townsend, October 5, 1861, 595.
318. Hawkins, papers, W.L. Brown to Hawkins, October 2, 1861, 66.
319. Secretary of the Navy, *Official Reports*, Rowan report to Welles, October 5, 1861, 275–6.
320. Ibid., Rowan to Chauncey, September 30, 1861, 273.
321. Moore, *Rebellion Record*, Vol. 3, 156.
322. U.S. Office of Naval Records, Secretary of the Navy Gideon Welles orders to Lieutenant Pierce Crosby, September 24, 1861.
323. U.S. Office of Naval Records, Lieutenant Peirce Crosby to Secretary of the Navy Gideon Welles, October 1, 1861, 32; *Daily National Intelligencer*, "The Capture of the Transport Fanny," October 8, 1861. Even as late as October 5, informed persons relating the account of the *Fanny* capture were noting that the disaster occurred "in the absence of her commander, Lieutenant Crosby, who for some days has been upon a furlough."
324. Moore, *Rebellion Record*, 156.
325. Hawkins, papers, Wool orders to Hawkins, September 26, 1861.
326. U.S. National Archives and Records Administration, Returns from U.S. Military Posts.

327. *Daily National Intelligencer*, "From Fortress Monroe," October 4, 1861.
328. Johnson, *Long Roll*, 53–4.
329. Graham, *Ninth Regiment*, 631.
330. Jeffrey, *Richmond Prisons*, 103.
331. Whitney, *Hawkins Zouaves*, 212.
332. Ely, *Journal of Alfred Ely*, 196.
333. Jeffrey, *Richmond Prisons*, 33.
334. Hawkins, papers, F.M. Peacock to R.C. Hawkins, March 8, 1864, 110. Peacock wrote Hawkins on March 8, 1864, on his departure to Europe from New York City, stating, "I cannot leave here without expressing my ever most admiration for you."
335. French, *1864 Field Artillery Tactics*, 58
336. Johnson, *Long Roll*, 6; Ibid, 54–5.
337. Secretary of the Navy, *Official Records*, Morrison statement to Rowan, October 1, 1861, 276.
338. Hawkins, papers, Commissary J. Clark report to Hawkins, October 2, 1861, 64.
339. Ibid., W.L. Brown to Hawkins, October 2, 1861, 66.
340. Ibid.
341. Duyckinck, *National History*, 548.
342. *Lafayette Journal*, January 11, 1862.
343. Duyckinck, *National History*, 548.
344. Secretary of the Navy, *Official Records*, Morrison statement to Rowan, October 1, 1861, 276.
345. U.S. National Archives, Case Files of Approved Pension Applications, Hiram A. Unruh, private, Company C, Twentieth Indiana Infantry, approved pension Certificate No. 1,142,378.
346. Burdette, *American Biography*, 387
347. Duyckinck, *National History*, 548.
348. Hawkins, papers, Commissary J. Clark report to Hawkins, October 2, 1861, 64.
349. *New York Times*, "The Indiana Twentieth on the North Carolina Coast," October 20, 1861.
350. U.S. National Archives, Case Files of Approved Pension Applications, Charles H. White, approved pension Certificate No. 209.509.
351. *New York Times*, "The Indiana Twentieth on the North Carolina Coast," October 20, 1861.
352. "Boston Courier," *Book Buyer*, 70.
353. *Baltimore Sun*, "The War News," October 8, 1861.
354. U.S. National Archives, Case Files of Approved Pension Applications, Lucius L. Bennett, approved pension Certificate No. 393,405.
355. *New York Tribune*, "From North Carolina," October 19, 1861.
356. *New York Times*, "The Indiana Twentieth on the North Carolina Coast," October 10, 1861.
357. Gilbreath, manuscript, 10.
358. Secretary of the Navy, *Official Records*, Morrison statement to Rowan, October 1, 1861, 276.
359. Ibid.
360. *New York Herald*, "Our Fortress Monroe Correspondence," October 9, 1861.
361. Hawkins, papers, Commodore Lynch report to S.R. Mallory, October 3, 1861.

362. *New York Times*, "The Indiana Twentieth on the North Carolina Coast," October 10, 1861.

363. Olson, "Curlew," 26.

364. *Philadelphia Press*, "How the Propeller Fanny was Captured," October 10, 1861; Merrill, *Soldier of Indiana*, 488; *New York Herald*, "Our Fortress Monroe Correspondent," October 9, 1861; Merrill, *Soldier of Indiana*, 488; *New York Tribune*, "From North Carolina," October 19, 1861; Hawkins, papers, F.M. Peacock report to Hawkins, October 8, 1861, 68.

365. Merrill, *Soldier of Indiana*, 488.

366. *Miami Union*, "Hart, Captain Isaac W.," March 22, 1873.

367. "Colonel James Harvey Hart," Troy Historical Society; Ohio General Assembly, Roster Commission, 43. Hart's brother James's regiment, the Seventy-first Ohio Infantry, had been organizing in September. On October 7, just as news was released in the papers of Quartermaster Hart's capture, James was commissioned first lieutenant and adjutant of the Seventy-first Ohio Volunteers.

368. *Miami Union*, "Hart, Captain Isaac W.," March 22, 1873.

369. Corcoran, *Captivity of General Corcoran*, 87.

370. *New York Times*, "Prison Life in Richmond," February 27, 1862.

371. Merrill, *Soldier of Indiana*, 488.

372. Moore, *Rebellion Record*, 157.

373. *Baltimore Sun*, "The Capture of the Fanny—Statement of a Passenger," October 7, 1861.

374. *New York Tribune*, "From North Carolina," October 19, 1861.

375. Merrill, *Soldier of Indiana*, 488.

376. *Covington News*, "Mr. Moss's Diary," June 15, 1916.

377. *New York Herald*, "Our Fortress Monroe Correspondence," October 9, 1861.

378. Hawkins, papers, F.M. Peacock report to Hawkins, October 8, 1861, 68.

379. Spencer, Wiggins and Cone, *My Dear Friend*, 35.

380. Lindsey and Andrews, "Third Georgia Regiment."

381. Gilbreath, manuscript, 10.

382. Wyllie, *Confederate States Navy*, 327.

383. *Richmond Daily Dispatch*, "From Norfolk," October 7, 1861; ibid., "The Norfolk Day Book, of Friday…," October 28, 1861. Langhorne returned to Norfolk on Wednesday, October 23, aboard the CSS *Raleigh*, which had returned under Midshipman Gregory for repairs. Langhorne is noted as the acting paymaster of the Confederate States navy. Captain Alexander was temporarily detached from the *Raleigh*.

384. Scharf, *History of the Confederate States Navy*, 277.

385. *Richmond Daily Dispatch*, "The Capture of General Butler's Flag-ship Fanny," October 8, 1861.

386. Spencer, Wiggins and Cone, *My Dear Friend*, 35.

387. *New York Times*, "The Indiana Twentieth on the North Carolina Coast," October 10, 1861.

388. Stephens, *Civil War Diary*, 14.

389. Clif Hinds, e-mail message to the author, November 18, 2003.

390. *New York Herald*, "Our Fortress Monroe Correspondence," October 9, 1861.

391. Merrill, *Soldier of Indiana*, 490.

392. *New York Tribune*, "From North Carolina," October 19, 1861.

393. Hawkins, papers, Commissary J. Clark report to Hawkins, October 2, 1861, 64.

394. *New York Tribune*, "From North Carolina," October 19, 1861.

395. Lindsey and Andrews, "Third Georgia Regiment."

396. Hawkins, papers, Commodore Lynch report to S. R. Mallory, October 3, 1861.

397. Johnson, *Long Roll*, 54.

398. *New York Times*, "The Loss of the Propeller Fanny," October 7, 1861.

Chapter Eight

399. U.S. War Department, *War of the Rebellion*, Wright report to Huger, October 2, 1861, 596–7.

400. Lindsey and Andrews, "Third Georgia Regiment."

401. Ibid.

402. *Covington News*, "Mr. Moss's Diary," June 15, 1916.

403. Scharf, *History of the Confederate States Navy*, 379.

404. U.S. War Department, *War of the Rebellion*, Wright report to Huger, October 2, 1861, 596–7.

405. *Richmond Daily Dispatch*, "The Exploit at Chickamacomico," October 10, 1861.

406. *Philadelphia Press*, "How the Propeller Fanny was Captured."

407. *Richmond Daily Dispatch*, "The Exploit at Chickamacomico," October 10, 1861.

408. Duyckinck, *National History*, 548; *New York Tribune*, "From North Carolina," October 19, 1861.

409. *New York Herald*, "Our Hatteras Inlet Correspondence," October 13, 1861.

410. *Richmond Daily Dispatch*, "From Norfolk," October 7, 1861.

411. Turner, "3rd Georgia First Twelve Months," July 5, 1864; *Richmond Daily Dispatch*, "From Norfolk," October 8, 1861.

412. Ibid., "The Exploit at Chickamacomico," October 10, 1861; Yellowley, "8th NC Infantry Letter."

413. *Richmond Daily Dispatch*, "…rumored attempt to land on Roanoke Island, &c.," October 5, 1861; ibid., "From Norfolk," October 7, 1861.

414. U.S. War Department, Huger to Cooper, October 5, 1861, 726.

415. Ibid, Cooper to Huger, October 6, 1861, 726.

416. Ibid., Bledsoe Letter to Huger, October 8, 1861, 727–8.

417. Secretary of the Navy, *Official Records*, Tayloe report to Lynch, October 8, 1861, 738.

418. U.S. National Archives, Case Files of Approved Pension Applications, Michael Caspar [*sic*], approved pension Certificate No. 812,452.

419. U.S. Office of Naval Records and Library, Flag Officer William F. Lynch memo regarding the schooner *M.C. Sumner*; U.S. National Archives, Case Files of Approved Pension Applications, Hiram A. Unruh, private, Company C, Twentieth Indiana Infantry, Certificate No. 1,142,378.

420. *Richmond Daily Dispatch*, "From Norfolk," October 7, 1861.

Chapter Nine

421. Hawkins, papers, W.L. Brown to Hawkins, October 2, 1861, 63.

422. Ibid., Brown, General Order No. 11, October 2, 1861

423. Secretary of the Navy, *Official Records*, Rowan report to Welles, October 5, 1861, 275–6.

424. Ibid., Goldsborough orders to Lardner, September 28, 1861, 260.

425. Ibid., Rowan Report to Welles, October 5, 1861, 275–76.

426. Merrill, *Soldier of Indiana*, 488.

427. Duyckinck, *National History*, 549

428. Secretary of the Navy, *Official Records*, Rowan report to Welles, October 5, 1861, 275–6.

429. *Daily National Intelligencer*, "The Capture of the Transport Fanny," October 8, 1861.

430. Merrill, *Soldier of Indiana*, 488.

431. Hawkins, papers, W.L. Brown report to Hawkins, October 6, 1861, 68;

432. *The Independent*, "An Attempt to Retake Hatteras," New York, October 17, 1861.

433. Merrill, *Soldier of Indiana*, 488.

434. Gilbreath, manuscript, 10.

435. Merrill, *Soldier of Indiana*, 488.

436. Hawkins, papers, W.L. Brown report to Hawkins, October 6, 1861, 68.

437. *The Independent*, "An Attempt to Retake Hatteras," October 17, 1861.

438. Hawkins, papers, W.L. Brown report to Hawkins, October 6, 1861, 68. Hawkins's plan to send Jardine up to Live Oak preceded the Bankhead Expedition. According to Brown's report dated October 6, Jardine went with retreat orders from Hawkins dated October 2.

439. Graham, *Ninth Regiment*, 75–7.

440. *New York Tribune*, "From North Carolina," October 19, 1861.

441. *Philadelphia Press*, "From Fortress Monroe," October 8, 1861.

442. *New York Tribune*, "Our Hatteras Correspondence," October 11, 1861.

CHAPTER TEN

443. *Daily National Intelligencer*, "A Brush in North Carolina," October 10, 1861.

444. Brown to George Winter, November 4, 1861, George Winter Collection.

445. Turner, "3rd Georgia First Twelve Months," July 19, 1864.

446. "Address by Colonel Claiborne Snead," Third Georgia Volunteer Infantry Website.

447. Yellowley, "8th NC Infantry Letter."

448. *Covington News*, "Mr. Moss's Diary," June 15, 1916.

449. *Richmond Daily Dispatch*, "From Norfolk," October 9, 1861.

450. Secretary of the Navy, *Official Records*, Rowan to Stringham, September 12, 1861, 198.

451. *Richmond Daily Dispatch*, "From Norfolk," October 9, 1861. Ironically, this landing craft was used in the first Federal amphibious landing of the Civil War and later in the first Confederate amphibious assault of the Civil War.

452. *New York Times*, "The Affair at Chicamacomico," October 24, 1861.

453. Lindsey and Andrews, "Third Georgia Regiment."

454. *Richmond Daily Dispatch*, "From Norfolk," October 9, 1861; North Carolina, Mitchells, 229C. The "Colonel Solomon Cherry" noted here is not clearly connected with any of the North Carolina regiments at Roanoke Island. The colonel, most certainly, is from the Cherry/Chearry family of Bertie County, in eastern North Carolina.

455. *Richmond Daily Dispatch*, "From Norfolk," October 9, 1861.

456. *New York Herald*, "Our Hatteras Inlet Correspondence," October 13, 1861.

457. Hawkins, papers, W.L. Brown report to Hawkins, October 6, 1861, 68; *Logansport Journal*, "Letter From Hatteras," October 19, 1861.

458. Ibid.

459. Lewis, manuscript, 9.

460. Hawkins, papers, W.L. Brown report to Hawkins, October 6, 1861, 68.

461. Ibid.

462. *New York Times*, "The Affair at Chicamacomico," October 24, 1861.

463. Hawkins, papers, W.L. Brown report to Hawkins, October 6, 1861, 68.

464. *Logansport Journal*, "Letter from Hatteras," October 19, 1861.

465. *New York Times*, "The Indiana Twentieth on the North Carolina Coast," October 20, 1861.

466. Moore, *Rebellion Record*, 168.

467. Brown to George Winter, November 4, 1861, George Winter Collection.

468. Merrill, *Soldier of Indiana*, 488.

469. Brown to George Winter, November 4, 1861, George Winter Collection.

470. *New York Times*, "The Indiana Twentieth on the North Carolina Coast," October 20, 1861.

471. Hawkins, papers, W.L. Brown report to Hawkins, October 6, 1861, 68.

472. *Rihcmond Daily Dispatch*, "Yankee Encampment at Chickonocomac [*sic*]," October 9, 1861.

473. Turner, "3rd Georgia First Twelve Months," July 5, 1864.

474. Cotton Plant," *Dictionary of American Fighting Ships*.

475. Turner, "3rd Georgia First Twelve Months," July 5, 1864.

476. Ibid.

477. Yellowley, "8th NC Infantry Letter."

478. *New York Times*, "The Affair at Chicamacomico," October 24, 1861.

479. *New York Tribune*, "From North Carolina," October 19, 1861.

480. Secretary of the Navy, *Official Records*, Stellwagen report to Welles, October 2, 1861, 279–80.

481. Duyckinck, *National History*, 549.

482. *New York Herald*, "Our Hatteras Inlet Correspondence," October 13, 1861.

483. Duyckinck, *National History*, 549.

484. Merrill, *Soldier of Indiana*, 488.

485. Johnson, *Long Roll*, 56; *New York Tribune*, "From North Carolina," October 19, 1861.

486. Duyckinck, *National History*, 549.

487. Graham, *Ninth Regiment*, 94.

488. Johnson, *Long Roll*, 56.

489. Hawkins, papers, W.L. Brown report to Hawkins, October 6, 1861, 68.

490. Turner, "3rd Georgia First Twelve Months," July 5, 1864.

491. *New York Times*, "The Affair at Chicamacomico," October 24, 1861.

492. Yellowley, "Chicamacomico," 55–6.

493. *New York Times*, "The Affair at Chicamacomico," October 24, 1861.

494. Merrill, *Soldier of Indiana*, 488.

495. *New York Times*, "The Affair at Chicamacomico," October 24, 1861.

496. Yellowley, "8th NC Infantry Letter."

497. *New York Times*, "The Affair at Chicamacomico," October 24, 1861.

498. Ibid; Turner, "3ʳᵈ Georgia First Twelve Months," July 5, 1864; *New York Times*, "The Affair at Chicamacomico," October 24, 1861.

499. Turner, "3ʳᵈ Georgia First Twelve Months," July 5, 1864; Yellowley, "8ᵗʰ NC Infantry Letter;" *Covington News*, "Mr. Moss's Diary," October 4, 1861; Lindsey and Andrews, "Third Georgia Regiment."

500. U.S. National Archives, Case Files of Approved Pension Applications, Abraham Van Horn, private, Company H, Twentieth Indiana Infantry, approved pension Certificate No. 282,704.

501. Ibid., Charles M. Gross, private, Company G, Twentieth Indiana Infantry, approved pension Certificate No. 233,988.

502. Ibid., Leonard Riley, private, Company E, Twentieth Indiana Infantry, approved pension Certificate No. 525,136.

503. Dunn, *Harvestfields of Death*, 5.

504. Gilbreath, manuscript, 11.

505. *New York Times*, "The Indiana Twentieth on the North Carolina Coast," October 20, 1861.

506. Merrill, *Soldier of Indiana*, 488.

507. *New York Times*, "The Indiana Twentieth on the North Carolina Coast," October 20, 1861.

508. Hawkins, papers, W.L. Brown report to Hawkins, October 6, 1861, 68.

509. *Richmond Daily Dispatch*, "Yankee Encampment at Chickonocomac [*sic*]," October 9, 1861; ibid., "The Exploit at Chickamacomico," October 10, 1861; ibid., "Yankee Encampment at Chickonocomac [*sic*]," October 9, 1861.

510. Stephens, *Civil War Diary*, 15.

511. Hawkins, papers, W.L. Brown report to Hawkins, October 6, 1861, 68.

512. Powell, *History of Cass County Indiana*, 674.

513. Hawkins, papers, W.L. Brown report to Hawkins, October 6, 1861, 68.

514. *New York Times*, "The Indiana Twentieth on the North Carolina Coast," October 20, 1861.

515. Hawkins, papers, W.L. Brown report to Hawkins, October 6, 1861, 68.

516. *New York Times*, "The Fight at Hatteras," October 11, 1861.

517. *The Independent*, "An Attempt to Retake Hatteras," October 17, 1861.

518. Secretary of the Navy, *Official Records*, Werden to Lardner, October 4, 1861, 289–90.

519. Ibid.

520. Johnson, *Long Roll*, 56.

521. Secretary of the Navy, *Official Records*, Lardner Report to Goldsborough, October 6, 1861, 291.

522. *New York Times*, "The Fight at Hatteras," October 11, 1861.

523. Secretary of the Navy, *Official Records*, Lardner Report to Goldsborough, October 6, 1861, 291.

524. Johnson, *Long Roll*, 56.

525. *New York Tribune*, "From North Carolina," October 19, 1861.

526. Merrill, *Soldier of Indiana*, 488–9.

527. *Marshall County Republican*, "Letter from a Prisoner," November 7, 1861.

528. Hover, Barnes, Jones, Conover, Wright, Leiter, Bradford and Culkins, *Memoirs*, 144.

529. U.S. Congress, Senate, *Journal of Executive Proceedings*, 358.

530. Ibid, 491.

531. U.S. National Archives, Case Files of Approved Pension Applications, William Stickley, private, Company C, Twentieth Indiana Infantry, Certificate No. 685.560.

532. *Marshall County Republican*, "Letter from a Prisoner," November 7, 1861.

533. Merrill, *Soldier of Indiana*, 489.

534. Kansas, Fort Scott, 3A.

535. Baird and Brown, *Catalogue of Beta Theta Pi*, 566.

536. *Howard Tribune*, "From the Coast of North Carolina," October 29, 1861.

537. *Marshall County Republican*, "Letter from a Prisoner," November 7, 1861.

538. Turner, "3rd Georgia First Twelve Months," July 5, 1864.

539. *New York Times*, "The Affair at Chicamacomico," October 24, 1861.

540. *Marshall County Republican*, "Letter from a Prisoner," November 7, 1861.

541. *New York Times*, "The Affair at Chicamacomico," October 24, 1861.

542. Turner, "3rd Georgia First Twelve Months," July 19, 1864.

543. *New York Times*, "The Affair at Chicamacomico," October 24, 1861.

544. Lindsey and Andrews, "Third Georgia Regiment."

545. U.S. National Archives, Case Files of Approved Pension Applications, William Stickley, private, Company C, Twentieth Indiana Infantry, Certificate No. 685,560.

546. *New York Times*, "Prisoners of the Twentieth Indiana Regiment," October 13, 1861.

547. Hoffman, "Journal of 1853."

548. U.S. National Archives, Case Files of Approved Pension Applications, John C. Drury, private, Company I, Twentieth Indiana Infantry, Certificate No. 996,484.

549. *Baltimore Sun*, "Youthful Prisoners of War," October 17, 1861.

550. *Marshall County Republican*, "Letter from a Prisoner," November 7, 1861.

551. Moore, *Rebellion Record*, 171.

552. *Marshall County Republican*, "Letter from a Prisoner," November 7, 1861.

553. Turner, "3rd Georgia First Twelve Months," July 5, 1864.

554. *Richmond Daily Dispatch*, "The Exploit at Chickamacomico," October 10, 1861.

555. Lindsey and Andrews, "Third Georgia Regiment."

556. Gilbreath, manuscript, 11.

557. Ibid, 10.

558. *Logansport Journal*, "Letter from Hatteras, Fort Clark, Hatteras Inlet, October 7, 1861," October 19, 1861.

559. Suther, "George E. Ritchie," 1; Scharf, *History of the Confederate States Navy*, 381; Suther, "George E. Ritchie," 1; Lindsey and Andrews, "Third Georgia Regiment;" U.S. Office of Coast Survey, "U.S. Coast Survey Map," Sheet No. 377.

560. Long, "CSS Appomattox."

561. "Empire," *Dictionary of American Fighting Ships*.

562. Hawkins, papers, W.L. Brown report to Hawkins, October 6, 1861, 68.

563. Ibid.

564. Gilbreath Manuscript, 11.

565. Hawkins, papers, W.L. Brown report to Hawkins, October 6, 1861, 68.

566. Ibid.

567. Hawkins, papers, General Rush C. Hawkins Speech of Welcome Before the Veterans of the Ninth New-York and Third Georgia Regiments, April 20, 1891, 4.

568. Wright, "Addresses Thirty Years After," 567–8. The Ninth New York invited members of the Third Georgia Regiment to attend their annual reunion in New

York. Reverend Clark Wright, a Hawkins Zouave, spoke and shared a poetic narrative of the events of that first week in October 1861.

569. Suther, "George E. Ritchie," 1.

570. Yellowley, "8th NC Infantry Letter."

571. *New York Times*, "The Affair at Chicamacomico," October 24, 1861.

572. Suther, "George E. Ritchie," 1.

573. Yellowley, "8th NC Infantry Letter."

574. Yellowley, "Chicamacomico," 55–6.

575. Callahan, "Cabarrus Phalanx," 40.

576. A definitive source for this appellation is elusive, though a number of local and regional historians recall hearing this was the name used by some North Carolina Volunteers for the "Chicamacomico Affair."

577. Merrill, *Soldier of Indiana*, 489.

578. "Phases of the Moon," *NASA*.

579. Brown to George Winter, November 4, 1861, George Winter Collection.

580. *New York Times*, "The Fight at Hatteras," October 11, 1861.

581. Gilbreath, manuscript, 12.

582. *New York Herald*, "Our Hatteras Inlet Correspondence," October 13, 1861.

583. Merrill, *Soldier of Indiana*, 489.

584. Turner, "3rd Georgia First Twelve Months," July 5, 1864.

585. Ibid.

586. U.S. National Archives, Case Files of Approved Pension Applications, Hiram A. Unruh, Certificate No. 1,142,378. Unruh received his Civil War pension based on his service with the First U.S. Marine Artillery, not the Twentieth Indiana Infantry. However, in a letter to the pension board, he demanded that his service to the Twentieth be included as his "due."

587. U.S. National Archives, Case Files of Approved Pension Applications, Eli Snyder, private, Company E, Twentieth Indiana Infantry, Certificate No. 779,899.

588. Merrill, *Soldier of Indiana*, 490.

589. Johnson, *Long Roll*, 57.

590. Ibid, 56–7

591. Gilbreath, manuscript, 12. In fact, only a portion of the Eighth North Carolina made shore—forty men of Company G, Captain Edward C. Yellowley and First Lieutenant Amos J. Hines returned by land to Chicamacomico to complete the loading of the captured Twentieth Indiana property.

Chapter Eleven

592. Gilbreath, manuscript, 12.

593. Hawkins, papers, W.L. Brown report to Hawkins, October 6, 1861, 68.

594. Stephens, *Civil War Diary*, 15.

595. Gilbreath, manuscript, 12.

596. Turner, "3rd Georgia First Twelve Months," July 5, 1864.

597. Hawkins, papers, General Rush C. Hawkins Speech of Welcome Before the Veterans of the Ninth New-York and Third Georgia Regiments, April 20, 1891, 5.

598. Turner, "3rd Georgia First Twelve Months," July 5, 1864.

599. *New York Times*, "The Affair at Chicamacomico," October 24, 1861.

600. Turner, "3rd Georgia First Twelve Months," July 5, 1864.

601. Andrews, "Condensed History."

602. Ibid.

603. Turner, "3rd Georgia First Twelve Months," July 5, 1864.

604. Secretary of the Navy, *Official Records*, Braine report to Lardner, October 5, 1861, 291–2.

605. *New York Times*, "The Fight at Hatteras," October 11, 1861.

606. Secretary of the Navy, *Official Records*, Braine report to Lardner, October 5, 1861, 291–2.

607. Spencer, Wiggins and Cone, *My Dear Friend*, 37.

608. Secretary of the Navy, *Official Records*, Braine report to Lardner, October 5, 1861, 291–2.

609. Spencer, Wiggins and Cone, *My Dear Friend*, 37.

610. Turner, manuscript, "Dear Farther."

611. Secretary of the Navy, *Official Records*, Braine report to Lardner, October 5, 1861, 291–2.

612. Spencer, Wiggins and Cone, *My Dear Friend*.

613. Turner, "3rd Georgia First Twelve Months," July 5, 1864.

614. Ibid.

615. *New York Times*, "The Fight at Hatteras," October 11, 1861.

616. Secretary of the Navy, *Official Records*, Braine report to Lardner, October 5, 1861, 291–2.

617. *New York Times*, "The Fight at Hatteras," October 11, 1861.

618. Secretary of the Navy, *Official Records*, Braine report to Lardner, October 5, 1861, 291–2.

619. Moore, *Rebellion Record*, 169.

620. *The Republican*, "Warren O'Haver," September 3, 1908.

621. U.S. Department of the Interior, United States Board of Pension Appeals, 208.

622. Moore, *Rebellion Record*, 169.

623. Secretary of the Navy, *Official Records*, Braine report to Lardner, October 5, 1861, 291–2.

624. U.S. National Archives, Case Files of Approved Pension Applications, Lucius L. Bennett, Certificate No. 393,405.

625. Secretary of the Navy, *Official Records*, Braine report to Lardner, October 5, 1861, 291–2.

626. There were lieutenants named "Wilson" in both Company C and Company G of the Third Georgia Regiment, but no "Wilson" found among the officers of the Seventh North Carolina.

627. Moore, *Rebellion Record*, 169.

628. Ibid.

629. Secretary of the Navy, *Official Records*, Braine report to Lardner, October 5, 1861, 291–2.

630. *Covington News*, "Mr. Moss's Diary," June 15, 1916.

631. Secretary of the Navy, *Official Records*, Braine report to Lardner, October 5, 1861, 291–2.

632. *New York Times*, "The Fight at Hatteras," October 11, 1861.

633. U.S. National Archives, Case Files of Approved Pension Applications, Charles H. White, Certificate No. 209.509.

634. Ibid.; U.S. Department of the Interior, United States Board of Pension Appeals, 208. Private Warren O'Haver was discharged from the Twentieth

Indiana on November 15, 1861 at Camp Hamilton, Fort Monroe, due to chronic erysipelas

635. Yellowley, "8ᵗʰ NC Infantry Letter."

636. "Col. E. C. Yellowley," *Cyclopedia*, 107–9.

637. *New York Times*, "The Affair at Chicamacomico," October 24, 1861.

638. Turner, manuscript, "Dear Farther."

639. "Muster Roll of Company D;" Lindsey and Andrews, "Third Georgia Regiment;" "Muster Roll of Company E;" Lindsey and Andrews, "Third Georgia Regiment;" "Muster Roll of Company E;" Moore, *Rebellion Record*, 171; Lindsey and Andrews, "Third Georgia Regiment."

640. Yellowley, "8ᵗʰ NC Infantry Letter."

641. Frank Leslie's *Illustrated Newspaper*, November 2, 1861.

642. *New York Tribune*, "From North Carolina," October 19, 1861. Note that "Goodin" is the correct spelling, as in the article.

643. *New York Herald*, "Our Hatteras Inlet Correspondence," October 13, 1861.

644. Lindsey and Andrews, "Third Georgia Regiment."

645. MacNeill, *Hatterasman*, 159ff. Ben Dixon MacNeill tells the story of a deaf man, Johnny Barnes, age fifty-three, who was shot and killed in Little Kinnakeet, September 2, 1861. MacNeill wrote that Barnes was the only Banker to die by gunfire during the Civil War, when he started running after a Zouave sentry called him to halt. Whatever truth there is to this story, if any, may possibly be rooted in the account of the shooting during the Chicamacomico Affair.

646. *Covington News*, "Mr. Moss's Diary," June 15, 1916.

647. *New York Times*, "The Affair at Chicamacomico," October 24, 1861.

648. Ibid.

649. *Richmond Daily Dispatch*, "Yankee Encampment at Chickonocomac [*sic*]," October 9, 1861.

650. Yellowley, "Chicamacomico," 55–6.

651. *Richmond Daily Dispatch*, "Yankee Encampment at Chickonocomac [*sic*]," October 9, 1861.

652. Yellowley, "Chicamacomico," 55–6.

653. Spencer, Wiggins and Cone, *My Dear Friend, 40.*

654. Yellowley, "8ᵗʰ NC Infantry Letter."

655. Yellowley, "Chicamacomico," 55–6.

656. Yellowley, "8ᵗʰ NC Infantry Letter."

657. Spencer, Wiggins and Cone, *My Dear Friend*, 40.

658. Yellowley, "Chicamacomico," 55–6.

659. Lindsey and Andrews, "Third Georgia Regiment."

660. *New York Times*, "The Affair at Chicamacomico," October 24, 1861.

661. Lindsey and Andrews Papers, "Third Georgia Regiment."

662. Folsom, *Heroes and Martyrs*, 4.

663. *Covington News*, "Mr. Moss's Diary," June 15, 1916.

664. Ibid.

665. Folsom, *Heroes and Martyrs*, 4.

666. Stephens, *Civil War Diary*, 15.

667. *New York Tribune*, "From North Carolina," October 19, 1861.

668. *Valparaiso Republic*, "All Safe," October 24, 1861.

669. Johnson, *Long Roll*, 59.

670. *Valparaiso Republic*, "All Safe," October 24, 1861.

671. *New York Tribune*, "From North Carolina," October 19, 1861.
672. Hawkins, papers, List of Missing Men of the 20th Ind. Regt., 70.

CHAPTER TWELVE

673. *Daily National Intelligencer*, "The Late Affair on Hatteras Beach," October 18, 1861.
674. U.S. War Department, Mansfield to Scott, October 14, 1861, 626–7.
675. *Harper's Weekly*, "The Monticello Shelling the Rebels," October 26, 1861. See also the image on the cover of this volume, original to Frank *Leslie's Illustrated Newspaper*, November 2, 1861, and reprinted in *Leslie's Pictorial History of the War of 1861*, 178.
676. Porter, *Naval History*, 49–50.
677. Scharf, *History of the Confederate States Navy*, 382.
678. *New York Times*, "The Affair at Chicamacomico," October 24, 1861.
679. "Address by Colonel Claiborne Snead." Third Georgia Volunteer Infantry Website.
680. *New York Herald*, "The Exploits at Chicamacomico," October 14, 1861.
681. *New York Times*, "The Late Affair Near Hatteras Inlet…Effect of the Hatteras Victory," October 11, 1861.
682. *New York Tribune*, "From North Carolina," October 19, 1861.
683. There were actually two cooks hired by the Twentieth from the Baltimore area while the regiment was on duty in Cockeysville, Maryland, guarding the Northern Central Railroad. Citizen Nathan Brady, attached to Company D, was from Baltimore. He was not aboard the *Fanny* but was captured during the retreat from Camp Live Oak on the fourth or fifth.
684. Johnson, *Long Roll*, 57–8.
685. *New York Times*, "Important from Hatteras Inlet," October 10, 1861.
686. Brown to George Winter, November 4, 1861, George Winter Collection.
687. *Valparaiso Republic*, "Fort Hatteras," October 24, 1861.
688. *Logansport Journal*, "Letter From Hatteras," October 19, 1861.
689. Stephens, *Civil War Diary*, 20.
690. *New York Times*, "The Indiana Twentieth on the North Carolina Coast," October 20, 1861.
691. *The Independent*, "An Attempt to Retake Hatteras," October 17, 1861.
692. Brown to George Winter, November 4, 1861, George Winter Collection.
693. Yellowley, "8th NC Infantry Letter."
694. Ibid.
695. U.S. War Department, *War of the Rebellion*, Hawkins Letter to Wool, October 8, 1861, 623–4.
696. Ibid., Mansfield report to Townsend, October 5, 1861, 595.
697. *Lancaster Intelligencer*, "Important News from Fortress Monroe," October 8, 1861.
698. U.S. War Department, *War of the Rebellion*, Mansfield Report to Townsend, October 5, 1861, 595.
699. Ibid., General Orders No. 21, Whipple by Command of Wool, October 5, 1861, 620.
700. *New York Herald*, "Our Fortress Monroe Correspondence," October 9, 1861.
701. Moore, *Rebellion Record*, 157.
702. "Joseph K.F. Mansfield," *Biographical Register*, 287.
703. Eicher and Eicher, *Civil War High Commands*, 85.

704. O'Brien, and Diefendorf, *General Orders of the War Department*, 125.

705. U.S. War Department, *War of the Rebellion*, General Orders No. 21, Whipple by Command of Wool, October 5, 1861, 620.

706. U.S. War Department, *War of the Rebellion*, Mansfield report to Wool, October 8, 1861, 624–5.

707. Graham, *Ninth Regiment*, 103.

708. *New York Herald*, "Our Hatteras Inlet Correspondence," October 13, 1861.

709. U.S. War Department, *War of the Rebellion*, Mansfield report to Wool, October 8, 1861, 624–5.

710. Ibid.

711. *Daily National Intelligencer*, "The Late Affair on Hatteras Beach," October 18, 1861. Originally in the *New York Tribune*, dated "Fort Monroe, October 9, 1861."

712. U.S. War Department, *War of the Rebellion*, Wool Report to Scott, October 6, 1861, 621.

713. Ibid.

714. *New York Times*, "The Battle," October 20, 1861. Colonel Brown, according to Adjutant Stiles, was proud of all his field and staff officers in the way they conducted themselves. Standing six-foot-two-inches tall, Surgeon Orpheus Everts was described by Stiles as "one of the best men, cool, calm, a thorough scholar, and an efficient surgeon." It was said of Everts's assistant surgeon, Anson Hurd, that "a better man for the service cannot be found." Major Benjamin H. Smith, and Adjutant Israel N. Stiles all were noble and gallant and each did his duty, "seconding the efforts of their chief." Stiles, noted that Sergeant Major Charles Hammond Comly was "taken prisoner while trying to save the stragglers." "A finer man," Stiles praised, "never marched with a regiment." Of course, the men of the ranks, with endurance and courage, "bore fatigue and privation without a murmur."

715. U.S. War Department, *War of the Rebellion*, William D. Whipple Orders to Brigadier General Thomas Williams, October 8, 1861.

716. U.S. Adjutant General Office, Records, General Thomas Williams to Adjutant General S. Thomas, October 8, 1861; *Brooklyn Daily Eagle*, "From Fortress Monroe," October 10, 186.1

717. Ibid., "The Recent Engagement at Hatteras," October 12, 1861; *Howard Tribune*, "From the Coast of North Carolina," October 29, 1861; *New York Herald*, "Important from Fortress Monroe," October 14, 1861.

718. U.S. War Department, *War of the Rebellion*, Major General John E. Wool to Lieutenant General Winfield Scott, October 11, 1861.

719. Ibid., Hawkins to Wool, October 8, 1861, 623–4.

720. Ibid.

721. Ibid.

722. *Baltimore Sun*, "The Capture of the Fanny—Statement of a Passenger of the Pawnee," October 7, 1861.

723. *New York Tribune*, "Our Fortress Monroe Correspondence," October 12, 1861.

724. Secretary of the Navy, *Official Records*, Rowan report to Welles, October 5, 1861, 275–6.

725. Ibid., Morrison statement to Rowan, October 1, 1861, 276; ibid., Ridgely statement to Rowan, October 2, 1861, 276–7.

726. Ibid., Rowan report to Welles, October 5, 1861, 275–6.

727. U.S. War Department, *War of the Rebellion*, Hawkins to Wool, October 8, 1861, 623–4.

728. Hawkins, "Early Coast Operations," 638.

729. *New York Times*, "Affairs at Fortress Monroe," September 13, 1861. Correspondent wrote from Fort Monroe on Sunday, September 8, 1861.

730. Greeley, *American Conflict*, 600; Whitney, *Hawkins Zouaves*, 59.

731. Graham, *Ninth Regiment*, 103; *New York Herald*, "Our Hatteras Inlet Correspondence," October 13, 1861; Graham, *Ninth Regiment*, 9.

732. Whitney, *Hawkins Zouaves*, 63.

733. Graham, *Ninth Regiment*, 1–20.

734. Marshall, *Private and Official Correspondence*, 255.

735. U.S. War Department, *War of the Rebellion*, Whipple orders to Williams, October 8, 1861, 622.

736. Ibid., Mansfield Letter to Scott, October 14, 1861, 626–7.

737. Graham, *Ninth Regiment*, 95

738. *Brooklyn Daily Eagle*, "From Fortress Monroe," October 15, 1861.

739. U.S. Adjutant General Office, Records, Major General John Wool to Lieutenant General W. Scott, October 2, 1861.

740. *Howard Tribune*, "From the Coast of North Carolina," October 29, 1861.

741. *Valparaiso Republic*, November 28, 1861.

742. Graham, *Ninth Regiment*, 96.

743. *Harper's Weekly*, "Traitors in Government Service," September 7, 1861.

744. *New York Times*, "Views from the Capital—Startling Developments of the Report of the Treason Committee," August 26, 1861.

745. Ibid., "Disloyalty of Government Employees," January 20, 1862.

746. *Baltimore Sun*, "Important Naval Engagement at Hatteras," October 10, 1861.

747. Whitney, *Hawkins Zouaves*, 60.

748. Moore, *Rebellion Record*, 157

749. Secretary of the Navy, *Official Records*, Stringham report to Welles, September 2, 1861, 120–3.

CHAPTER THIRTEEN

750. *Covington News*, "Mr. Moss's Diary," June 15, 1916.

751. Long, "Why the 3rd Georgians."

752. *Weekly Columbus Enquirer*, "Fine Regiment," June 10, 1862. See rare photo on back cover. It includes three Third Georgia Regiment soldiers from Company D, each wearing a blue Union overcoat, who were captured from the Twentieth Indiana Regiment aboard the U.S. gunboat *Fanny* on October 1, 1861. Columbus C. Taylor, *far left*, and James D. Jackson, *middle*, were both killed at Malvern Hill, July 1, 1862. James H. Porter, "detailed for railroad service," was discharged January 1862. The photo was taken near Richmond during the winter of 1861–2. *Courtesy of the Museum of the Confederacy*.

753. "Muster Roll of Company E;" *Richmond Daily Dispatch*, "Yankee Encampment at Chickonocomac [*sic*]," October 9, 1861.

754. *Covington News*, "Mr. Moss's Diary," June 15, 1916.

755. Lindsey and Andrews, "Third Georgia Regiment."

756. *Baltimore Sun*, October 14, 1861, 1.

757. U.S. War Department, *War of the Rebellion*, Huger to Cooper, October 15, 1861, 729.

758. Ibid., Cooper to Huger, October 16, 1861, 730.

759. U.S. National Archives, Case Files of Approved Pension Applications, Michael Caspar [*sic*], Certificate No. 812,452.

760. U.S. Congress, House, William Abbott testimony, 932–4.

761. Jeffries, *Richmond Prisons*, 32.

762. U.S. Congress, House, William Abbott testimony, 932–4.

763. Jeffries, *Richmond Prisons*, 32; U.S. Congress, House, William Abbott testimony, 932–4. U.S. Navy master's mate and acting lieutenant William A. Abbott shared that train, having also shared an upstairs prison cell with Ninth New York sergeant major Francis Peacock in the Norfolk jail. He would later report on this sighting after release in early 1862.

764. *Richmond Daily Dispatch*, October 21, 1861,

765. U.S. Congress, House, William Abbott testimony, 932–4.

766. U.S. War Department, *War of the Rebellion*, Benjamin to Moore, October 23, 1861, 730; ibid., Benjamin to Brown; ibid., Benjamin to Pickens; ibid., Benjamin to Moore, October 25, 1861, 730–2.

EPILOGUE

767. U.S. National Archives, Case Files of Approved Pension Applications, Elias Oxford, Certificate No. 140,676. Elias Oxford's Record of Death and Interment and Burial Register entries are in conflict. The former states Oxford entered the hospital on the eighteenth, then died and was buried on the nineteenth. The Burial Register, however, indicates he died on the eighteenth and was buried on the nineteenth.

768. *Indianapolis Daily Journal*, "Elias Oxford, Co. H, 20th Indiana," May 29, 1862.

769. Turner and Turner, *Mary Todd Lincoln*, 130–1.

770. Strong, *Diary of the Civil War*, 507.

771. Burlingame, *Dispatches*, 82.

772. Pinsker, *Lincoln's Sanctuary*, 54–71; ibid., 140–1. On June 18, 1862, the president and Vice President Hannibal had dinner together at the Soldiers' Home, where Lincoln, later that night in the library, shared a draft of the completed Emancipation Proclamation with Hamlin.

773. Strong, *Diary of the Civil War*, 507.

Bibliography

MANUSCRIPTS, DIARIES AND LETTERS

Andrews, Charles H. "Condensed History of the 3rd Georgia Volunteer Infantry." Circa 1885. Georgia Archives. http://www.3gvi.org/ga3hist1.html (accessed March 23, 2013).

Brown, William L., to George Winter. November 4, 1861. George Winter Collection. Tippecanoe Historical Association, Lafayette, IN.

Corcoran, Michael. *The Captivity of General Corcoran.* Philadelphia: Barclay & Co., 1864.

Dennis Tuttle Papers, 1862–3. Pearce Civil War Collection. Navarro College, Corsicana, TX.

Ely, Alfred. *The Journal of Alfred Ely: A Prisoner of War in Richmond.* Edited by Charles Lanman. New York: D. Appleton and Co., 1862.

George Weber Papers, 1861–2. South Carolina Library. University of South Carolina, Columbia.

Gilbreath, Erasmus C., Manuscript S2594. January 16, 1898. Indiana State Library Manuscript Division. Indianapolis, IN.

Hawkins, Rush Christoper. Files. Correspondence with the *National Cyclopedia of American Biography* in 1917. Norwich University Archives and Special Collections. Northfield, VT.

———. Papers, 1861–1920. John Hay Library, Brown University. Providence, RI.

Hoffman, William. "Journal of 1853 Travel Across the Plains and the Rocky Mountains from Covington, IN to Jacksonville, OR—Diary of William Hoffman." Vertical file 7049. Transcribed typescript copy by Frederick Keith. [n.d]. Rogue Valley Genealogical Society & Library, Phoenix, Oregon.

Jeffrey, William H. *Richmond Prisons 1861–2.* St. Johnsbury, VT: Republican Press, 1893.

Johnson, Charles F. *The Long Roll: Being A Journal of the Civil War, as Set Down During the Years 1861–3.* East Aurora, NY: Roycrofters, 1911.

Lewis, Joshua. Manuscript. S861. [n.d.]. Indiana State Library Manuscript Division. Indianapolis, IN.

Lindsey, Daniel McDonald. *Report on Coastal Defenses to Colonel James G. Martin, Adjutant General N.C. State Troops, September 3, 1861*. Manuscript. Henry Toole Clark Governor's Correspondence. Collection of Governor's Papers. North Carolina State Archives, http://digital.ncdcr.gov/cdm/ref/collection/p15012coll8/id/8661/ (accessed April 4, 2013).

Lindsey, John W., and Charles H. Andrews. "Third Georgia Regiment: History of its Campaigns from April 26th, 1861 to April 9th, 1865." Charles H. Andrews Papers 2849. Southern Historical Collection. Wilson Library. University of North Carolina. Chapel Hill, NC.

Main, Jonathan. "Civil War Record of Jonathan H. Main." Transcript of September 1, 1861 letter dated Cockeysville, [MD], by Karen J. Mayo Barrow, [n.d.].

Spencer, Alva Benjamin, Clyde G. Wiggins, and Margaret Lucinda Cone. *My Dear Friend: The Civil War Letters of Alva Benjamin Spencer, 3rd Georgia Regiment, Company C*. Macon, GA: Mercer University Press, 2007.

Stephens, Thomas White. *The Civil War Diary of Thomas White Stephens, Sergeant, Company K, 20th Indiana Regiment of Volunteers*. Edited and Annotated by Paul E. Wilson and Harriet Stephens Wilson. Lawrence, KS: Privately published, 1985.

Turner, J.G., Manuscript. "Dear Father." October 8 [?], 1861. Ann C. Poe Collection. Greenville, SC.

Turner, Justin G., and Linda Levitt Turner, editors. *Mary Todd Lincoln: Her Life and Letters*. New York: Knopf, 1972.

Turner, William W. "3rd Georgia First Twelve Months." Compiled by Johnnie P. Pearson and Mary A. Pearson. Article series originally appearing in the [Putnam County, Georgia] *Countryman*, 1864. From microfilm at University of Georgia, Athens, Georgia. [n.d.]. *Third Georgia Volunteer Infantry Website*. http://www.3gvi.org/ga3hist3.html (accessed March 23, 2013).

Welles, Gideon, to Prize Commissioner Henry Flanders, Esq., July 9, 1862. Naval Historical Collection. Naval War College. Newport, RI.

Yellowley, Edward C. "Chicamacomico, 4 October 1861." Letter dated Roanoke Island, 8 October 1861. *Histories of the Several Regiments and Battalions from North Carolina in the Great War 1861–'65*. Vol. 5. Edited by Walter Clark. Goldsboro, NC: Nash Brothers, 1901.

———. "8th NC Infantry Letter on Early Coastal Operations Performed by the South." Camp Raleigh, Roanoke Island, October 8, 1861. Transcript of hand-written letter. Outer Banks History Center Collection. Manteo, NC.

GOVERNMENT PUBLICATIONS AND FILES

Hawkins, Dexter. Headstone. Burns Cemetery. Pomfret, Windsor County, VT. Created by Clint Black. Findagrave.com, 2011. http://www.findagrave.com/cgi-bin/fg.cgi?page=gr&GRid=77419933/ (accessed March 23, 2013).

Indiana. Jefferson. Cass County. 1880 U.S. census. Population schedule. Enumeration district 31. Family History Film 1254268, roll 268, page 388A, image 0412. Ancestry.com.

Indiana. Jefferson. Cass County. 1900 U.S. census. Population schedule. Enumeration district 18. NARA microfilm publication roll T623_362, page: 7A. Ancestry.com.

Kansas. Fort Scott Ward 2. Bourbon County. 1910 U.S. census. Population schedule. Family History Library microfilm 1374445, roll T624_432, page 3A. Ancestry.com.

Lincoln, Abraham. "Proclamation 80: Calling Forth the Militia and Convening an Extra Session of Congress." April 15, 1861. Online by Gerhard Peters and John T. Woolley. *American Presidency Project.* http://www.presidency.ucsb.edu/ws/?pid=70077/ (accessed March 24, 2013).

Maryland. Vansville. Prince George's County. 1850 U.S. census. Population schedule. NARA microfilm publication M432_295, page 43A, image: 352. Ancestry.com.

"Muster Roll of Company D: 3rd Regiment, Georgia Volunteer Infantry, Army Northern Virginia, C.S.A., Madison County, Georgia, ('Clarke County Rifles')." Excerpted from roster of Confederate soldiers of Georgia 1861–5. Compiled by Lillian Henderson. Circa 1900. *Third Georgia Volunteer Infantry Website.* http://www.3gvi.org/ga3rosterd.html (accessed March 23, 2013).

"Muster Roll of Company E: 3rd Regiment, Georgia Volunteer Infantry, Army Northern Virginia, C.S.A., Houston County, Georgia, ('Governor's Guard')." Excerpted from roster of Confederate soldiers of Georgia 1861–5. Compiled by Lillian Henderson. Circa 1900. *Third Georgia Volunteer Infantry Website.* http://www.3gvi.org/ga3rostere.html (accessed March 23, 2013).

"Muster Roll of Company L: 3rd Regiment, Georgia Volunteer Infantry, Army Northern Virginia, C.S.A., Clarke County, Georgia, ('Madison Home Guards')." Excerpted from roster of Confederate soldiers of Georgia 1861–5. Compiled by Lillian Henderson. Circa 1900. *Third Georgia Volunteer Infantry Website.* http://www.3gvi.org/ga3rosterl.html (accessed March 23. 2013).

Naval Records. U.S. Naval Historical Center. U.S. Navy Yard. Washington, D.C.

New York Adjutant General's Office. Annual Report of the Adjutant General of the State of New York For the Year 1893. "Registers of the 6th, 7th, 7th Veterans & 8th–11th Regiments of Infantry." Vol. 2. Albany, NY: James B. Lyon, 1894.

North Carolina. Adjutant General's Department. *Register of North Carolina Troops.* Raleigh, NC: Adjutant General's Office, 1861. http://archive.org/details/registerofnorth00nort/ (accessed January 21, 2013).

North Carolina. Mitchells. Bertie County. 1880 U.S. census. Population schedule. Family History Library microfilm 1254953, roll 953, page 229C, image 0102. Ancestry.com.

North Carolina. State Legislature. *Report of the Adjutant General of North Carolina to the State Convention.* June 1861. Raleigh, NC: Symme & Hall, Printers, 1861. http://archive.org/details/volunteertroops00nort/ (accessed March 3, 2013).

O'Brien, Thomas M., and Oliver Diefendorf. General Orders of the War Department: Embracing the Years 1861, 1862 and 1863 Adapted Specially for the Use of the Army and Navy of the United States. 2 vols. New York: Derby & Miller, 1864. http://archive.org/details/generalordersofw00unit/ (accessed January 21, 2013).

Ohio General Assembly. Roster Commission. *Official Roster of the Soldiers of the State of Ohio in the War of the Rebellion.* Vol. 6. Cincinnati: Wilstach, Baldwin, 1886. http://www.civilwarindex.com/armyoh/rosters/71st_oh_infantry_roster.pdf (accessed March 24, 2013).

Secretary of the Navy. *Official Records of the Union and Confederate Navies in the War of the Rebellion.* 30 vols. Washington, DC: GPO, 1894–1922. http://ebooks.library.cornell.edu/m/moawar/ofre.html (accessed January 21, 2013).

U.K. House of Commons. *Accounts and Papers of the House of Commons.* 38 Vols. London, 1862.

U.S. Adjutant General's Office. Records of the Adjutant General's Office, 1780s–1917. Letters Received by the Office of the Adjutant General. Mail Series 1861–1870, 619. Roll 69, 890 W. 61. Record Group 94. National Archives and Records Administration, Washington, D.C.

U.S. Congress. *Biographical Dictionary of the United States Congress, 1774–Present. United States Congress Website.* http://bioguide.congress.gov/ (accessed January 21, 2013).

U.S. Congress. House. *Report of the Treatment of Prisoners of War by the Rebel Authorities, during the War of the Rebellion: To Which Are Appended the Testimony Taken by the Committee, and Official Documents and Statistics, etc. H.R. Doc. No. 45.* 40ᵗʰ Cong., 3ʳᵈ sess., 1869: 932–4. http://memory.loc.gov/cgi-bin/ampage?collId=llss&fileNa me=1300/1391/llss1391.db&recNum=8/ (accessed February 20, 2013).

U.S. Congress. Senate. *Journal of Executive Proceedings of the Senate of the United States of America, from December 6, 1858, to August 6, 1861, Inclusive.* Vol. 11. Washington, DC: GPO, 1887.

U.S. Department of the Interior. United States Board of Pension Appeals. *Decisions of the Department of the Interior in cases relating to pension claims, and the laws of the United States granting and governing pensions.* Vol. 4. Washington, D.C.: GPO, 1891.

U.S. National Archives. Burial Registers of Military Posts and National Cemeteries, compiled circa 1862–circa 1960. Records of the Office of the Quartermaster General, 1774–1985. Record Group 92. Archive number 44778151. Series A1 627. Washington, D.C.

U.S. National Archives. Case Files of Approved Pension Applications of Veterans Who Served in the Army and Navy Mainly in the Civil War and the War with Spain ("Civil War and Later Survivors' Certificates"), 1861–1934; Civil War and Later Pension Files; Records of the Department of Veterans Affairs. Record Group 15. Washington, D.C.

U.S. National Archives and Records Administration. Returns from U.S. Military Posts, 1800–1916. Microfilm Serial: M617. Microfilm Roll: 465. Post Return of Hatteras Inlet & Vicinity, commanded by Colonel Rush C. Hawkins, for the month of September, 1861. Washington, D.C.

U.S. Naval Academy Graduates' Association. *First Annual Reunion June 10–11, 1886.* Baltimore, MD: Isaac Friendenwald, 1887.

U.S. Navy. *Dictionary of American Naval Fighting Ships.* Online version provided by the Naval History and Heritage Command Website. http://www.history.navy.mil/danfs/ (accessed January 20, 2013).

U.S. Office of Coast Survey. "U.S. Coast Survey Map of the Eastern Coast of North Carolina." Sheet No. 14. A.D. Bache, superintendent. Topography surveyed by Hull Adams, esq. March and April 1852. Historical Map & Chart Collection. National Oceanographic and Atmospheric Administration. http://historicalcharts.noaa.gov/historicals/preview/image/T00367-00-1852/ (accessed April 1, 2013).

U.S. Office of Coast Survey. "U.S. Coast Survey Map of the Eastern Coast of North Carolina." Sheet No. 377. A.D. Bache, superintendent. Topography surveyed by Hull Adams, esq. March and April 1852. Historical Map & Chart Collection. National Oceanographic and Atmospheric Administration. http://historicalcharts.noaa.gov/historicals/preview/image/T00377-00-1852/ (accessed April 1, 2013).

U.S. Office of Naval Records and Library, 1691–1945. Naval Records Collection. Subject Files for the Confederate States Navy, compiled circa 1924–circa 1929, documenting the period 1861–1865. NARA M1091. Roll 0029. Category O. Operations of Naval Ships and Fleet Units, file OX. Records from the Confederate Navy during the Civil War, organized by subjects ranging from ships to prisoners of war. Record Group 45. *www.fold3.com.*

U.S. War Department. *Supplement to the Official Records of the Union and Confederate Armies.* 4 parts. 100 vols. Edited by Janet B. Hewett, et al. Wilmington, NC: Broadfoot, 1994–2001.

U.S. War Department. *The War of the Rebellion: A Compilation of the Official Records of the Union and Confederate Armies.* 70 vols. Washington: GPO, 1880–1901. http://ebooks.library.cornell.edu/m/moawar/waro.html (accessed January 21, 2013).

Vermont. Pomfret. Windsor County. 1830 US census. Population schedule. Family History Library microfilm 0027453, page 21. NARA series M19, number 187. Ancestry.com.

"Vermont, Vital Records, 1760-1954." Index and images. FamilySearch.org. https://familysearch.org/pal:/MM9.1.1/XFVF-179/ (accessed December 29, 2012).

Wisconsin. Bayfield. Bayfield County. 1900 U.S. census. Family History Library microfilm 1241778, roll 1778. Family History Library microfilm: 1241778. Ancestry.com.

Newspapers, Journals and Magazines

Baltimore Sun
Boca Raton News
Brooklyn Daily Eagle
The Countryman
Covington (GA) *News*
Daily National Intelligencer
Frank Leslie's Illustrated Newspaper
Harper's Weekly: A Journal of Civilization
Howard (IN) *Tribune*
The Independent
Lafayette (IN) *Journal*
Logansport (IN) *Journal*
Marshall County (IN) *Republican*
The Miami (OH) *Union*
Nashville Union and American
New York Herald
New York Times
New York Weekly Tribune
Philadelphia Press
The (Danville, IN) *Republican*
Richmond Daily Dispatch
Scribner's Magazine
Valparaiso (IN) *Republic*
Vermont Chronicle
Weekly Columbus (GA) *Enquirer*

ARTICLES, ESSAYS AND INTERVIEWS

"Address by Colonel Claiborne Snead at the Reunion of the Third Georgia Regiment at Union Point on the 31st July, 1874." *History of the 3rd Georgia Volunteer Infantry.* http://www.3gvi.org/ga3history.html (accessed March 23, 2013).

Ancestry.com. U.S. Army. Register of Enlistments, 1798–1914. From Adjutant General's Office. Records. National Archives Microfilm Publication M233, 81 rolls. Washington, D.C.

Atkinson, Matt. "We Are Now Complete Masters of the Field: Ambrose Wright's Attack on July 2." In *Papers of the 2006 Gettysburg National Military Park Seminar.* Gettysburg National Military Park. Gettysburg, PA: National Park Service, 2008: 211–30. http://www.nps.gov/history/history/online_books/gett/gettysburg_seminars/11/essay7.pdf (accessed March 28, 2013).

"Biographies in Naval History: Captain William Francis Lynch, 1 April 1801–17 October 1865." *Naval History and Heritage Command.* http://www.history.navy.mil/bios/lynch_wmf.htm (accessed March 25, 2013).

"The Boston Courier. From 1824 to 1884. Extracts from a Sketch of the History of the Paper." In *Book Buyer: A Summary of American and Foreign Literature.* Vol. 1. February 1884–January 1885. New York: Charles Scribner's Sons, 1884: 70.

Callahan, Ben F. "The Cabarrus Phalanx: Company H, 8th NC Regiment, CSA." Unpublished essay. N.d.

"Ceres." *Dictionary of American Fighting Ships.* http://www.history.navy.mil/danfs/c5/ceres.htm (accessed March 24, 2013).

"Col. E.C. Yellowley." *Cyclopedia of Eminent and Representative Men of the Carolinas of the Nineteenth Century.* Vol. 2. Edited by Samuel A'Court Ashe. Madison, WI: Brant & Fuller, 1892: 107–9.

"Colonel James Harvey Hart." *Troy Historical Society.* http://www.thetroyhistoricalsociety.org/stories/biograph/biog-fl/2004.htm (accessed March 24, 2013).

"Cotton Plant," *Dictionary of American Fighting Ships.* http://www.history.navy.mil/danfs/cfa2/cotton_plant.htm (accessed March 25, 2013).

Dawson, Scott. "Coastal Algonquian Vocabulary: Croatan Words." *Coastal Carolina Indian Center.* 2010. http://www.coastalcarolinaindians.com/research/algonquian/croatoan_words.htm (accessed March 22, 2013).

Delaney, Norman C. "Charles Henry Foster and the Unionists of Eastern North Carolina." *North Carolina Historical Review* 37, no. 35 (July 1960): 244–5.

Fearing, John Bartlett. "Federal Attack on Hatteras." *Pasquotank Historical Society Year Book, 1956–1957*, Vol. 2. Edited by John Elliott Wood. Elizabeth City, NC: Pell Paper Box Company, 1957.

Gerhardt, Jason. "Permaculture Design on the Edge: Coastal Settlement and Regeneration." November 27, 2012. http://permaculturenews.org/2012/11/27/permaculture-design-on-the-edge-patterns-of-coastal-settlement-and-regeneration/ (accessed March 23, 2013).

Hawkins, General Rush Christopher. "Early Coast Operations in North Carolina." *Battles and Leaders of the Civil War: Being for the Most Part Contributions by Union and Confederate Officers.* Vol 1. New York: Century Company, 1887: 632–59. http://archive.org/details/battlesleadersci01underich/ (accessed January 20, 2013).

Johnson, Reinhard O. "The Liberty Party in Vermont, 1840–8: The Forgotten Abolitionists." *Vermont Historical Society* 47, no. 4 (Fall 1979): 258–75. http://www.vermonthistory.org/journal/misc/LibertyParty.pdf/ (accessed December 29, 2012).

Johnson, Rossiter, ed. *Twentieth Century Biographical Dictionary of Notable Americans*. Vol. 5. Boston: Biographical Society, 1904.

"Joseph K.F. Mansfield." In *Biographical Register of the Officers and Graduates of the United States Military Academy*. Vol. 1. 3rd edition. Edited by George W. Cullum. Boston: Houghton, Mifflin, 1891: 287.

"Junaluska." *Dictionary of American Fighting Ships*. http://www.history.navy.mil/danfs/cfa6/junaluska.htm (accessed March 23, 2013).

Lincoln, Abraham. "Proclamation 85: Proclaiming a Day of National Humiliation, Prayer, and Fasting." August 12, 1861. Online by Gerhard Peters and John T. Woolley. *The American Presidency Project*. http://www.presidency.ucsb.edu/ws/?pid=69979/ (accessed March 23, 2013).

Long, Bruce. "CSS Appomattox." *Civil War Links for Northeastern North Carolina*. http://rblong.net/ncsquadron/Appomattox.htm (accessed March 24, 2013).

———. "Why the 3rd Georgians Wore Blue Coats at the Battle of South Mills." *Battle of South Mills*. http://southmillsbattle.home.coastalnet.com/Blue%20Uniforms%20Anecdote.htm (accessed March 23, 2013).

Muenchausen, Nancy Andrews. John Henry Andrews Family Group Sheet and Notes. October 3, 2000.

Olson, Christopher. "The Curlew: The Life and Death of a North Carolina Steamboat, 1856–1862." The North Carolina Historical Review 83, no. 2 (April 2006): 26 http://www.academia.edu/901326/The_Curlew_The_Life_and_Death_of_a_North_Carolina_Steamboat_1856-1862/ (accessed March 25, 2013).

"Our Washington Correspondence." *Unknown newspaper publication*. Washington, May 20, 1862. www.secondwi.com/fromthefront/2d%20wis/1862/may.htm (accessed February 15, 2013).

Owens, Margaret Dawson. "The Story of the Confederate Flag (8th Regimental Flag)." *Tuttle Tattler: A Tuttle-Dawson Family Website*. http://www.tuttletattler.com/ancestors.cfm (accessed January 21, 2013).

"Phases of the Moon: 1801–1900." *NASA*. http://eclipse.gsfc.nasa.gov/phase/phases1801.html (accessed March 28, 2013).

Pollard, Alfred W. "General Rush C. Hawkins." *Library Fourth Series* 1, no. 5 (June 1920): 171–8.

"Raleigh." *Dictionary of American Fighting Ships*. http://www.history.navy.mil/danfs/cfa8/raleigh.htm (accessed March 25, 2013).

Sons of the Revolution, New York Society. "Membership Roll: Hawkins, Rush Christopher." *Constitution of the General Society of the Sons of the Revolution and the Constitution and By-laws of the Society of the Sons of the Revolution in the State of New York, with the Membership Roll of the New York Society*. New York: Exchange Printing Company, 1891: 80.

Spears, John R. "Sand-Waves at Henlopen and Hatteras." *Scribner's Magazine* 8, no. 4 (October 1890).

Stillwell, Margaret Bingham, "General Hawkins as He Revealed Himself to His Librarian." *The Papers of the Bibliographical Society of America*. Vol. 16. Part 2. Chicago: University of Chicago Press, 1923: 69–106.

Suther, David. "George E. Ritchie and the Boys of Cabarrus County in the War Between the States." Two-page transcript from Ritchie Family News. No. 2 (Spring 1990). Privately published.

Symonds, Craig. "The Battle of Hampton Roads, Then & Now: An Interview with Naval Historian Craig Symonds." By Civil War Trust staff. *Civil War Trust* (2012).

http://www.civilwar.org/battlefields/hampton-roads/hampton-roads-history/the-battle-of-hampton-roads.html (accessed March 22, 2013).

Tayloe, W. Randolph. *The Tayloes of Virginia and Allied Families*. Berryville, VA: Privately published, 1963. http://worldconnect.rootsweb.ancestry.com/cgi-bin/igm.cgi?op=GET&db=adgedge&id=I390/ (accessed February 16, 2013.)

"William Ambrose Wright." From *Georgia's Public Men 1902–1904*. Thomas W. Loyless. Atlanta: Byrd Printing Co., 1902. *Third Georgia Volunteer Infantry Website*. http://www.3gvi.org/ga3vetwawright.html (accessed March 28, 2013).

"William Ambrose Wright." *Memoirs of Georgia: Containing Historical Accounts of the State's Civil, Military, Industrial and Professional Interests, and Personal Sketches of Many of Its People*. Vol. 1. Edited by Southern Historical Association. Atlanta: Southern Historical Association, 1895: 965–6.

"William G. Putnam." *Dictionary of American Fighting Ships*. http://www.history.navy.mil/danfs/w8/william_g_putnam.htm (accessed March 24, 2013).

Wood, John Taylor. "The First Fight of Iron-Clads." *Century Illustrated Monthly Magazine* 29 (November 1884–April 1885): 738–54.

Wright, Clark. "Addresses Thirty Years After" in "Memorial Day." Chap. in *Holydays and Holidays: A Treasury of Historical Material, Sermons in Full and in Brief, Suggestive Thoughts, and Poetry, Relating to Holy Days and Holidays*. Edited by Edward Mark Deems. New York: Funk & Wagnalls, 1906: 567–8.

BOOKS

Aldrich, Lewis Cass, and Frank R. Holmes, editors. *History of Windsor County, Vermont, with Illustrations and Biographical Sketches of Some of Its Prominent Men and Pioneers*. Syracuse, NY: D. Mason & Co., 1891. http://www.archive.org/details/historyofwindsor00aldr/ (accessed December 30, 2012).

Baird, James, and Taylor Brown, editors. *Catalogue of Beta Theta Pi*. 7th ed. Galesburg, IL: Mail Printing Company, 1905.

Barrett, John Gilchrist. *Civil War in North Carolina*. Chapel Hill: University of North Carolina Press, 1963.

Branson, Levi, editor. *Branson's North Carolina Business Directory for 1872*. Raleigh, NC: J.A. Jones, 1872.

Burdette, Robert J., editor. *American Biography and Genealogy, California Edition*. Vol. 1. Chicago: Lewis Publishing Company, 1910.

Burlingame, Michael, editor. *Dispatches from Lincoln's White House: The Anonymous Civil War Journalism of Presidential Secretary William O. Stoddard*. Lincoln, NE: University of Nebraska Press, 2002.

Butler, Benjamin F. *Butler's Book*. Boston: A.M. Thayer & Company, 1892.

Casstevens, Frances Harding. *Clingman's Brigade in the Confederacy, 1862–5*. Jefferson, NC: McFarland, 2002.

Clark, Rufus Wheelwright. *The Heroes of Albany: A Memorial of the Patriot-Martyrs of the City and County of Albany....Brief Histories of the Albany Regiments*. Albany, NY: S.R. Gray, 1867. http://archive.org/details/theheroesofalb00clar/ (accessed January 20, 2013).

Clark, Walter, editor. *Histories of the Several Regiments and Battalions from North Carolina in the Great War 1861–'65*. 5 vols. Goldsboro, NC: Nash Brothers, 1901.

Coggins, Jack. *Arms and Equipment of the Civil War*. North Chemsford, MA: Courier Dover Publications, 2004.

Dana, Henry Sawn. *History of Woodstock, Vermont*. Boston: Houghton, Mifflin, 1889.

Davis, Varina Howell. *Jefferson Davis: Ex-President of the Confederate States of America; A Memoir by His Wife in Two Volumes.* Vol. 2. New York: Belford Company, 1890.

Duffus, Kevin P. *The Lost Light: The Mystery of the Missing Cape Hatteras Fresnel Lens.* Raleigh, NC: Looking Glass Productions, Inc., May 2003.

Dunn, Craig L. *Harvestfields of Death: The Twentieth Indiana Volunteers of Gettysburg.* Carmel, IN: Guild Press, 1999.

Duyckinck, Evert A. *National History of the War for the Union: Civil, Military and Naval; Founded on Official and Other Authentic Documents.* 3 vols. New York: Johnson, Fry and Company, 1861. http://archive.org/details/historyofwarforu02duyc/ (accessed January 20, 2013).

Eicher, John H., and David J. Eicher. *Civil War High Commands.* Palo Alto, CA: Stanford University Press, 2001.

Ellis, William Arba, compiler and editor. *Norwich University, 1819–1911: Her History, Her Graduates, Her Roll of Honor.* 3 vols. Montpelier: Capital City Press, 1911.

Folsom, James M. *Heroes and Martyrs of Georgia: Georgia's Record in the Revolution of 1861.* Macon, GA: Burke, Boykin & Company, 1864.

French, William Henry. *The 1864 Field Artillery Tactics.* Mechanicsburg, PA: Stackpole Books, 2005.

Gaff, Alan D. *On Many a Bloody Field: Four Years in the Iron Brigade.* Bloomington: Indiana University Press, 1999.

Genealogy and Biography of Leading Families of the City of Baltimore and Baltimore County Maryland, Including Portraits of Many Well Known Citizens of the Past and Present. New York: Chapman Publishing Company, 1897.

Gilman, M.D., editor. *The Bibliography of Vermont; or, A List of Books and Pamphlets Relating in Any Way to the State with Bibliographical and Other Notes.* Burlington: The Free Press Association, 1897.

Graham, Lieutenant Matthew J. *The Ninth Regiment, New York Volunteers (Hawkins' Zouaves).* New York: E.P. Coby & Company, 1900.

Greeley, Horace. *The American Conflict: A History of the Great Civil War in the United States of America, 1860–4; Its Causes, Incidents and Results....To the Close of the War for the Union.* 2 vols. Hartford, CT: O.D. Case & Company, 1864. http://books.google.com/books?id=fS2V04gM2kgC&printsec=frontcover&source=gbs_ge_summary_r&cad=0#v=onepage&q&f=false (accessed March 23, 2013).

Hattaway, Herman, Archer Jones and Jerry A. Vanderlinde. *How the North Won: A Military History of the Civil War.* Champaign: University of Illinois Press, 1991.

Hill, Daniel Harvey. *History of North Carolina in the War Between the States: From Bethel to Sharpsburg.* 2 vols. Raleigh: Edwards-Broughton, 1926.

Hover, John C., J.D. Barnes, W.D. Jones, C.R. Conover, W.J. Wright, C.A. Leiter, J.E. Bradford and W.C. Culkins, editors. *Memoirs of the Miami Valley.* Vol. 2. Chicago: Robert O. Law Company, 1919. http://archive.org/details/memoirsmiamival00unkngoog/ (accessed January 19, 2013).

Leslie, Frank. *Leslie's Pictorial History of the War of 1861.* Edited by Ephraim George Squier. New York: Frank Leslie, 1862.

Lynch, William Francis. *Narrative of the United States' Expedition to the River Jordan and the Dead Sea.* 9th edition, revised. Philadelphia: Blanchard and Lea, 1853. http://archive.org/details/narrativeunited01lyncgoog/ (accessed March 23, 2013).

———. *Naval Life; or, Observations Afloat and Ashore, The Midshipman.* New York: Charles Scribner, 1851. http://books.google.com/books?id=AMUYAAAAYAAJ/ (accessed March 23, 2013).

MacNeill, Ben Dixon. *The Hatterasman.* Winston-Salem: J.F. Blair, 1958.

Marshall, Jessie Ames, editor. *Private and Official Correspondence of General Benjamin F. Butler During the Period of the Civil War*. 5 vols. Privately issued. Norwood, MA: The Plimpton Press, 1917. http://archive.org/details/privateofficialc01inbutl/ (accessed January 21, 2013).

Merrill, Catharine. *The Soldier of Indiana in the War for the Union*. Indianapolis: Merrill & Company, 1869.

Moore, Frank, editor. *Rebellion Record: A Diary of American Events with Documents, Narratives, Illustrative Incidents, Poetry, Etc.* 12 vols. New York: D. Van Nostrand, 1861–8.

Paine, Ralph D. *The Ships and Sailors of Old Salem*. Chicago: A.C. McClurg, 1912.

Parker, Captain William Harwar. *Recollections of a Naval Officer, 1841–65*. New York: Charles Scribners' Sons, 1883. http://archive.org/details/recollnavalofficer00parkrich/ (accessed January 20, 2013).

Pinsker, Matthew. *Lincoln's Sanctuary: Abraham Lincoln and the Soldiers' Home*. New York: Oxford University Press, 2003.

Porter, David D. *The Naval History of the Civil War*. New York: The Sherman Publishing Company, 1886.

Powell, Jehu Z., editor. *History of Cass County Indiana*. Vol. 1. Chicago: Lewis Publishing Company, 1913.

Powell, William S., editor. *Dictionary of North Carolina Biography*. Vol. 5. Chapel Hill: University of North Carolina Press, 1994.

Rennie, David Field, M.D. Peking and the Pekingese during the First Year of the British Embassy at Peking. 2 Vols. London: John Murray, 1865.

Roberts, Bruce, and Cheryl Shelton-Roberts. *North Carolina Lighthouses: Stories of History and Hope*. Guilford, CT: Globe Pequot, 2011.

Ross, John Foster George. *A History of the Coldstream Guards, from 1815 to 1895*. London: A.D. Innes & Company, 1896.

Scharf, J. Thomas. *History of the Confederate States Navy from Its Organization to the Surrender of Its Last Vessel*. New York: Rogers & Sherwood, 1887.

Stegeman, John F. *These Men She Gave: Civil War Diary of Athens, Georgia*. Athens: University of Georgia Press, circa 1964.

Stick, David. *The Outer Banks of North Carolina, 1584–1958*. Chapel Hill: University of North Carolina Press, 1958.

Strong, George Templeton. *Diary of the Civil War: 1860–1865*. Vol. 3. Allan Nevins, editor. New York: Macmillan, 1952.

Warner, Ezra J. *Generals in Gray: Lives of the Confederate Commanders*. Baton Rouge: Louisiana State University Press, 1959.

Whitman, Walt. *Notebooks and Unpublished Prose Manuscripts*. Vol. 2: Washington. Edited by Edward F. Grier. New York: New York University Press, 1984. From the *Collected Writings of Walt Whitman*. 17 vols. Edited by Gay Wilson Allen and Sculley Bradley. New York: New York University Press, 1961–84.

———. *The Wound Dresser: A Series of Letters Written from the Hospitals in Washington During the War of the Rebellion*. Edited by Richard Maurice Bucke, M.D. Boston: Small, Maynard & Company, 1898.

Whitney, J.H.E. *The Hawkins Zouaves (Ninth N.Y.V.) Their Battles and Marches*. New York: Privately published, 1866. http://archive.org/details/cu31924030908937/ (accessed January 21, 2013).

Wyllie, Arthur. *The Confederate States Navy*. Whitefish, MT: Kessinger, 2007.

Index

About the Author

Lee Thomas Oxford is the proprietor of Lee Oxford Books and Antiquarian Newspapers in Salisbury, Maryland. Oxford is a historian and Civil War conference speaker, having presented at the Flags Over Hatteras Civil War Sesquicentennial Conference commemorating the Hatteras Invasion of August 1861. Oxford was also the keynote speaker at the Museum of the Albemarle's Civil War Sesquicentennial of the Battle of Elizabeth City. He received a bachelor of arts in sociology from Frostburg University and a master of divinity from Columbia Biblical Seminary. Married with three adult children, Oxford makes his home on Maryland's Eastern Shore. Oxford leads an international organization he founded in 2011 to fight poverty in Africa and throughout the world. His website is www.leeoxford.com.